BLACK HISTORIANS

A Critique

BLACK HISTORIANS

A Critique

(a revision of *Negro Historians in the United States*)

Earl E. Thorpe

WILLIAM MORROW AND COMPANY, INC.   NEW YORK 1971

TO THE MEMORY OF CARTER G. WOODSON

Preface

Literature on American historiography has had almost nothing to say about black historians. Aside from the statements interspersed in Vernon Loggins's volume, *The Negro Author, His Development in America until 1900;* a brief unpublished master's thesis by Joseph Grimes; and a few articles on individual black historians, there has not been —until now—an analysis of the black historian and his contribution to American historiography.

This is a study of the black historian in the broadest and most inclusive sense. Any Afro-American who wrote history, as distinct from other literary forms such as poetry, drama, fiction and autobiography, has been included.

These historians have been grouped into four schools. The first, entitled "The Beginning School," covers the general period from 1800 to 1896. The second, entitled "The Middle Group," covers the period from 1896 to 1930; the third, "The Modern Laymen," in many ways an adjunct of the Middle Group, covers the period from about 1896 to date. Finally, the last group, entitled "The New School," covers the general period from about 1930 to 1960. Also included is a section on writers of Church History.

Writers discussed have been studied in terms of the following general criteria:

1. Quantity of their writings.
2. Literary merits of their writings.
3. Training in historical methodology, especially thoroughness in use of sources and documentation.
4. Philosophy of history.
5. Breadth and soundness of their interpretations of historical events and movements.
6. Objectivity.
7. Impact which their writings have had on people of their own and subsequent periods.

In my opinion, the black historians of greatest stature (according to the above-listed criteria) were: for the nineteenth century, William Wells Brown and George Washington Williams; and, for the twentieth century, W. E. B. Du Bois and Carter Woodson. This is not to say that these men have been the "best" black historians. Excluded from this judgment are all contemporary historians who may reasonably be considered still primarily engaged in their craft.

Readers may wonder why more space has been allotted to some earlier, less qualified and less known historians than to some of the outstanding contemporary scholars. The answer lies in the fact that I studiously avoided saying much about contemporaries, other than listing their published works. This is due to my conviction that any evaluation of the work of persons still living might be off-set by subsequent productions of these individuals.

I have used the terms *Black* and *Negro* synonymously and have not made the distinction that some historians are now making between Black History and Negro History.

Acknowledgments

I am indebted to all persons who have published observations concerning Negro historians and their writings. Especially valuable were the several bibliographies on Negro literature, Vernon Loggins' volume, *The Negro Author*, and the few articles on individual historians which were available. Of course the books produced by the Negro writers of history constituted the greatest source of information. The next most extensive source used was probably the volumes of the *Journal of Negro History*.

A study of any aspect of Negro life and history is facilitated by the Negro collections at such schools as Fisk University, Tuskegee Institute, Hampton Institute, Atlanta University, Howard University, and the Schomburg Collection, New York Public Library. To the library staffs at these schools, as well as at the Ohio State University Library, Columbus, Ohio, the St. Louis Public Library, St. Louis, Missouri, and several others, I am especially grateful.

It is impossible to express acknowledgments directly to

all persons whose helpfulness goes into the making of such a work as this. In addition to those mentioned above, I feel a debt of gratitude to all of my many teachers—especially those of the Department of History at Ohio State University and Dr. Helen G. Edmonds of North Carolina College—for their inspiration and encouragement. Perhaps even greater is the debt owed my wife and daughters, without whose patience and forbearance this study would not have been completed.

For permission to quote from works published by them especial appreciation is hereby extended to the following: *The Quarterly Review of Higher Education Among Negroes;* the Columbia University Press; Harcourt, Brace and Company; University of North Carolina Press; Prentice-Hall; the Association for the Study of Negro Life and History and the Associated Publishers; *Phylon; The American Historical Review; Mississippi Valley Historical Review;* and *The Southern University Bulletin.*

And finally, because of his example of promptness, efficiency and exactness, and the courtesy and encouragement which he has always extended to me, I am deeply indebted to my last academic adviser, Dr. Henry H. Simms.

E. E. THORPE

CONTENTS

JOHN HOPE FRANKLIN
LAWRENCE D. REDDICK
WILLIAM M. BREWER
CLINTON EVERETT KNOX
ERIC E. WILLIAMS

BLACK HISTORY

Overleaf:
"Chapin rescues Solomon from hanging,"
from *Solomon Northup: Twelve Years a Slave*

1

THE CENTRAL THEME OF BLACK HISTORY

Black history, like southern history, is largely a product of the twentieth century. While it is generally agreed that southern historiography drew much of its initial impetus from the desire of southerners to change the unfavorable picture given to them by historians of the Nationalist School, no effort has been made to evaluate the basic ideas which have produced and inspired black historiography or even to define black history.

Black history is American history with the accent and emphasis on the point of view, attitude, and spirit of Afro-Americans, as well as on the events in which they have been either the actors or the objects of action. Because black people have been forcibly kept in a subordinate status, their portion of America's wealth and power has been smaller than their numbers would command. This necessarily means that their point of view, attitude, and spirit are different from those of white Americans.

Black history is that American history which, until the 1960s, was viewed by white America with contempt and disdain or ignored altogether, just as black people themselves were viewed and treated. Men tend either to deny or force out of consciousness the evil that they do. Much of black history, then, is the story of the cruelties and inhumanities which a powerful white majority has inflicted on a defenseless black minority.

As fields of historical specialization, before 1945 Afro-American history and the history of Africa shared the common fate of not having won wide respectability and acceptance. In Service Center for Teachers of History Pamphlet No. 56, entitled *African History,* Philip Curtin makes the statement: "Before the Second World War, most of the important contributions to African history were made by non-historians." Today, the fact that one can earn the Ph.D. with a specialty in African or black history is perhaps the strongest proof that these fields have won wide acceptance. This has been a source of pleasure and concern for the pioneers in these fields. At annual meetings of the Association for the Study of Negro Life and History, lengthy discussions have centered about the question of whether the new acceptance of Negro history makes the work of the Association obsolete.

The black scholars who pioneered in establishing Afro-American history as a respectable field of historical endeavor had motivations which stemmed in large part, but by no means completely, from the condition and status of the black man in this nation. Negro history is still studied by both white and black Americans, partly for these reasons. But more than ever, black history is studied, taught, and written for the same academic reasons as other fields of historical specialization.

The central theme of black history is the quest of Afro-Americans for freedom, equality, and manhood. It is not necessary to cite the many instances where black spokesmen before 1865 used the words *freedom* or *liberty. Free Negroes* and *freedom* were terms of pride. The first Negro newspaper was called *Freedom's Journal*—and more recently, the Freedom Riders had their buses burned as they made sacrifices in the cause of advancing civil rights. *Freedom* has been one of the black American's most often-used words.

Nor is it necessary to recite the many instances before slavery and after slavery when black spokesmen used the word *equality*. In Georgia, near the opening of this century, Negroes called one of their organizations the Equal Rights League. Among other things and along with other groups, the National Association for the Advancement of Colored People has fought for equality before the law, while the National Urban League has sought equal employment opportunities. *Equality* has been among the words most often used by black Americans. The same is true of the word *manhood*.

Throughout the United States, both in ideology and practice, the black male has been denied the right and opportunity to play the role of a man, to be aggressive, competitive, and to hold high positions. If manhood means freedom, pride, the opportunity for maximum growth, self-expression, and personal and social health, then slavery is manhood's greatest subverter.

A Kentucky court ruled that "a slave by our code is not a person, but a thing." But the law of slavery was ambiguous. Another judge, this time in Georgia, declared:

. . . it is not true that slaves are only chattels, . . . and therefore, it is not true that it is not possible for them to be prisoners. . . . The Penal Code has them in contemplation . . . in the first division . . . as persons capable of committing crimes; and as a consequence . . . as capable of becoming prisoners.

A few years later, another southern judge declared:

Because they are rational *human beings,* they are capable of committing crimes; and, in reference to acts which are crimes, are regarded as *persons.* Because they are *slaves,* they are . . . incapable of performing civil acts; and in reference to all such, they are *things;* not persons.

By law, a male slave was a more degraded being than a female slave, for the latter could be legally recognized as a mother. Since marriage between slaves had no legal standing, no offspring of slaves was ever recognized as having a legal father.

The speeches and other statements of black Americans reveal the extent to which they have felt that slavery and compulsory racial segregation and discrimination constituted denials of their manhood.

Concern about manhood is seen in Frederick Douglass's description of slaves as "beings deprived of every right, stripped of every privilege, ranked with four-footed beasts and creeping things, with no power over their own bodies and souls, . . . compelled to live in grossest ignorance, herded together . . . without marriage, without God, and without hope." The same is true of the statement by Douglass that nothing could keep the Negro satisfied in slavery. "Give him a *bad* master," Douglass declared, "and he aspires to a *good* master; give him a good master, and he wishes to become his *own* master."

In his famous 1829 appeal, David Walker admonished white America, several times, to "Treat us like men." At one point Walker added to this: "Treat us like men and we will like you more than we do now hate you." In an 1843 address to the slaves, made at the National Convention of Colored Citizens convening in New York, Henry Highland Garnet said: "You had far better all die—*die immediately,* than live slaves." To this he added, "Let your motto be resistance! *Resistance!* RESISTANCE!" Many times he recounted the evils borne by the slave. "In the name of God," Garnet cried, "we ask, are you men?"

Although the Thirteenth Amendment to the federal constitution lifted black Americans above the level of property, they were far from their goal of equality of status and opportunity.

In an article entitled "The Relation of the Whites to the Negroes," published in the July, 1901, issue of *The Annals of the American Academy of Political and Social Science,* the president of North Carolina's white land-grant college expressed the long-prevailing views of many white Americans when he said, "The Negro is a child race . . . bound to be under the tutelage and control of the whites." He continued:

It would be a cruelty greater than slavery to leave this help-less race, this child race, to work out its own salvation . . . the Negro . . . must aim at white civilization, and must reach it through the support, guidance, and control of the white people among whom he lives.

It is noteworthy here that, in such minds as this one, the Negro had progressed from being classified as chattel —along with horses, cows, and barns—to the classification of a *child.* How much good would it have done to point out to this college president that there never has been any such thing as child and adult races—and that during the ninth, tenth, and eleventh centuries of the Christian era, highly civilized, independent, affluent black kingdoms and empires existed in Africa? How much good would it have done to tell this college president that he—and many other persons who thought as he did—was rationalizing to jus-tify the exploitation of black Americans?

The black educator, J. C. Price, declared: "Freedom implies manhood." In his 1903 book, *The Souls of Black Folk,* W. E. B. Du Bois attacked Booker T. Washington's philosophies of education and racial progress, and based his case on Negro manhood. He said that Washington's thinking overlooked the "higher aims of life" in favor of making money. On this, Du Bois declared:

If we make money the object of man-training, we shall develop money-makers but not necessarily men: if we make technical skill the object of education, we may possess artisans but not, in nature, men. Men we shall have only as we make manhood the object of the work of the schools.

In his last speech in Congress, delivered in 1900, George White, the last black Reconstruction congressman, urged his white colleagues to stop maligning the Afro-American and to help him in his efforts to rise. "Treat him as a man," White urged.

Restoring to health the crippled manhood of many Negro males has been a central concern of the Black Muslims and other nationalist-oriented groups. When in his great eulogy at the funeral of Malcolm X, the actor Ossie Davis sought the central meaning of the life of this remarkable man, he found that meaning in Afro-American manhood. Davis declared: "Malcolm was our . . . living, black manhood!" But, as was Marcus Garvey before him, Elijah Muhammed was also a symbol of manhood to thousands of black Americans. In this regard Malcolm and his mentor "made each other." The big objection which many young blacks had with the non-violent philosophy of Martin Luther King, Jr., was their conviction that not to strike back when hit is unmanly. Even though many felt that Dr. King compromised when he would not strike back, he too, because he fearlessly, willingly, and continuously offered his body to be bruised, arrested, and murdered, was a true symbol of manhood to millions of black Americans.

Some persons contend that the young black male of the ghetto participates in riots because he is not allowed other means of asserting his manhood. Consider also the "Deacons" of the South, and the Black Panthers, and their concern with black manhood. Also, note Eldridge Cleaver's great concern with black manhood in his book, *Soul on Ice*.

Even a superficial reading of the documents of Afro-American history reveals that the central theme of black history is the quest of black Americans for freedom, equality, and manhood. This can be further seen when one surveys the development of written Negro history.

There are at least three basic reasons for the development of the Negro History Movement. The first is related to the fact that historical writing has been slow to shed its aristocratic tradition and bias of being almost exclusively concerned with the affairs of the ruling class or elite. Even after written history shifted from its aristocratic-political emphasis, it long neglected numerous segments of society. Even today there is little written on the role of women in history. So it is, too, that the Negro History Movement came into being because blacks, as human beings, had been left out of written history. Dr. Carter Woodson, the father of Negro history, called the Association for the Study of Negro Life and History "the first systematic effort . . . to treat the records of the race scientifically and to publish the findings to the world." He gave this same justification for the founding of the *Journal of Negro History,* but to this he added that the *Journal* was also dedicated to "the promotion of harmony between the races by acquainting the one with the other."

A second reason that the Negro History Movement came into being was to combat the prominence of racial prejudice and stereotypes. To justify slavery and the system of degradation which followed emancipation, many people found it convenient to argue that blacks belonged in a degraded social position because they were biologically inferior. A highly articulate and influential segment of Western civilization long has depicted blacks as being emotional, impulsive, nonrational, childish creatures. This, of course, was the judgment which was pronounced by the antebellum slave owners and their apologists, and it has been the judgment of numerous social scientists who have written in more recent times. James Schouler, a noted American historian of the Nationalist School, described Negroes as being "a black servile race, sensuous, stupid, brutish, obedient . . . and childish." Ulrich Bonnell

Phillips described the Negro as being innately stupid, docile, submissive, unstable, and negligent. William A. Dunning, John Fiske, J. G. Randall, and Claude H. Van Tyne are also among the sizable number of American historians who have depicted blacks in this vein. Well-known is the manner in which such European writers as Houston Stewart Chamberlain and Count de Gobineau told the world that such was indeed the scientifically verified picture of the mentality, personality, and character of blacks.

The Negro History Movement came into being to combat this image and to correct a serious sin of omission made by Caucasian historians. Disbelief of this so-called science, plus a desire to round out and complete the record, and to set the record straight, caused Drs. Woodson and Du Bois, among other scholars, to concentrate on studying and popularizing the truth about the Afro-American past.

In a multi-ethnic society like the United States of America, every public school and college graduate should know that when white Christian Europe was living in her Dark Ages, there were great black kingdoms and empires and high civilizations in sub-Sahara Africa; and that the successful revolt of black people led by Toussaint L'Ouverture was a major reason Napoleon I sold the Louisiana Territory to the United States. They should know that this nation probably would have lost its War for Independence if George Washington had stuck to his early decision not to use black soldiers, and that Abraham Lincoln admitted that the Union could not have been preserved without the service of the black soldier. They should know that black men and women have made outstanding contributions not only in music, entertainment, and sports, but in literature, medicine, and science; and they should know the names and achievements of some of these men and women.

They should know that in recent years a number of books have been published which not only revise old views and attitudes, but fill gaps in our knowledge of the history of this nation. So it is, for example, that there now exists a book on the Negro cowboy, and a volume on slavery in the cities. So it is, too, that Kenneth Stampp, John Hope Franklin, and others, have caught the spirit of W. E. B. Du Bois's book, *Black Reconstruction,* and have assaulted the old myth that black people and so-called Radical Republicans were responsible for all of the evils of a supposedly bleak and barren Reconstruction period.

History is the memory of mankind, and all men need and use it. The question is not *whether* men know some history and use it, but rather *how well* they understand and use history. Especially are professional historians aware that, because everyone needs and uses history, everyone should not only seek a fuller understanding of it, but should be concerned that the history he knows is as free as possible from class, racial, religious, and national bias.

A third reason the Negro History Movement came into being was to inspire blacks to high achievement. People always have sought to inspire the young by telling them of the outstanding qualities of their ancestors. Evidence that leaders of the Negro History Movement hoped and sought to use history to bolster the race's self-esteem and self-confidence is abundant. This is seen in the fact that until around 1920, many black history books were largely biographies of outstanding black persons. In the preface to his *History of the Negro Race in America,* George Washington Williams stated that one of his reasons for writing the book was to "incite the Negro people to greater effort in the struggle of citizenship and manhood." While he is not generally known as a historian, Booker T. Washington produced a two-volume history which has been widely read. In the preface, Washington expressed the hope that the book would "inspire" some Negro "to make himself useful and successful in the world."

Carter G. Woodson's life was devoted to correcting the false image of blacks so that, as he put it, his race might "escape the awful fate of becoming a negligible factor in the thought of the world." In the introduction to his little book entitled *The Mis-Education of the Negro*, Dr. Woodson said: "When you control a man's thinking you do not have to worry about his actions." One of Dr. Woodson's often-repeated themes was the power and importance of faith and self-affirmation. In effect, he said to his race: "Yes, your ancestors were slaves, but they had a distinguished history *before America was discovered,* and even as slaves, they never stopped loving freedom!" And Woodson was right, for in spite of the long dark night of bondage, they still produced the poetry of Phillis Wheatley, Paul Laurence Dunbar, James Weldon Johnson, Margaret Walker, Gwendolyn Brooks, Langston Hughes, and LeRoi Jones; the scientific genius of Benjamin Banneker, George Washington Carver, Daniel Hale Williams, Ernest Just, and Charles Drew; the novels of Richard Wright, Ralph Ellison, Ann Petry, and James Baldwin; and the eloquence and saintliness of Frederick Douglass, Medgar Evers, and Martin Luther King, Jr. Dr. Woodson reminded men that the Afro-American has been much more in history than a hewer of wood and drawer of water, and that there is nothing wrong with black affirmation.

The popularity of certain aspects of history has some relationship to social conditions and usefulness. When it was true that the sun never set on British soil, the history of England was more popular than it is now. When President Franklin D. Roosevelt was promoting the Good Neighbor Policy, the history of Latin America acquired greater popularity. In 1970 the fact that the "Black Revolution" is one of the nation's major domestic issues presents an added reason why both white and black Americans should look to Afro-American history for whatever inspiration, mutual respect, and sense of direction they can acquire from this history.

Both black and white Americans need an acquaintance with black history. Unless they, too, can endorse the Black

History Movement, white Americans of this generation cannot have respect for black Americans of this generation. It is impossible to think positively about any group whose past is viewed negatively. The negative view can never predominate if we will always keep in mind that the central theme of black history is the Afro-American's quest for freedom, equality, and manhood.

2

THE WHY AND WHAT OF BLACK HISTORY

Many historians have felt the urge to justify their concentration in black history, seemingly a narrow field of endeavor. George Washington Williams, regarded as the first serious student of Negro history,[1] states his reasons for writing his celebrated work, *History of the Negro Race in America from 1619 to 1880*, thusly:

. . . because Negroes had been the most vexatious problem in North America from the time of its discovery down to the present day; because that in every attempt upon the life of the nation . . . the Colored people had always displayed a matchless patriotism and an incomparable heroism in the cause of Americans; because such a history would give the world more correct ideas of the Colored people, and incite the latter to greater effort in the struggle of citizenship and manhood. The single reason that there was no history of the Negro race would have been a sufficient reason for writing one.[2]

For Williams, black history would serve to elevate the Negro in American society by educating the whites concerning the true value of the Negro. Similarly, he felt that black history would stimulate the Negro to greater achievement. "Race prejudice is bound to give way," he wrote, "before the potent influence of character, education and wealth." [3]

Not until the appearance of W. E. B. Du Bois's *Suppression of the African Slave Trade* in 1896 was any other black historian to produce works of such magnitude as those of Williams. Du Bois was the first black American to receive a Ph.D. in any of the social sciences,[4] and he inaugurated a new era in scholarship in general.[5] Together with Carter G. Woodson, Du Bois deserves rank as a leader and maker of the field of Negro history.[6] But like Williams before him, Dr. Du Bois studied and wrote history because he felt that to do so would help elevate the position of the Negro through reeducating both black and white Americans toward a greater respect for the nation's largest minority group. Moreover, it would, he felt, inspire the latter to greater achievement. "The world was thinking wrong about race," he thought, "because it did not know. The ultimate evil was stupidity. The cure for it was knowledge based on scientific investigation." [7] Again he wrote that he held a "firm belief that race prejudice was based on wide-spread ignorance. My long-term remedy was truth: carefully gathered scientific proof that neither color nor race determined the limits of a man's capacity or desert." [8]

Upon completion of his pioneer sociological study, *The Philadelphia Negro*, Dr. Du Bois recommended that such studies be made of other leading American cities with large Negro populations. Such studies, he asserted, are a prerequisite for this education of the races.

Only a few years lapsed between the time when Du Bois first catapulted into the limelight of the scholarly world and the appearance of Carter G. Woodson, another Harvard University Ph.D. Dr. Du Bois, for the time being, had continued his work in the field of sociology, and it was Dr. Woodson who was to get Negro history generally recognized as an area for serious study. He gave up the class-room after a short period and became America's first scholar to devote his full time to collecting and publicizing the history of the Negro.

Dr. Woodson, like Williams and Du Bois, wrote history because he believed it would elevate the position of the Negro in American society by reeducating both Caucasians and Negroes to a greater appreciation of race and would inspire the latter to greater achievement.[9] It was, he believed, the job of the historian of the Negro to prove that the race had a creditable past. On this point, he wrote:

The American Indian left no continuous record. He did not appreciate the value of tradition; and where is he today? The Hebrew keenly appreciated the value of tradition, as is attested by the Bible itself. In spite of worldwide persecution, therefore, he is still a great factor in civilization.[10]

Dr. Woodson is equally clear in the expression of his belief that race prejudice in America was the result of mis-education of both races. He felt that a different type of education which presented the Negro in a more favorable light was the basic solution to the so-called color problem. Race prejudice, he argued, "is not something inherent in human nature. It is merely the logical result of tradition, the inevitable outcome of thorough instruction to the effect that the Negro has never contributed anything to the progress of mankind. The doctrine has been thoroughly drilled into the whites and the Negroes have learned well the lesson themselves." Woodson denied the validity of the doctrine of white supremacy. "One race has not accomplished any more good than any other race," he wrote, "for God could not be just and at the same time make one race the inferior of the other." Emphasizing his faith in education as the proper solution, he wrote, that "just as thorough education in the belief in the inequality of races brought the world to the cat-and-dog stage of religious and racial strife, so may thorough instruction in the equality of races bring about a reign of brotherhood through an appreciation of the virtues of all races, creeds and colors." [11]

Throughout his life, Woodson continuously reaffirmed his convictions (1) that race prejudice was the result of historical writing and teaching which either ignored the Negro's achievements or said that they were nonexistent, (2) that the Negro must be shown that he does have a creditable past or he will lack "inspiration" and, (3) that Caucasians must be educated to this conclusion or they will lack respect for the race. Woodson's entire life became devoted to accomplishing these ends that his race might "escape the awful fate of becoming a negligible factor in the thought of the world." [12]

Negro historians who have become prominent since Woodson launched his great work, in general, have not differed substantially with his interpretation of the efficacy of Negro history (and its need) in effecting a great change for good in the thinking and acting of black and white Americans. On the contrary, many have agreed with Dr. Woodson and have been inspired and directed by these convictions, convictions that have played a prominent role in making black historians determined to reinterpret the topics of slavery, Civil War, and Reconstruction in American history.

There are other motivating factors responsible for Negro historiography which are not so obvious. Concomitant with the New Colonialism of the late nineteenth century there was a swelling tide of nationalism which affected people in all quarters of the globe. Everywhere racial and cultural groups became intensely interested in their pasts. Many sought a folk genius of some kind which would explain their achievements or promises of achievement and serve as a stimulus to group pride. Well does the twentieth century know that, in some quarters, this absorbing interest was perverted into master-race theories.

Furthermore, as the number of Negro college graduates

swelled, Negro scholars became aware of the work of archaeologists and anthropologists in their discovery and reevaluation of the pottery, metal arts, and other artifacts of African peoples. These latter scholars, largely Europeans, were proving what the Negro historian had long contended on moral grounds—namely, that Africans have made a substantial contribution to cultural progress and civilization. While a student, Carter Woodson had sensed this fact. Franz Boas was to bring it to the attention of W. E. B. Du Bois.

Writing in *The New Negro,* published in 1925, the volume's editor, Alain Locke, showed a keen awareness of these developments. The same may be said for Arthur A. Schomburg, who wrote an article for this volume entitled "The Negro Digs Up His Past." So, for a number of reasons, the Negro historian came to insist that the history of the United States be rewritten to include the positive contributions of the Negro and that world history be rewritten to give recognition to Africa's gift to civilization.

This summary herein makes it quite clear that some of the most outstanding black historians have been influenced by the conception of black history *as a weapon in the fight for racial equality.* An analysis of the reasons they have believed history to be an essential weapon in this fight will show some of the strengths and weaknesses of this argument.

A GLORIOUS AND WONDERFUL PAST IS NECESSARY FOR RACIAL ACHIEVEMENT

From the foregoing it is clear that several black historians have felt that a glorious and wonderful past is a prerequisite stimulus for racial achievement, and that such a past would produce greater achievement. As Dr. Woodson put it, the race that "has no history . . . becomes a negligible factor in the thought of the world, and it stands in danger of being exterminated." [13]

This motivating idea is suspect simply because there is no convincing proof of its truthfulness. There is much to deny such an assertion. In contradistinction to the Woodson view, the American Indian was not vanquished because "he did not appreciate the value of tradition," but rather because the technological and cultural levels of development of the Indian were below those possessed by Europeans. And, despite persistent statements to the contrary, there is no general agreement that the explanation for survival ability of the Hebrew is due to the fact that he "keenly appreciated the value of tradition." Similarly, the remarkable rise of western Europeans to world domination despite the fact that they had no glorious past (as Dr. Woodson and others constantly point out in their efforts to show African superiority to Europeans during the Middle Ages) belies the contention that the race that "has no history . . . becomes a negligible factor in the thought of the world, and . . . stands in danger of being exterminated." The same might be said for the barbaric Greek invaders of the Aegean, or any other group which is "on the make" for the first time. The first rise to prominence of any race or peoples must of necessity take place without a prior "history." [14]

There is even evidence that the reverse position from that taken by Woodson and others is true, that is, that the possession of a "history" negates the possibility of future achievement and survival of a race or peoples by causing them to "rest on their oars." [15] And it is a fact of common observation that many individuals strive all the more to create a present if their past is dim.

THE DOCTRINE OF WHITE SUPREMACY SPRINGS FROM AN OVER-EMPHASIS OF ACHIEVEMENTS BY EUROPEANS AND UNDER-EMPHASIS OF ACHIEVEMENTS BY NON-EUROPEANS

Many black historians have believed that race prejudice springs primarily from historical writing and teaching which depicts the Negro as an inferior being, or ignores him entirely. This belief has stimulated many of these scholars to present the story of the Negro as a teaching device for the improvement of race relations.

While there is little doubt that a "filio-pietistic bias" [16] contributes to the tenacity of the doctrine of white supremacy, it seems clear that, as Dr. Du Bois came to see, this doctrine has been primarily a rationalization of a *de jure* and *de facto* situation. Since the sixteenth century, Europeans have held actual economic, political, and military superiority or supremacy in almost every quarter of the globe. Thus, the doctrine of biological supremacy of Caucasians grows from no mere verbalization or educational system, but springs primarily from the existence of a concrete situation. And, it is perhaps reasonably accurate to say that inroads made on this doctrine owe the greater part of their success to inroads made on European hegemony of the world.[17] Many black historians have indicated little appreciation of the true basis for the doctrine in question. They have generally shown, as Dr. Lawrence Reddick states, too little awareness of economic forces in history.[18] Their philosophy of history has been largely a moral one. Thus, too frequently such institutions as slavery and colonialism disappear simply because they were sinful and immoral, and wars are explained as God's punishment for wrongdoing. It is this type of thinking which explains the general failure of many historians to see that the concept of racial inferiority stems primarily from and feeds on the actual economic, political, and social degradation of the masses of Negroes.

Along the way to this realization, Du Bois wrote: "My own panacea in earlier days was flight of class from mass through the development of a Talented Tenth, but the power of this artistocracy of talent was to lie in its knowledge and character and not in its wealth." [19] After this change of outlook, Du Bois placed the emphasis on race consumer and producer cooperatives and the utilization of improved means of organization to advance directly the *economic* position of the Negro.[20] "My whole attitude toward the social sciences began to change," he wrote. "The studies which I had been conducting . . . I saw as fatally handicapped because they represented so small a part of the total sum of occurrences; were so removed in time and space as to lose the hot reality of real life. . . . I saw before me a problem that could not and would not await the last word of science." [21]

SCIENTIFIC STUDIES ARE ESSENTIAL TO RACIAL PROGRESS

As shown, several of these historians have been imbued with the idea that the prerequisite to an elevation of the position of the race in America was studies designed to show the "scientific" position and condition of the race. The famed Atlanta University Studies which were inaugurated and carried out by Du Bois, and many of those conducted by the Association for the Study of Negro Life and History, were made specifically to provide such data.[22] This belief has provided a powerful stimulus to this historiography.

It would seem that in their earnest desire to serve the cause of advancement of the Negro, and their effort to serve the cause of knowledge for which their training and scholarly proclivities fitted them, several of these men have succeeded in convincing themselves that their training and abilities were *sine qua non* for the advancement of the black man. As Du Bois first believed: "Until he [the scholar] has prepared the ground by intelligent and discriminating research, the labors of philanthropist and statesman must continue to be, to a large extent, barren and unfruitful." [23]

I do not contend that black history as an educational device has not contributed to better race relations, or that scientific studies have not also contributed. The position here is simply that several of the foremost black historians have misconstrued the significance of these things as justifications for black history, and that, even if these motivating ideas were completely sound, they do not constitute the total justification for the field.

It is a normal trait for individuals and groups to want to discover and publish, with the emphasis on favorable aspects, the facts of their racial and cultural backgrounds; especially when there is some reason either for being especially proud or not-so-proud of that background. As southern historiography drew its primary inspiration from the desire to redraw the unfavorable picture given of that section's role in the Civil War and Reconstruction, so Negro historiography drew its primary inspiration out of the desire to redraw the unfavorable picture which many scholars have presented of this American minority. Still, of all forces which combined to give rise to this body of literature, the racial uplift theme stands out prominently among those given by most black historians.

ANOTHER JUSTIFICATION FOR
BLACK HISTORY

This leads to the question, What is the proper justification for black history? It does not need to seek its justification only in the contribution it has made to the "advancement of the race" (and undoubtedly it has made a contribution to this cause). It may well be that it is unnecessary for a race to have a creditable past for achievement, despite the fact that the ability to make such a boast swells the pride and inflates the ego. It may well be that scientific studies are not a prerequisite to the progress of the Negro. Another justification for black history, as with any other area of scholarly endeavor, is that *it constitutes a contribution to the knowledge and understanding of mankind.* The only inspiration really necessary for the scholar is that he, through his researches and writings, is giving to his generation, and to posterity, knowledge and understanding. Any other outlook is detrimental to scholarship.

Considered from this frame of reference, Black History is not simply biography of great men and the chronicling of noble achievements. It becomes a record, viewed in the light of conditioning circumstances, of the Negro's achievements and failures, dreams *and* lack of dreams. While cause-serving on the part of the scholar has merits, it also rings up a score of demerits. The large and creditable body of literature produced by black historians would be more convincing (hence a greater contribution) had the work been conceived in an outlook farther removed from cause-serving of a racial nature.

Du Bois admitted that writings by black Americans on the Reconstruction period were too one-sided and suffered from an attitude of "striking back." [24] His own historical writings have been crticized for this same reason. Dr. Woodson launched the *Journal of Negro History* with the belief "that facts properly set forth will speak for themselves," [25] but one has only to read many of his reviews for this organ to wish that he had not insisted so often on using a review to proselytize. His more lengthy writings have also been criticized, to some extent, because of this characteristic.

Still, all America owes the black historian great homage and respect for the splendid manner in which he has uncovered and ordered the facts of the Negro's past and published them to the eternal edification and enlightenment of all mankind. This has been a "solid service . . . rendered not merely to the Negro race, but to historical scholarship generally . . . in a difficult and still largely unworked field." [26] *This is another well-earned justification for black history.*[27]

THE BLACK HISTORIAN:
The Beginning School, Justifiers of Emancipation, 1800–1896

Introduction

Since at least 1800 the Negro's attitudes and thoughts about himself have vacillated between, and been mixtures of, an image of inferiority painted by nineteenth-century slaveholders and a picture of equality painted by traditional Christianity and modern liberalism. For a number of reasons some slaves felt and thought about themselves in conformity with the image painted by their masters. However, other bondsmen related to the equalitarian view, outlined in the Bible and the platitudes of nineteenth-century abolitionists. Like the underprivileged masses under ancient Roman rule, Negro slaves found in tenets of the Christian religion powerful justification for the view of themselves which they wished to have. They were the ancient Israelites whose natural God-given rights were being negated by Egyptian or Babylonian captivity. And just as God freed the Israelites, so in His own good time would He free them. The slaves were to wait on the Lord and not grow weary. That some did not believe this very strongly is evidenced by the numbers who absconded, committed suicide, or rebelled against the institution and their plight.

Slaves admired and respected the slaveowner because of his power and wealth. This caused many to be confused. In spite of their desire to view themselves as equals of any race, admiration and respect for the planter and the dominant culture, plus their own easily observable shortcomings, caused them to accept the planter's derogatory picture. According to this picture, the black man was inferior and childish, and possessed no rights which the white man was bound to respect. From slavery to the present there has been this dichotomy and polarization in the Negro's thought about his group. Persons who held the equalitarian view have tended to be antagonistic toward contrary opinions. Those who accepted the planter's preachments of inferiority have thought and acted in a manner of accommodation which was popularized by Booker T. Washington. The bands of slaves who surreptitiously or openly rebelled against slavery adhered vigorously to the equalitarian picture. This includes the early writers of Negro history, who were mostly ex-slaves. Until his death in 1895, Frederick Douglass was the best-known protagonist of his race's equalitarian sentiments and efforts. After Douglass's death, W. E. B. Du Bois and the NAACP assumed the position which Douglass had held. The Negro historian always has fitted in this equalitarian tradition.

The social philosophies with which Afro-Americans have been identified have been dependent to a large extent on the conceptions which they have held of their racial group. Those who accepted the planter's picture have tended toward a conservative fatalism. They have neither dreamed of nor believed in a bright future for their race. Hence they have devised no programs or activities to elevate its position *in the social order*. Still, though they believed in and largely sought mere personal survival and pleasure, their labors have contributed greatly to the building of the nation.

That majority of Negroes who have accepted the equalitarian ideal have dreamed of a bright future for their group. The programs of action which this conception has inspired have varied with the degree of patience and objective realism possessed by the proposer. While the majority of these programs have involved working faithfully with the democratic tools of party, ballot, pen, forum, and court action, a small minority, less hopeful and patient, has sought to realize the dream in schemes of immigration to a black republic, or of changing this one to a Marxist-type socialist order.

Members of the Beginning School of Negro historians had faith in a bright future for the Negro. Against frightful odds they believed constantly in the Christian religion, the Declaration of Independence, the Constitution, and the American people. Though they lived and wrote at a time when the main concern of their race was for freedom and the main weapon an appeal to the nation's conscience, they never lost their faith that ultimately democracy would triumph.

These writers differ, sometimes greatly, in the historical and literary qualities of their works. Despite this, there is enough of a pattern among them to justify classifying them as the Beginning School of black historians. These writers:

1. Wrote in the period from about 1830 to 1890.
2. Wrote history only incidentally, not as a major interest.
3. Wrote to justify emancipation by showing that some members of their race had committed distinctive acts in the past, and that the numbers of such individuals could be multiplied many times by giving the race better opportunities. They did not directly attack the sociological arguments of the slavocracy. This is due perhaps to their lack of formal education. They argued indirectly and by historical examples taken from their race.
4. Wrote only one or two historical works each. None of them was employed in the teaching of history. They

usually had no formal training in history or historical methodology, did superficial research, and documented poorly.

Although the quality of his writings far excels that of any other member of this School, George Washington Williams is placed in the Beginning School because he displays more of the above characteristics than he does those of the Middle Group. Actually, in some ways Williams represents the terminal point and the flowering of the Beginning School. Although the same high praises cannot be sung for his history, Booker T. Washington is also listed with this group for the same reasons. Adhered to in general, however, is a chronological grouping of writers.

The writers of this School wrote their histories when the status of the Negro was one of the dominant questions of the day. The period from 1830 to 1890 saw the great debates and compromises, Civil War, Reconstruction and the end of Reconstruction. It is only natural that such writings as American Negroes would produce during this period would be deeply influenced by these movements and events. The writers of Negro history, most of whom were ministers, pointed to the violation of Christian tenets which was inherent in slavery and racial discrimination, and expressed the hope of all Christians that some day injustices of man to man would disappear from the earth. History was a theodicy to most members of the Beginning School.

It is significant that these writers set the pattern of thought which almost all Negro historians were to follow until around 1930. This first group advanced the argument that slavery was doomed in America because it was a violation of God's will. Their moralistic approach to this problem shows almost no appreciation of the economic or political forces which militated against the continuance of the institution. They saw no violation of American democracy in Radical Reconstruction, and attempted to establish for the American Negro his cultural and historical inheritance from Africa.

These early writers, as also has been the case with almost all Negro historians, praised the positive contributions of the Afro-American while giving almost no attention to negative aspects of his life in America. Also, they had little appreciation for the anti-Negro feelings of whites. Whether later Negro historians wrote in this vein because of the precedents set by this first school, or not, is impossible to ascertain. It is probable, however, that the pattern of this historiography was fixed to a large extent by the actual social, economic and cultural conditions of the Negro.

Despite their shortcomings, much is owed to this first group. They started the movement of interest in the background of the black man which was later to bear such commendable fruit with the work of Du Bois, Woodson, and others. It was this group which pointed up for the first time such neglected aspects of American history as the participation of Negro soldiers in the Revolutionary War, the War of 1812 and the Civil War. It is this group which began to convince America that Negroes as slaves had not been entirely complacent, happy, willing chattel. They made it known that there was a considerable antislavery movement constantly going on. Many members of this group were collectors of Negro records. Without their works, many sources of black history would probably be unavailable today.

Of the writers before 1830, only two wrote anything which might be called history. Paul Cuffee, an affluent free Negro from Massachusetts, published in 1812 his *Brief Account of the Settlement and Present Situation of the Colony of Sierra Leone in Africa.*[1] The work was subtitled: "As Communicated by Paul Cuffee . . . to his friend in New York: also, an Explanation of the object of his visit, and some advice to the people of Colour in the United States." This very brief work of only twelve pages, written in good prose, can scarcely be called history.

The other person in this period who wrote history was Prince Saunders. Born free in Vermont, Saunders received an education in the public schools of Vermont and taught school for a while in New England. In 1807 he went to Haiti and was hired to improve the school system there. Although he returned to the United States, where he served as a minister in the city of Philadelphia, Saunders later returned to Haiti and became Attorney-General of that country.[2]

The most important publication by Saunders, and his only work of history, was his *Haitian Papers: A Collection of Very Interesting Proclamations and other Official Documents, Together with Some Account of the Rise, Progress and Present State of the Kingdom of Haiti*.[3] Of his style, Dorothy Porter says, "At times his writings were very figurative." [4] This is a characteristic of almost all Negro writers of history until very recently. There is only a small amount of actual history in this brief work, which is primarily "A Collection of the Very Interesting Proclamations and Other Official Documents." Saunders published this work "to give the Britons a better understanding of Haiti's greatness." [5]

Other than these two writers, Negro literature before 1835 is comprised of sermons, the scientific writings of Benjamin Banneker, the poetry of Phillis Wheatley and Jupiter Hammon, personal narratives, and similar materials.

PIONEERS IN PROTEST

ROBERT BENJAMIN LEWIS

Little is known of the early life of Robert Benjamin Lewis. He was born in Boston of Negro and Indian parentage. The historical production of Lewis is confined to one volume, which was copyrighted in 1836 bearing the title *Light and Truth*. It was published in 1844.[1] In this work Lewis tried to prove that many civilizations of antiquity were offshoots of Ethiopian civilization, and he asserted that many outstanding personalities of antiquity were Negroes. Included in this classification were: Solon, Plato, Hannibal, Pompey, Epictetus, Homer, and Euclid. Lewis, like several other black historians of his period, attempted to tell the story of the Negro from the Creation. Sources for these early years he listed as Herodotus, Gibbon, Pliny, Anacharsis's *Ecclesiastical History,* Joseph Milner's *History of the Church of Christ,* Bruce's *Scottish Travels,* and the Bible. Uncritical, sermonistic, replete with errors of fact and interpretation, this work is important only because it was the initial effort of an Afro-American to tell the story of his race. Loggins calls it the "first extensive effort of an American Negro to dig into the story of his past." [2]

The subtitle of the volume read: *Containing the Universal History of the Colored and Indian Race, from the Creation of the World to the Present Time.* Lewis conceived of this work not so much as narrative history but as "collections from sacred and profane history." It was published "with a determination that a correct knowledge of the Colored and Indian people, ancient and modern, may be extended freely, unbiassed by any prejudicial effects from descent or station." [3]

This volume carries fourteen chapters bearing the following titles:

The History of Man [all data here is taken from the Old Testament]
Ancient Cities and Kingdoms
Ancient Kings and Wars
Antiquity of America
Colored Generals and Soldiers [such men as Hanno, Hamilcar, Hannibal and Pompey]
Destruction of Jerusalem
The Present State of Judah and Israel
The Arts and Sciences
Modern Eminent Colored Men
The Great Historical Ages
The Ancient Arabians
History of the Prophets
Periods, & C.
St. Domingo or Hayti

The Bible is the primary source for Lewis's information and the volume carries almost nothing on the Negro and Indian in America. Most of the volume is an effort to substantiate the thesis that American Indians are descendants of the lost tribes of Israel.

Since this volume was published by a "Committee of Colored Gentlemen," one may surmise that there was considerable interest among northern Negroes of this period in showing that the race had produced men of eminence. It also shows that Negroes "did their own thing" even then.

JAMES W. C. PENNINGTON

James W. C. Pennington, an ex-slave, by the age of twenty-one had become a minister, abolitionist, and Underground Railroad worker. Largely self-educated until he reached manhood, Pennington published an autobiography in 1849.[4] Entering the abolitionist movement in New England, Pennington's activities took him to Europe, and in 1851 he had become the first Negro to receive a Doctor of Divinity degree from a European university. This degree was awarded to him by the University of Heidelberg.[5] Returning to the United States, Pennington served as pastor of a New York church and as an antislavery orator.

In 1841 he published a volume entitled *A Text Book of the Origin and History, &c. &c. of the Colored People.*[6] The book is written in a question-and-answer style and concerns the origin of the Negro (Chaps. I–III), how he came to be enslaved in Western Christendom (Chaps. IV–V), his intellect compared to white people (Chap. VI), the nature of American prejudice (Chap. VII), and the complexion of the Negro (Chap. VIII). The volume was intended "for families and to students and lecturers in history," and involved no scholarly presentation. Pennington stated his purpose thusly:

Prejudices are to be uprooted, false views are to be corrected, and truth must be unveiled and permitted to walk forth with her olive branch.

I have met with not a few colored persons who held historical views as prejudicial to the truth in our case as the whites do.[7]

Despite its being poor history, within a year after its initial appearance, the work was in its third edition. Helen

Boardman says that this book was "possibly the most successful of the early attempts to popularize Negro history."

JAMES THEODORE HOLLY

Negro authors, and prospective authors, felt for a long time that white publishers were prejudiced against their work. Lewis's *Light and Truth* was published by a "Committee of Colored Gentlemen," and in 1857 an all-black organization was formed for the sole purpose of publishing the writings of black authors. This group, the Afric-American Printing Co., apparently sponsored only one publication, a lecture by a free Negro, James Theodore Holly (1829–1911). Bearing the lengthy title, *A Vindication of the Capacity of the Negro Race for Self-Government, and Civilized Progress, as Demonstrated by Historical Events of the Haitian Revolution; and the Subsequent Acts of That People since Their National Independence,*[8] this work is another effort to prove the equality of blacks to whites. Forty-eight pages in length, it began as "a lecture . . . prepared and delivered before a Literary Society of Colored Young Men," in New Haven, following Holly's return from Haiti in the autumn of 1855. The language and historical allusions used in this volume show Holly to have been well-read and temperate in tone, although William Wells Brown said that Holly made "Negro nationality" a matter of much thought. A minister when he wrote the vindication, Holly moved to Haiti and became a bishop.

WILLIAM COOPER NELL

William Cooper Nell (1816–1874) was a free person, born and reared in Boston.[9] Although he possessed only an elementary education, he sent letters to Garrison's *Liberator,* and was advertised in that journal as an accountant, copyist and collector. He later became Garrison's personal friend, and one of the reporters for his newspaper. Nell was also an acquaintance of Frederick Douglass and helped him with the publication of his paper, the *North Star.* It was during this period with Douglass that Nell became interested in writing a history of the Negro in the military services. This interest was due primarily to John Greenleaf Whittier's published regret that no one had yet produced such a treatise. In 1851 Nell published in Boston a twenty-four-page pamphlet entitled *Services of the Colored Americans in the Wars of 1776 and 1812.* It was well received and enlarged the next year to forty pages, with an introduction by Wendell Phillips. "The following pages are an effort," wrote Phillips in the introduction, "to stem the tide of prejudice against the colored race."

With his interest aroused in this aspect of Negro history, and spurred on by the reception his pamphlet received, Nell published, in 1855, his *The Colored Patriots of the American Revolution,* a full-sized study. This volume carried an introduction by Harriet Beecher Stowe, and bore the subtitle *With Sketches of Several Distinguished Colored Persons: to which Is Added a Brief Survey of the Condition and Prospects of Colored Americans.*

The title of the volume belies the contents somewhat, for also included is an account of the story of the black man in the United States beyond his military service. This latter portion is largely biographical. For the story of the American Revolution, chapters are arranged by state, with one for each of the thirteen original colonies as well as for Kentucky, Ohio, Louisiana, and Florida. Nell quotes at length from a wide range of documents, including national and state papers, antislavery works, and military records. Hence, the volume is a good source for documentary materials. However, direct quotations are generally too long and too frequent. There are sections in which ten successive pages of quoted material are given. The failure to para-phrase or condense source material is a marked characteristic of most members of the Beginning School. The volume is written in a temperate vein and has a conversational style. Of the members of the Beginning School, only William Wells Brown, Joseph T. Wilson, and George Washington Williams were to equal the quality of research done by Nell in this volume.[10]

WILLIAM WELLS BROWN

William Wells Brown (1814–1884) was born a slave in Lexington, Kentucky. Yet he became the "first American Negro to attempt seriously the novel, the drama, and travel literature, and at the time he ceased writing he was the best historian that the colored race had produced in America." His mother was reputed to have been a daughter of Daniel Boone.[11]

While still in bondage, Brown worked in the office of Elijah P. Lovejoy at the plant of the St. Louis *Times,* of which Lovejoy was then editor. While hired out on a boat which ran the Mississippi and Ohio Rivers, Brown, then about twenty years of age, escaped near Cincinnati, Ohio. Befriended by a Quaker, he took the last name of his bene-factor. He worked for a time on the Great Lakes, and while so doing, used his job as a link in the Underground Railroad.

Brown joined the abolitionist movement in 1843 and be-came a lecturer and writer. During the next decade, he gave over one thousand lectures in the United States and in Europe. He attended a Peace Congress in Paris, and lec-tured widely in the British Isles between 1849 and 1854. The England of Gladstone, Disraeli, Palmerston, Cobden, and Bright made a profound impression on him.[12]

One of Brown's earliest efforts in Negro history, *St.*

Domingo: Its Revolution and Its Patriots, appeared in 1855. This was a reprint in pamphlet form of a speech which he had given earlier in London and Philadelphia. Although its title seemed large, actually the work centered around the rise and fall of one man, Toussaint L'Ouverture. Even in his initial years as a writer, Brown had a tendency to indulge in moralizing, sentimental, or philosophical digressions, which was to become even more serious with the passing years.

His most outstanding historical productions were *The Black Man,* published in 1863, and *The Rising Son,*[13] published in 1874.

The Black Man appeared in the same year as the Emancipation Proclamation. Undoubtedly this helped the popularity of his work. Before the end of the year, the volume appeared in an enlarged edition, and was reprinted until 1867. Apart from a brief sketch denying the black man's inferiority, this volume follows the pattern set by Nell. *The Black Man* carries fifty-three biographical sketches of prominent Negroes. The tone is laudatory.

The 1863 edition is divided into three parts, with no chapter divisions. Part I is a "Memoir of the Author." Part II is entitled "The Black Man and His Antecedents." Misnamed, this section does not treat the African background historically as one might expect. Rather, it is a naive polemic against the stereotypes of black people which had been popularized by the defenders of slavery. Here Brown asserts a belief which George Washington Williams later called "The Unity of Mankind." Part III is entitled "The Black Man, His Genius and His Achievements." This section consists of biographical sketches of Negroes who had risen to prominence in the Western world and the United States. Treated briefly are such men as Dessalines, Alexandre Dumas, Henri Christophe, Nat Turner, William Still, William C. Nell, and Frederick Douglass.

"Aside from attempting to defend the Negro and plead

his cause," writes Coleman of this work, "it never misses an opportunity to praise the Anti-Slavery Movement, to boost the cause of religion, and it is somewhat patriotic in character." [14] Brown's writings, apart from being examples of the early efforts to write history, are good as source material. He was a participant in many of the events which he attempted to chronicle, and showed a true understanding of the events of his day.

Although *The Black Man,* as his other works, carries almost no documentation, Brown occasionally uses Latin phrases and quotes such men as Herodotus and Macaulay. The direct quotations are far too long. In telling of births, deaths, and other such events he almost never gives dates, not even the year. In all fairness, it must be noted that some dates were simply not attainable.

His purpose in writing *The Black Man* is again typical of much Negro historiography. In a word, it is to refute the charge that the race is biologically inferior to other groups. He writes:

The calumniators and traducers of the Negro are to be found, mainly, among two classes. The first . . . are those who have [been] . . . instrumental in their enslavement and consequent degradation. . . . The second class are those who are ignorant of the characteristics of the race, and are the mere echoes of the first. To meet and refute these misrepresentations, and to supply a deficiency, long felt in the community, of a work containing sketches of individuals who, by their own genius, capacity and intellectual development, have surmounted the many obstacles which slavery and prejudice have thrown in their way . . . this volume was written. The characters represented in most of these biographies are for the first time put in print. The author's long sojourn in Europe, his opportunity of research amid the archives of England and France, and his visit to the West Indies, have given him the advantage of information respecting the blacks seldom acquired.[15]

William Wells Brown was probably the first Afro-

American author to receive lucrative remuneration from his writings. His books were extremely popular. "This is just the book for the hour," wrote Lewis Tappan of *The Black Man.* "It will do more for the colored man's elevation than any work yet published." The *Boston Transcript* called it "the best account of the ability of the Negro ever put in print." The *New York Herald* commented: "Mr. Brown has given us an interesting work. The subjects of the biographies are well chosen to exhibit the versatility and range of the genius of the African race. Science and Philosophy, Literature and the Arts, are shown to be richly indebted to it. Mr. Brown's book is an incontestable argument." [16] Writing in his monthly newspaper, Douglass observed:

Though Mr. Brown's book may stand alone upon its own merits, and stand strong, yet while reading its interesting pages, —abounding in fact and argument, replete with eloquence, logic, and learning,—clothed with simple yet eloquent language, it is hard to repress the inquiry, whence has this man this knowledge? He seems to have read and remembered nearly everything which has been written or said respecting the ability of the Negro, and has condensed and arranged the whole into an admirable argument, calculated both to interest and convince.[17]

Brown's largest work, *The Rising Son,* appeared in 1874 and was published as a general history of the Afro-American from his African beginnings. Although better organized than *The Black Man* and a more comprehensive history, this book still indicates Brown's lack of training. His sources are generally unreliable and too few. The work is sermonistic and uncritical. Fourteen chapters, one hundred pages, are taken to discuss the Negro in Haiti, whereas only one chapter of three pages is used by Brown to discuss the Negro in South America. Many of the chapters are of three, five, or six pages. The work is almost devoid of documentation. Yet, *The Rising Son* sold over 10,000 copies its first year.[18]

In *The Rising Son,* Brown portrays (1) an African background, (2) the slave trade, (3) the black republics of Liberia and Haiti, (4) the black man in the Revolutionary War and the War of 1812, (5) slavery in the Caribbean Islands and Latin America, (6) slavery in colonial North America, and (7) the rise of abolitionism and the Civil War. However, after the sketch of the new era, the period after the Civil War, the rest of *The Rising Son* consists of a repetition of the biographical sketches, many of which had already appeared in *The Black Man. The Rising Son* contains fifty unbalanced chapters. The interpretation, such as it is, follows the well-known abolitionist viewpoint of the unhappy slave and his cruel master. Brown dwelt on the darker aspects of slavery: beatings, sufferings, murders, rape, slave trading, and slave breeding. There is no indication that there was another aspect to slavery. Brown's history, like so much of that produced by this group, while good propaganda, is considerably below the standards of scholarship which many scholars of the period were producing.

Between the appearances of *The Black Man* and *The Rising Son,* Brown wrote *The Negro in the American Rebellion: His Heroism and His Fidelity.*[19] In this volume there is a résumé of the military services of Negroes in the American Revolutionary War, the War of 1812, and the Civil War. For his facts on the Civil War, Brown relied largely on newspapers. His data on the Revolutionary War and the War of 1812 added nothing to what Nell had already found. In the introduction he stated: "I waited patiently, before beginning this work, with the hope that someone more competent would take up the subject in hand, but up to the present, it has not been done, although many books have been written upon the rebellion."

As previously stated, Brown's writings were very popular. "He had no true historical perspective on his material," writes Loggins, "but he treated it in an informal and gossipy style," thus enhancing his readability. *The Rising*

Son, at the time it was published, "was the most complete and thorough general history of the Negro which had been produced in America, and such it remained until it was superseded in 1883." [20] One, however, should not dwell on Brown's faults as a historian. For him, "the value of history consisted primarily not in what it was but in what it did—in the extent to which it influenced the course of human affairs." [21]

WILLIAM STILL

William Still (1821–1902) was born in Burlington County, New Jersey, of parents who were ex-slaves. He became a participant in the Underground Railroad and served as a secretary for the Pennsylvania Anti-Slavery Society. In 1871 this organization disbanded and authorized Still to write an account of his experiences as a Secretary of its Vigilance Committee (its Underground Railroad arm). The result was Still's volume, *The Underground Railroad,* which appeared the next year.[22] For this work Still used letters which had been sent to him by slaves his organization had helped to escape. Many of these letters are quoted in the volume, making it a good source collection. However, it is poorly organized and crude in style. It bears interest primarily as a source from the pen of a firsthand observer of the Underground Railroad.

Still states that he first decided to begin preserving such records when his own fugitive-slave brother, looking for his parents who had escaped the South earlier, turned up in Philadelphia at the antislavery office where Still happened to be working. After hearing his brother's story of his life in bondage, Still decided to begin preserving such stories.

JOSEPH T. WILSON

After the Civil War, Joseph T. Wilson (1836–1891) became intensely interested in the past of his race. This epic
struggle in American history impressed many Negroes of
the period. Union victory was the long-sought day of Jubilee—the answer to millions of prayers, and a manifestation
that "the judgments of the Lord are true and righteous altogether." There can be little wonder that this war bred a
crop of Negro historians who used the moralistic judgments
of slavery and the war which had been characteristic of the
abolitionists.

Wilson published his first historical work in 1882. It
bore the imposing title of *Emancipation: Its Course and
Progress, from 1481 B.C. to A.D. 1875.*[23] *Emancipation* was
a very crude effort to trace some aspects of Negro history
back to what he apparently thought was the Exodus. Wilson
was honored this same year in being chosen by the Grand
Army of the Republic to write a history of his regiment in
the War. Obviously, his chances of succeeding in producing
a creditable work were greater in this area than his first
effort to cram over three thousand years of history into a
book of only two hundred and forty-two pages.

In 1888, after six years of work, *The Black Phalanx*[24] was
published. It carried a general account of the services of
black troops in the Revolutionary War, the War of 1812,
and the Civil War. Despite its many faults, two other editions appeared, a fact which attests to its success.[25]

The Black Phalanx contains nineteen chapters, fifty-six
illustrations, and an appendix. Interspersed with the chronicle of the military services is information concerning the
general economic, social, political and cultural status of
the Negro at varying times. Like most histories of the period, this work also contains lengthy sketches of outstanding Negroes. Apart from two rather long chapters which
treat the military services of Negroes in the Revolutionary

War and the War of 1812, *The Black Phalanx* is essentially
a study of the military services of Negroes during the Civil
War. The information in the first two chapters adds nothing new to the facts already revealed by Nell and Brown.

Wilson's sources are creditable. He used documents
from leading city libraries, including those at Boston, New
York, Cincinnati and New Bedford, and from various private libraries, records from the War Department, letters,
and newspapers. Wilson's lack of formal education reveals
itself in misspelled words, incorrect grammar, and poor
organization. The direct quotations are far too long and
frequent, ranging sometimes to fourteen continuous pages.
Approximately one-half of the volume consists of direct
quotations. The work carries no index. There are sixteen
chapters, with three chapters of miscellany. The chapters
are entitled:

Part I. The Wars for Independence

The War of 1775
The War of 1812

Part II. The War between the
States
Public Opinion
Recruiting and Organizing
Recruiting and Organizing in
South Carolina
Officers of the Phalanx
Department of the Gulf
The Army of the Frontier

Department of the South
The Army of the Cumberland
The Phalanx at Marion, Ten-
nessee
The Black Flag
The Phalanx in Virginia
The Roll of Honor
The Roster of the Black Pha-
lanx
The Confederate Service

Part III. Miscellany

The Phalanx at School
Benevolence and Frugality
Bibliography

Despite the high praise which the work accords the military services, one feels that this praise was deserved, and
that *The Black Phalanx* was in general rather temperately
written. The volume was well received by the public, although it was very soon superseded by George Washington
Williams's study on this topic.

GEORGE WASHINGTON WILLIAMS

George Washington Williams (1849–1891) was born at Bedford Springs, Pennsylvania, of racially mixed parentage. With scant formal education, he served in the Union Army by falsely raising his age to the minimum required. He was mustered from the service in 1865 with the rank of Sergeant-Major. Having come to like military life, he re-enlisted in the American Army and later served in the war against the usurping Maximilian.

In 1868 Williams graduated from Howard University and became a theology student at Newton Theological Seminary. He graduated in 1874. A good student, Williams was chosen to deliver a graduation oration. He spoke on the topic, "Early Christianity in Africa." Here can be seen his early interest in the background of the Negro.[26]

Within the next few years, Williams served as a Baptist minister, newspaper editor, and government clerk. Moving from New England to Cincinnati, Ohio, he served as a minister and also studied law. He was admitted to the bar and then entered politics. In 1879 he was elected to the Ohio legislature and later became Judge Advocate of the Grand Army of the Republic.

Williams became interested in writing on Negro history while doing research for an oration he was to deliver at Avondale, Ohio, on a program celebrating the one hundredth anniversary of the Declaration of Independence. His topic was to be the services of the Negro to the United States. Williams states that he was surprised to discover the abundance of material which existed on the Negro. After this oration was given, he retired from public life in order to devote all of his time to writing a general history of the Negro in the United States. After seven years of assiduous effort, he brought out his first and best work, *A History of the Negro Race in America from 1619 to 1880.*[27]

As his purpose for writing *A History of the Negro Race,* Williams wrote:

I became convinced that a history of the colored people in America was required, because of the ample historically trustworthy material at hand; because the Colored people themselves have been the most vexatious problem in North America, from the time of its discovery down to the present day; because that in every attempt upon the life of the Nation, whether by foes from without or within, the Colored people had always displayed a matchless patriotism and an incomparable heroism in the cause of Americans; and because such a history would give the world more correct ideas of the Colored people, and incite the latter to greater effort in the struggle of citizenship and manhood. The single reason that there was no history of the Negro race would have been a sufficient reason for writing one.[28]

The work, in two volumes, is divided into nine parts, with a total of sixty chapters. The first volume contains 481 pages, the first portion of which is concerned with the African background of the Negro. The second part deals with the Negro in colonial America. The remainder is concerned with the colonial era and the Revolutionary War, and carries biographical sketches of leading figures in this early part of the nation's history. The second volume treats the nineteenth century, with its sectional problems, antislavery agitation, Civil War and Reconstruction. In each volume several chapters are devoted to social and cultural history.

Some of Williams's sources were documents from the Congressional Library, Washington, D.C., the Lenox Library, New York, the Public Library, Columbus, Ohio, the War Department, the African Methodist Episcopal Church, and the Boston Public Library; the *Congressional Record* and *Congressional Globe, Journal of the Confederate Congress,* Executive Documents of the several states, manuscript information furnished by War Offices of foreign governments, orderly books of general officers, the principal histories of the war, newspapers, various other private libraries, and conversations with persons who could give him information. Williams states that he consulted over twelve thousand volumes, of which over one thousand are mentioned in *A History of the Negro Race*.[29] It can be readily seen that his was a high level of research, the like of which no Negro historian had attempted to that date. It is likely that Williams's training in law and theology helped impress upon him the need for documentation and the seeking of evidence to prove his assertions. It is doubtful whether he could have produced such good historical works without his legal and theological specialization.

In presenting his work to the public, Williams stated:

Some persons may think it irreverent to tell the truth in the plain, homely manner that characterizes my narrative; but, while I have nothing to regret in this particular, I can assure them that I have been actuated by none other spirit than that of candor. Where I have used documents it was with a desire to escape the charge of superficiality. If, however, I may be charged with seeking to escape the labor incident to thorough digestion, I answer, that, while men with the reputation of Bancroft and Hildreth could pass unchallenged when disregarding largely the use of documents and the citation of authorities, I would find myself challenged by a large number of critics.[30]

Williams made much of his desire to be objective and to tell nothing but the truth. "Not as a blind panegyrist of my race," he wrote, "nor as a partisan apologist, but from a love for '*the truth of history*,' I have striven to record the truth, the whole truth, and nothing but the truth. I have not striven to revive sectional animosities or race prejudices. . . . My whole aim has been to write a thoroughly trustworthy history; and what I have written, if it have no other merit, is reliable." [31]

He entitled the first chapter "The Unity of Mankind." This eleven-page chapter is based almost completely on the story of creation as recorded in the Book of Genesis, and is an effort to prove that all of mankind springs from "one flesh, one blood." The next ten chapters are devoted to the Negro in antiquity. These are good chapters which carry information about the Ashanti Empire, African languages and customs, the kingdoms of Benin, Dahomey, Yoruba, The Republic of Liberia, and Sierra Leone. This section on the ancient period is included "to explain and explode two erroneous ideas,—the curse of Canaan, and the theory that the Negro is a distinct species,—that were educated into our white countrymen during the long and starless night of the bondage of the Negro." [32]

Williams reveals his moralistic conception of history when he attempts to explain the condition of the Negro in the modern period. "It is our firm conviction," he writes, ". . . that the Creator gave all the nations arts and sciences. Where nations have turned aside to idolatry they have lost their civilization. The Canaanites, Jebusites, Hivites, etc. . . . were the descendants of Canaan; and the only charge the Lord brought against them when he commanded Joshua to exterminate them was, that they were his enemies . . ." Applying this reasoning, Williams finds that throughout history, the Negro has played no commanding role. On this, he writes:

His [the Negro] position, it is true, in all history up to the present day, has been accidental, incidental and collateral; . . . His brightest days were when history was an infant; and, since he early turned from God, he has found the cold face of hate and the hurtful hand of the Caucasian against him. The Negro type is the result of degradation. It is nothing more than the lowest strata of the African race. . . . His blood infected with the poison of his low habitation, his body shrivelled by disease, his intellect veiled in pagan superstitions, the noblest yearnings of his soul strangled at birth by the savage passions of a nature abandoned to sensuality,—the poor Negro of Africa deserves more our pity than our contempt.[33]

It is precisely the above type of reasoning and thinking

which reveals Williams, despite his commendable researches, as a scholar who belongs with the earlier writers. Only in the area of research does Williams represent a maturation or coming of age of Negro historiography. He accepts the idea that the Afro-American is very religious and explains this religious nature as the result of a reaction against extreme paganism. "And now that he is an American citizen,—the condition and circumstances which rendered his piety appropriate abolished,—he is likely to move over to an extreme rationalism." [34]

Williams's condemnation of slavery is eloquent.

> Slavery was . . . "the sum of all villanies"—the blackest curse that ever scourged the earth. To buy and sell human beings; to tear from the famishing breast of the mother her speechless child; to separate the husband from the wife of his heart; to wring riches from the unpaid toil of human beings; to tear down the family altar and let lecherous beasts, who claim the name of "Christian," run over defenseless womanhood as swine over God's altar!—is there anything worse, do you ask? Yes! To work a human being from youth to old age, to appropriate the labor of that being exclusively, to rob it of the blessings of this life, to poison every domestic charity, to fetter the intellect by the power of fatal ignorance, to withhold the privileges of the gospel of love; and then when the hollow cough comes under an inclement sky, when the shadows slant, when the hand trembles, when the gait is shuffling, when the ear is deaf, the eye dim, when desire faileth,—then to turn that human being out to die is by far the profoundest crime man can be guilty of in his dealing with mankind. [35]

Williams was an anglophobe, probably because of Britain's role in the slave trade and because of British imperialism. After describing the exploit of Peter Salem killing Major Pitcairn at the battle of Bunker Hill, and the death of Crispus Attucks during the Boston Massacre, Williams writes:

> Significant indeed that a Negro was the first to open the hostilities between Great Britain and the colonies,—the first

to pour out his blood as a precious libation on the altar of a people's rights; and that here, at Bunker Hill, when the crimson and fiery tide of battle seemed to be running hard against the small band of colonists, a Negro soldier's steady musket brought down the haughty form of the arch-rebel, and turned victory to the weak! England had loaded the African with chains, and doomed him to perpetual bondage in the North American colonies.[36]

Williams takes the same view on the abolition of slavery which Du Bois later champions, that is, that slavery should have been abolished when the nation was founded. "It was then and there," writes Williams of the Constitutional Convention, "that the hydra of slavery struck its fangs into the Constitution; and, once inoculated with the poison of the monster, the government was only able to purify itself in the flames of a great civil war." [37]

Williams explained his exclusion of a thorough section on the Reconstruction Period on the grounds that he was preparing a two-volume work devoted exclusively to that period.[38] This separate study on the Reconstruction Period apparently was never published. His chapters on the thirteen colonies are very good, especially those which deal with New England. His great interest in religion is shown in frequent allusions to the Bible and to the fact that he devoted one chapter each to the three leading Negro denominations, the two black Methodist churches and the Baptists. It is probable, however, that Williams's preoccupation with things legal and military did not spring alone from his own experiences, as John Hope Franklin seems to think.[39] It must also be remembered that much of the history being produced by white historians in the late nineteenth century had a strong constitutional and military orientation.

This work was very well received. *The Magazine of American History* considered it as "perhaps the most creditable performance that has yet come from the pen of any representative of the African race in America," and stated that "It is the result of long and conscientious study by a vigorous and patient mind. It shows much labored research, and if there are those who could have performed the task better, few could have worked more enthusiastically or produced more acceptable general results." [40] The *Literary World,* of Boston, regarded the work as "upon the whole the most nearly satisfactory continuous account yet written of the African in America." [41] The *Atlantic Monthly* expressed special praise for Williams's chapters on slavery in colonial America.[42] Almost all reviewers criticized Williams for his florid style and generally poor documentation. *The Nation* was highly critical of the work on practically all counts, stating that "Its total effect is that of cramming without the power to digest or to arrange," and that the work "must be judged the crude performance of a mind in no way exceptionally endowed." [43] The *Kansas City Review of Science,* however, correctly observed that the work "will be an authority on the subject treated until a better one is produced, which is likely to be a long time." [44]

The work catapulted Williams into the national limelight, increasing his speaking engagements and leading to his appointment by President Arthur in 1885 as American Minister to Haiti. However, President Cleveland came into office before Williams had received his commission and refused to issue it.[45]

Encouraged by the success of this general history of the race, and with his interest in things military whetted by his own experiences and research, Williams turned to writing an account of the services of black troops in the Civil War. After five years of toil, during which he experienced dire financial straits because he gave up other profitable pursuits, Williams brought out *A History of the Negro Troops in the War of the Rebellion, 1861–1865.*[46] While laudatory of the Negro soldier, and written in his oratorical style, the work is heavily documented. His sources include documents from the Library of Congress, War Department, *Journal of the Confederate Congress,* State Executive documents, orderly books of general officers, conversations with both Negro veterans and officers under whom they served, leading newspapers, and published speeches.[47]

Knowing that he had allowed his emotions considerable sway in the volume, Williams wrote in explanation:

> I have spoken plainly, it is true, but I have not extenuated nor set down aught in malice. My language is not plainer than the truth, my philippic is not more cruel than the crimes exposed, my rhetoric is not more fiery than the trials through which these black troops passed, nor my conclusions without warrant of truth or justification of evidence.[48]

In committing this volume to the public, he hoped "that the day will hasten when there shall be no North, no South, no black, no white, but all be American citizens with equal duties and rights." [49]

This work has sixteen chapters. The first two treat the Negro soldier in antiquity and modern Europe. It was necessary, Williams felt, to "bring together in one work the necessary facts to understand their military capacity." [50] Other chapters are:

Antecedent Facts—Foreshadowing Events
Military Rendition of Slaves
The Negro Volunteer
Military Status of Negro Troops
Negro Idiosyncracies
The Outlook
Negro Troops in Battle—Department of the South

In the Mississippi Valley
In the Army of the Potomac
The Fort Pillow Massacre
In the Army of the Cumberland
In the Army of the James
As Prisoners of War
The Cloud of Witnesses

As with his general history, and as is characteristic of much of the history written by Negroes in the nineteenth century, Williams starts out documenting fairly thoroughly. After the first third of the volume, however, one finds almost no documentation at all.

A total of six chapters is devoted to the Civil War battle record of the Negro. Having served in many of the engagements himself, and having visited scenes and talked with participants in the battles, Williams is very vivid in description. The final two chapters of the volume are replete with statements from officers, the press, and public officials which praise the services of these troops.

Williams was aware that there is a danger of violating the canons of objectivity when writing on events in which one has participated. He stated that he had "relied very little on personal knowledge, preferring always to follow the official record." [51]

Negro Troops was well received by the critics. The author was again criticized for his flowery language and poor handling of materials. Since Joseph T. Wilson's *Black Phalanx* came off the press at about the same time as *Negro Troops* did, neither had the exclusive attention of the public. Reviewing both works together, *The Nation* said:

Both of these books show honest intentions and a certain amount of praiseworthy diligence . . . but both show a want of method and an inability to command their own materials, so that they leave the reader with a renewed interest in the subject, but with a very imperfect sense of clear comprehension. Each gives some facts and documents which the other omits. Of the two, Mr. Williams's book is the more grandiloquent, while Mr. Wilson is grandiloquent once for all by yielding to the whim of calling the troops a "phalanx." [52]

John Hope Franklin accuses Williams of "hypercriticism and iconoclasm" and states that he "viciously attacked the slightest inaccuracy which he happened to find in the writings of others." [53] This was due, according to Franklin, to Williams's "intense devotion to objectivity." However, since Williams, like so many of the other early black historians, was interested primarily in chronicling only the *achievements* of the race, his "intense devotion to objectivity" may be held suspect by some.

Vernon Loggins noted that only two Negro writers before Williams—and they were not historians—"stand out as better writers of prose," and that "emotional effect was Williams's highest stylistic achievement and at the same time his chief pitfall. He was too articulate." [54] One might add to this, that no historian has yet brought out a general history of the race in America of comparable scope and based on such broad research. Benjamin Brawley, a keen student of Negro literature and culture, writing in 1921, called Williams's general study "the epoch-making work in history," and stated that "some of its pages . . . have been superseded, but his work is even yet the great storehouse for students of Negro history." [55] Untrained in the field, it is only natural that Williams violated many of the canons of historical scholarship and writing. His documentation is faulty. Where we would expect him to cite his authority he frequently does not. His emotional and oratorical style frequently violates the objectivity which is expected of the historian. Yet, this penchant gave to his work an added readability and interest. His philosophy of history is unacceptable today. "In the interpretation of history," wrote Williams, "the plans of God must be discovered." [56] Still, his prodigious research set a standard of scholarship which *all* historians may well emulate. And many of his faults were characteristic of some of the best white scholars of his day, such as Channing and Bancroft.

BENJAMIN GRIFFITH BRAWLEY

Benjamin G. Brawley (1882–1939) was born in Columbia, South Carolina. His father is thought to have been the first person to write a history of the Negro Baptist Church, so Benjamin Brawley came somewhat naturally to his interest in history.

In 1901 Brawley graduated from Morehouse College. In 1906 he received another bachelor's degree, this time from the University of Chicago. Two years later he was awarded a master's degree in English Literature, from Harvard University. After teaching briefly at Shaw University, Raleigh, North Carolina, and Howard University, Washington, D.C., Brawley returned to Morehouse, his *alma mater*. He remained there from 1912 to 1932. In 1933 he moved back to Howard University as professor of English Literature.[57]

Although ordained a Baptist minister in 1920, Brawley was primarily a teacher and a scholar. In 1913 he published *A Short History of the American Negro.*[58] Using secondary sources almost exclusively, and documenting scantily, Brawley obviously was writing a "popular history."

In 1921, Brawley's most popular work was published, *A Social History of the American Negro.*[59] This volume was based on more extensive research than his *Short History.* Among his sources were documents from the New York Colonization Society, *The Crisis* magazine, *Journal of Negro History, Negro Year Book,* and many secondary sources and newspapers. The volume bore the subtitle: *Being a History of the Negro Problem in the U.S., Including a History and Study of the Republic of Liberia.* Brawley called this book "the first formal effort toward a History of the Negro Problem in America." [60] Yet, apart from lengthy discussions of Indian-Negro relations, and of northern and western migrations in the twentieth century and the resultant urban problems, this volume carries little that one would not then find in already published general histories.

In a review of *A Social History of the American Negro,* Carter Woodson called Brawley a "novice" in the field of history. He stated that too many novices were attempting to write on the history of the race, apparently with the belief that "it is an easy task to write a work" in this field. Scoring Brawley's lack of formal preparation in the field, Woodson states that neither in this work, nor in his earlier *Short History of the American Negro* and *The Negro in Literature and Art,* does Brawley "exhibit the knowledge required by the standards of present-day historiography." He further stated that Brawley's *Social History* "lacks proportion, style and accuracy." [61]

Despite the general truth of Woodson's assertions, one must be mindful that Woodson was judging Brawley's works from the standpoint of the university-trained specialist in history. It is a significant commentary on the growth of black history that by the end of the second decade of the twentieth century there should exist Afro-American scholars who would vociferously denounce historical writing which did not measure up to the most exacting criteria.

In organization, and largely content, Brawley imitated the pattern set by the writers we have so far discussed. His research was superficial and he indulged heavily in the biographical pattern of writing which was so characteristic of the Beginning School. Also, his philosophy of history was the same as that held by George Washington Williams. It is for these reasons that he is listed with this School, although chronologically his writings fall in the period of later historians.

Brawley's *The Negro in Literature and Art* had appeared in 1910 as a sixty-page pamphlet. In 1918 this work appeared, expanded to one hundred and seventy-six pages.[62] Even Woodson had praise for it.[63] The previous year Professor Brawley had published a history of his *alma mater,* Morehouse College,[64] and in 1918 he also published a brief work entitled *Africa and the World War.*[65] Here he traced the reshuffling of colonies in Africa which resulted from the war, and pleaded for a greater interest in Africa on the part of Afro-Americans. He also stated that the European colonial powers should improve the quality and quantity of education being offered to Africans.

Brawley was probably the first black historian to essay a non-Negro topic. In 1921 he wrote *A Short History of the English Drama*,[66] and in 1932 published a *History of the English Hymn*.[67] His *Short History of the English Drama* is a critical survey of this field which utilizes the biographical approach. The works of each dramatist are listed and analyzed. Brawley utilized the same approach in *The History of the English Hymn*, where two hundred and forty-five English hymns are handled.

Differing from the rather standard pattern of most Negro historians, Brawley produced two works of biography.[68] In this same biographical vein, he contributed sketches of outstanding Negroes to the *Dictionary of American Biography*,[69] and many articles to leading publications in the United States. Still utilizing the biographical approach, in 1919 Brawley brought out a small work entitled *Social History of American Negro Women of Achievement*,[70] and on the same pattern, he published in 1937 *Negro Builders and Heroes*[71] and *The Negro Genius: a New Appraisal of the Achievement of the American Negro in Literature and the Fine Arts*.[72]

In 1935 he published *Early Negro American Writers*, selections with critical introductions.[73] He also produced several other works which are nonhistorical in nature, and served as editor of the *Home Mission Review* from 1927–1930.

Perhaps the chief criticism that can be leveled at Benjamin Brawley as historian is his generally weak use of sources. This and other faults no doubt can be attributed to his lack of training in this discipline, as well as to the fact that he was prolific as a writer. He appears to have worked hurriedly. However, on the plus side, Brawley was detached and free from emotionalism, and was a skilled manipulator of the English language, something which cannot be said for most historians of any period, white or black. These attributes, plus the fact that he was prolific in the field of historical scholarship, and that he tried to examine new and unexplored areas, give Brawley a high place among Negro historians.[74]

BOOKER TALIAFERRO WASHINGTON

Booker T. Washington (1856–1915) is the most famous of all American Negroes. He is best known as the educator and spokesman for the race during the difficult days which succeeded the Reconstruction Period. Born a slave in Virginia near the middle of the nineteenth century, he finished Hampton Institute and shortly thereafter taught school in the state of Alabama. He founded Tuskegee Institute and championed an industrial-type education for the Negro and played down the race issue as a *modus vivendi* for the two races. This philosophy was classically expressed in his famed "Atlanta Exposition" Speech. This speech catapulted Washington into the national limelight.[75] Among the many things which Americans demanded of him was that he write a history of the Negro.

In 1900, Booker Washington's autobiography, *Up From Slavery*, appeared.[76] It is one of the most widely read autobiographies ever penned by any American. After the appearance of *Up From Slavery*, Washington wrote two other works which may be considered further chapters in his autobiography. They were *Working with the Hands* and *My Larger Education*.[77]

For the "American Crisis Biographies" series, edited by Ellis P. Oberholtzer, Washington wrote a biography of Frederick Douglass.[78] Using only sources already familiar to Douglass biographers, Washington added no new information to that already available. Still, it was a contribution to the literature on Douglass that a Negro of the stature of Booker T. Washington should endeavor to interpret his life. The volume is temperate and well written in Washington's always-appealing style.

Washington's most extensive attempt in the field of history was a two-volume work entitled *The Story of the Negro*,[79] which appeared in 1909. Loggins stated in 1931 that it was "probably the most widely read general history of the American Negro which has ever been published." [80] It is doubtful whether this assertion is valid considering the great reception accorded Carter Woodson's *The Negro in Our History*.

The experience of writing his autobiography had imbued Washington with the idea of writing a general history of the race.[81] Having little time to devote to the task, and perhaps realizing his lack of preparation, Washington admits that he did not essay either a formal or detailed history of the race.[82] He utilized freely the labor of various of his employees at Tuskegee in both the research and the writing of the volume.[83]

Washington's *Story of the Negro* has the organization typical of the earlier general histories of the Negro. First the African background is traced, then the period of slavery, and finally, the Civil War, Reconstruction, and post-Reconstruction periods. Volume One carries the story to the Civil War. Volume Two covers the Civil War, Reconstruction and post-Reconstruction periods. Written in characteristically straightforward and simple manner, *The Story of the Negro* is a chronicle of the continuous upward progress of an unfortunate people. Throughout the work may be discerned Washington's faith in America and in a final peaceful solution of the race problems.

The best social history of the Negro is found in Volume Two, where such topics as "Negro Crime," "Negro Secret Societies," "Negro Business," "Negro Literature," and the "Negro Church," are treated. These sections anticipate Brawley's *Social History of the American Negro* as well as the studies which Du Bois was to conduct at Atlanta University and Woodson was to carry out through the Association for the study of Negro Life and History.

The work is poorly documented and there is some evidence of carelessness in writing. Based largely on the history by George Washington Williams and other secondary works, *The Story of the Negro* added neither new information to this subject nor any new interpretation other than the pattern of continuous upward progress of the race. It was, however, less critical of the slave regime than had been the case with writings by previous Negro historians. Appearing at the height of Washington's popularity, the work was very well received by the public. Carter Woodson considered the effort, because of its emphasis on social and economic affairs, a valuable supplement to the history of George Washington Williams.[84]

Revealing his philosophy of history and the "race problem," Washington wrote: "The story of the negro, in the last analysis, is simply the story of the man who is farthest down. As he raises himself, he raises every other man who is above him. . . . We have had problems, it is true, but instead of despairing . . . we should, as a race, thank God that we have a problem. . . . It is only by meeting and manfully facing hard, stubborn and difficult problems that races, like individuals, are made strong." [85] Again he wrote in a chapter entitled "The Negro's Place in American Life," that "the Negro must, at all hazards and in all times and places, avoid crossing the colour line." "To me," he concluded, "the history of the Negro people in America seems like the story of a great adventure, in which . . . I am glad to have had a share." [86]

THE BLACK HISTORIAN:
The Middle Group, Builders of Black Studies, 1896–1930

Overleaf:
Top: Carter G. Woodson; bottom: W. E. B. Du Bois

Introduction

The last decade of the nineteenth century represents a turning point in the history of the black man in America. With the leadership of Booker T. Washington and the political disfranchisement of the freedmen in the South there was a subsiding of the fear by whites of Negro equality or domination. The previous generation of Afro-Americans had weathered successfully the critical period of adjustment to the new role of freedmen, and though the race was still beset with problems of poverty, poor health, bad housing, inadequate educational facilities, and racism, the economic wealth of the group had increased to surprising proportions.

Educational opportunities had also increased. In 1880 only thirteen Negro colleges existed in the South. These were largely colleges or universities in name only. A decade later the number of such institutions had increased to twenty-two, and each year saw an increasing number of college graduates. By 1936, 43,821 Negroes had received college degrees, 153 of which were Doctors of Philosophy. By

1945, 192 had been elected to Phi Beta Kappa, and by 1943, at least 381 had received doctorate degrees.[1]

Along with other forces, the mass migration to cities, southern and northern, during the period 1880–1920 produced an outburst of cultural activities, and various persons began to write of the "New Negro." Between 1900 and 1920 both the Urban League and The National Association for the Advancement of Colored People were born. Like Woodson's Association for the Study of Negro Life and History, each had its official journal. In the 1920s, pride of race helped produce not only the phenomenon known as "Garveyism," but the Harlem Literary Renaissance as well. Still, the "New Negro" was only the "old" with more education and maturity. "The younger generation," wrote Alain Locke in 1925, "has achieved an objective attitude toward life. Race, for them, is but an idiom of experience, a sort of added enriching adventure and discipline, giving subtler overtones to life, making it more beautiful and interesting even if more poignantly so." [2]

The turn of the century saw a tremendous upsurge in Negro progress. Alain Locke, first black Rhodes Scholar, urged the black intellectual and artist to be objective about race, to view their efforts not as utilitarian polemics, but in the final analysis as everlasting works of scholarship and art. He called for the highest devotion to truth and beauty. Yet Locke saw that even science and art, by revealing that Negro efforts could be successful on the highest planes of man's spirit, could and would be effective weapons in the fight for full citizenship. Du Bois had already become the first Afro-American holder of a doctorate in the social sciences, and his dissertation on the *Suppression of the African Slave-Trade to the United States* and his epic sociological study, *The Philadelphia Negro*, had won him praise from the nation's leading scholars. Booker T. Washington had achieved an international reputation as an educator and race spokesman, while Paul

Laurence Dunbar had won acclaim as a top-ranking poet. No longer were the productions of Afro-Americans to be considered good simply because they had been done by a member of a group recently emancipated from slavery. White America, and Negroes themselves, were demanding that the race measure up to the standards set for all scholars and artists, a standard many white scholars did not live up to. William Dean Howells, a leading literary critic of the period, expressed this point of view in introducing to the public a collection of poems by Paul Laurence Dunbar. "The world is too old now, and I find myself too much of its mood, to care for the work of a poet because he is black, because his father and mother were slaves." [3]

It was in this climate that *black scholars* began to uncover for the Negro his creditable past. While it is true that Nell, Brown, Wilson, Williams, and others of the earlier writers gave preeminent and almost sole consideration to the creditable aspects of the black man's history, they appear to have been motivated mainly by a desire to refute the prejudiced teachings of the slavocracy, and to justify their claims of equality. But they were not reacting against any large body of so-called scientific historical literature which was prejudicial against the race, as were members of the middle group.

By the first decade of the twentieth century, black scholars with graduate degrees in the social sciences were beginning slowly to emerge from American universities. Despite the fact that this was the era when the scientific history championed by Leopold von Ranke held sway, the biological and sociological teachings which these young Negro scholars received were deeply tinged with ideas of superior and inferior races. Rampant nationalism, Darwin's theories of natural selection, as well as the actual world supremacy of European civilization, all contributed to the prevalence of such notions. Count Joseph Arthur de Gobineau had given the idea of Aryan supremacy its classic expression in his famous *Essay on the Inequality of the Hu-*

man Races, published in 1853–55, and despite the fact that such Germanic writers as J. G. Cuno, Theodor Posche, and Carl Penka had all demonstrated during the last quarter of the nineteenth century the fallaciousness of most of Gobineau's premises, and that the American scholar W. Z. Ripley did the same thing in his *The Races of Europe,* published in 1899, the myth of a scientific basis for white supremacy persisted. That Mussolini and Hitler could gain such wide acceptance for this myth as late as the 1930s and 1940s is proof of the tenacity of some false notions.

Sensing that there was no basis in fact for these "scientific" proofs of the superiority and inferiority of races, the university-trained Negro reacted very strongly against this aspect of his education. White southern historians and historians of the South from other sections were just then delving into the slavery, Civil War, and Reconstruction questions in an effort to change the southern image projected by northern historians of the Nationalist School. Many views held by these historians of the South—led by such scholars as William Archibald Dunning and his students who left Columbia University with new inspiration, and Ulrich Bonnell Phillips and his students at the University of Michigan—aroused the ire of Negro historical scholars. These white historians either asserted or implied that, by and large, the bondsmen had been contented if not happy [thus inferring—at least to many Negro scholars— that slavery was a natural condition for the race], that the freedman had done practically nothing to acquire his freedom, and that the race had made no significant contribution to world civilization. Especially were these revisionist historians of the South vociferous in their condemnation of the effort made during the Reconstruction period to elevate the freedman to be the political equal of whites.

University training, together with the large body of racially biased literature which was then pouring from the press, had great influence in shaping the character and course of Negro historiography for almost three decades.

Beginning with W. E. B. Du Bois in 1896, until the Nazis gave all race-supremacy claims such a black eye, Negro historical scholars were primarily concerned with refuting these charges. In the absence of adequate scientific data in other fields for a strong refutation, these men sought in the field of history the needed evidence. While still a student at Harvard, Carter Woodson came to doubt the accuracy of some of these teachings and challenged them then and there.[4] He felt, even then, that there was enough scientific data to support a rebuttal of the claims of racial inferiority and superiority. Although Du Bois, with eloquent pride, doubted the truth of these assertions, it was not until some years after his student days that he became convinced that the scientific data for a successful refutation was available.[5] Both Woodson and Du Bois led an unrelenting crusade to overthrow all charges that the Negro was the inferior of any race, and to prove their case "from the record." After their initial successes in gaining a favorable audience, other young scholars, motivated by the same factors, but no longer doubting that in history a successful refutation could be found, became virtual disciples of the two leaders, especially of Woodson. While Du Bois went off into other pursuits, only to return now and then to history, Dr. Woodson stuck to this discipline and organized a movement. His leadership permeated to the grass roots of Negro life, and in his army marched not only a sizable number of university-trained scholars, but a large number of laymen as well.

These historians were convinced that their protestations were objective and scientific. Supported by footnotes, backed by doctorates from leading universities, they were sure that they proved their case on the equality of races. Though the writing was better in many particulars, their history was sometimes scarcely less propagandistic than that of the writers discussed earlier.

Because it now had the task of answering prejudiced scholars, black history took on a new perspective. Some readers tired of the bitterness and gloom which was to be found in what they felt should be dispassionate presentations of historical findings. Lawrence D. Reddick, a black historian, cried out for a cessation of interest in the "slavery theme." A very friendly and well-meaning professor once advised a black graduate student not to become a specialist in Negro history because it tends, he stated, to make one bitter. "You will be drinking your own poison." Yet it is highly doubtful that preoccupation with Negro history *per se* has made any scholar bitter. The assumed bitterness of some black historians sprang, not from Negro history itself, but from resentment at teachings and statements by "authorities" concerning the racial inferiority of the group.

Both Du Bois and Woodson followed somewhat the same approach in refuting the claims of racial superiority and inferiority. Both entered into a series of sociological-historical studies which covered almost every aspect of Negro life in the United States. Both sought in the African background something of a golden past. Both came to be keenly aware of economic forces in history, although moral forces continued to loom large in their *Weltanschauungen*. Both were far more prolific than any Negro historian before or since, and both felt it necessary to adhere rigidly to the canons of objectivity and scientific procedure. Together with their admirers and disciples, these two men "made" modern Negro historiography. They founded journals, wrote, and spoke in behalf of the newer outlook on race and the achievements of the Negro. They were remarkably successful.

By 1910 persons who dreamed of Negro participation in the mainstream of American life had placed their faith in a variety of means to effect this end. There had been an age of appeal to the national conscience and ideals, while the Civil War saw Americans of all colors resort to arms in an effort to realize some aspects of their social ideals. Confidence in the political path which rose and fell in many Negro breasts with the triumph and demise of Radical Reconstruction was followed by faith in education, emigration to the North or West, the Labor movement, socialism, or the Booker T. Washington-type Gospel of Wealth. Legal-redress organizations had been formed and proponents of a Talented Tenth ideal were to have their day. Throughout, there were many Afro-Americans who were sure that the best thing to do about the race problem was to "leave it in the hands of the Lord."

Thus it was in an atmosphere pregnant with proposals and programs for solving the nation's color problem that twentieth-century Negro historiography was born. While freedom was the primary aim of the Beginning School, equality of citizenship rights was to be a main goal of the writers now discussed—The Middle Group.

4

W. E. B. DU BOIS
Writing with a Sword in His Hand

For fifty years, with a pen dipped in gall, he has written in trenchant, classic English what he has deeply felt and deeply studied . . . his personal manner is purely scholarly. A little vanity perhaps appears in his neat, well-tailored clothes, in his nicely groomed hands and his carefully tended van dyke beard. But chiefly he is the dignified, restrained, almost shy, gentleman from New England. While he has hundreds of devoted admirers he has not attracted warm friends.[1]

Thus reads one reasonably accurate estimate of the personality and character of William Edward Burghardt Du Bois (1868–1963). The manner in which a scholar may attain such a large measure of notoriety and fame makes an interesting tale and reveals at the outset, perhaps, that such a person did not confine his activities solely, or even largely, to scholarship.

Du Bois was born in Great Barrington, Massachusetts, of black and French ancestry. There were few blacks in his home town and Du Bois was always proud of his ancestry.[2]

His mother died shortly after his graduation from high school, but Du Bois was able to enter Fisk University, Nashville, Tennessee, because a minister secured the necessary funds from his church members. Du Bois had dreamed of attending Harvard University, and went to Fisk only because this was the desire of the group financing his education.[3]

In his early years in Massachusetts, Du Bois was unaware of the prejudice to which black people were subjected in most parts of the United States. "Whatever of racial feeling gradually crept into my life," he later wrote, "its effect upon me in these earlier days was rather one of exaltation and high disdain. They were the losers who did not ardently court me and not I, which seemed to be proven by the fact that I had no difficulty in outdoing them in nearly all competition, especially intellectual." [4]

His experiences at Fisk University made Du Bois self-consciously a black man as his home town had never done. While there he even learned to "accept" segregation, and this, he states, helped him to accept the segregation which he later experienced at Harvard University.[5] At Fisk he also developed an interest in writing and public speaking, edited the school paper, became "an impassioned orator," and acquired an attitude of belligerence toward the color bar. This belligerence was to grow until it became the motor force of his entire life. "In my life," he writes in his autobiography, "the chief fact has been race—not so much scientific race, as that deep conviction of myriads of men that congenital differences among the masses of human beings absolutely condition the individual destiny of every member of a group. Into the spiritual provincialism of this belief I have been born and this fact has guided, embittered, illuminated and enshrouded my life." [6] Here lies the key to an understanding of the career of this genius.

The life of W. E. B. Du Bois is an outburst of literary and organizational genius, highly reminiscent of Voltaire, against the "race issue." In some ways this limited interest of such a born scholar represents a tragedy in the history of American letters.

Du Bois graduated from Fisk University in 1888. He wrote on Otto von Bismarck for his graduation paper. Bismarck was then his ideal because this leader had used force to make a nation out of a bickering people. Upon graduating, he applied for and received a scholarship to Harvard University. As a student there, he met such famous teachers as William James, George Santayana, Albert Bushnell Hart, and Justin Winsor. Majoring in history and the social sciences, Du Bois was one of Professor Hart's "favorite pupils." By this time the young scholar had become keenly conscious of race. He steered clear of members of the majority group. "In general," he writes, "I asked nothing of Harvard but the tutelage of teachers and the freedom of the library. I was quite voluntarily and willingly outside its social life. . . . For the most part, I do not doubt that I was voted a somewhat selfish and self-centered 'grind' with a chip on my shoulder and a sharp tongue." [7]

In 1890 he took his bachelor's degree from Harvard. One of six commencement speakers, he used the topic "Jefferson Davis," although this historic personage represented no hero to Du Bois. A fellowship made it possible for him to remain at Harvard, and the following year he received his M.A. degree. His thesis was "The Suppression of the African Slave Trade from Africa to the United States." At this time Du Bois received a Slater Fund Award to study abroad, and in 1892 he sailed for Germany. At the University of Berlin he studied under Treitschke, Weber, and Schmoller.[8] Thus Du Bois, at Harvard and later in Germany, had the opportunity to study under scholars who were inaugurating the era of "the Scientific School" of history. One cannot doubt that the stimulation derived from studying with such scholars as these fired his ever-present ambition to great heights.

Du Bois had not yet become an economic determinist.

Of the impact of his study abroad on his philosophy of history, he later wrote that it helped him begin "to see the race problem in America, the problem of the peoples of Africa and Asia, and the political development of Europe as one." "I began," he continues, "to unite my economics and politics; but I still assumed that in these groups of activities and forces, the political realm was dominant." [9]

After two years of study in Germany, and travel over most of Europe, he returned to the United States to utilize his thorough training as a college teacher. Writing his dissertation on the same topic which he used for his master's degree, he was awarded a Ph.D. from Harvard in 1895. His first teaching position was at Wilberforce University, a Negro college in Ohio. Here he remained for only two years. He left because his duties were largely limited to teaching classical languages, while he wanted to teach the social sciences.[10] Then followed a year as a graduate assistant at the University of Pennsylvania, a position awarded him in order that he might make a sociological study of Philadelphia's black population. This study appeared in 1899 as an epochal work, *The Philadelphia Negro*. Then followed thirteen years of teaching and scholarly activity at Atlanta University in Georgia.

At the beginning of his teaching career, Du Bois was gripped by the empirical method. "I was going to study the facts," he wrote, "any and all facts, concerning the American Negro and his plight, and by measurement and comparison and research, work up to any valid generalization which I could. I entered this primarily with the utilitarian object of reform and uplift; but nevertheless, I wanted to do the work with scientific accuracy." [11]

With an eighteenth-century faith in the efficacy of education, Du Bois began his teaching career with the hope of improving race relations through education. "The world was thinking wrong about race," he opined, "because it did not know. The ultimate evil was stupidity.

The cure for it was knowledge based on scientific investigation." Also, democratic principles and practices were a part of his articles of faith. "My attention from the first," he wrote, "was focused on democracy and democratic development and upon the problem of the admission of my people into the freedom of democracy." [12]

While at Atlanta University Du Bois had his greatest success as a teacher and scholar. There he annually edited the "Studies of Negro Problems," the famed Atlanta University Studies, which appeared from 1896 to 1914. Reminiscent of the surveys of Negro life which Carter G. Woodson was conducting through the Association for the Study of Negro Life and History, these researches covered reports on crime, health, business activities, landholding, professional groups, and education.

Criticism of his growing radicalism on the race issue slowly caused Dr. Du Bois to give up classroom teaching. He took a lead in differing with the preachments of Booker T. Washington to the effect that the education of the Negro should be centered largely on manual training and that the race should concentrate on achieving economic security almost to the exclusion of interest and participation in any movement for political and social equality. His outspoken opposition to these ideas brought Du Bois into conflict with what he termed the "Tuskegee Machine." According to Du Bois, this one-man "machine" of Mr. Washington dominated all major grants and other aid to Negro colleges. His opposition to the famed founder of Tuskegee Institute was dangerous business. "It seemed to many who cared for this iconoclast," writes a Du Bois biographer, "that his opposition to Washington would be his undoing. On the contrary it was his making. For he brought together the colored men and women of the country whose opinions he voiced." [13]

From classroom teaching, in 1910 Dr. Du Bois became Director of Publicity and Research of the newly founded National Association for the Advancement of Colored

People. He had aided greatly in the founding of this organization. "My career as a scientist," he wrote, "was to be swallowed up in my role as master of propaganda. This was not wholly to my liking. I was no natural leader of men. I could not slap people on the back and make friends of strangers. . . . Nevertheless, having put my hand to the plow, I had to go on." [14] He later said: "I did not hesitate because I could not. . . . My thoughts, the thoughts of Washington . . . and others, were the expression of social forces more than of our own minds." [15]

Du Bois slowly evolved in his thinking from a position of viewing the "race problem" as one peculiar to the Negro in the United States, to an internationalist outlook. On this point, he wrote: "At first . . . my criticism was confined to the relation of my people to the world movement. I was not questioning the world movement in itself. What the white world was doing, its goals and ideals, I had not doubted were quite right. What was wrong was that I and people like me and thousands of others who might have ability and inspiration, were refused permission to be a part of this world." [16] The success of the Russian Revolution of 1917, plus a visit to the Soviet Union by Du Bois, caused him to change this thinking.

Just as his earlier radicalism caused him to give up classroom teaching, after becoming a convert to the Marxist viewpoint, his now-altered ideas on the race issue caused Du Bois to give up his work with the NAACP. He states that by 1930 he had become convinced "that the basic policies and ideals" of the Association were in need of change. "In a world where economic dislocation had become so great as in ours," he continued, "a mere appeal based on the old liberalism, a mere appeal to justice and further effort at legal decision, was missing the essential need; that . . . essential need was to guard and better the chances of Negroes, educated and ignorant, to earn a living, safeguard their income, and raise the level of their employment. I did not believe that a further prolongation

of looking for salvation from the whites was feasible." [17]
To some extent, Booker Washington, with whom Du Bois
had disagreed so violently, had anticipated this economic
determinism in his own program for racial uplift.

Du Bois started advocating a movement in which all
Negroes in this country would organize their producing
and purchasing activities in nationwide cooperatives. He
was advocating socialism for the United States. The Negro
was to socialize his activities in conformity with the coming pattern. The success of the Russian Revolution of 1917
had convinced Du Bois that socialism represented, as Marx
had said, the next inevitable and desirable development
throughout the Western world. And it appears that post-
World War I conservatism, lynchings, and other manifes-
tations of racial antagonism directed Du Bois into thinking that the very existence of the black man in the United
States was threatened. He reversed his life-long struggle
for integration of the Negro into the mainstream of American life and started advocating an acceptance and strength-
ening of the fact of segregation. "We are now segregated
largely without reason," he wrote. "Let us put reason and
power beneath this segregation." [18] He had become an
economic determinist and was convinced that it was not
ignorance which bred race prejudice, but rather that
"economic exploitation of blacks was the greatest cause of
continued discrimination." [19]

A Russian family in America, possibly Red agents, Du
Bois thinks, had sought him out in 1927 and financed his
trip to Russia. "Since that trip," he wrote, "my mental
outlook and the aspect of the world will never be the
same." What significance may be attached to the fact that
the revised type of economic organization which he was
now championing for the black American coincided with
the Communist Party line in this country during the same
period is debatable. This scholar began to tell his people
of "things you must do for your own survival and self-
preservation." [20]

Feeling that he had correctly gauged the future, Du Bois now wanted to launch the NAACP and the American Negro into the socialistic movement. He wanted to use *The Crisis*, the organ of this Association which he had founded and edited continuously, as an educational and propaganda device for his new ideas. Unable to get the board of directors to go along with him, Du Bois resigned. His resignation accepted, the organization gave unstinted praise to him. His work with *The Crisis* was termed "an unprecedented achievement in American journalism." This commendation also stated that his efforts in general had been so effective "that the whole problem of the relation of the black and white races has ever since had a completely new orientation. He created, what never existed before, a Negro intelligentsia. . . . Without him the Association could never have been what it was and is." [21]

Upon leaving this organization, Du Bois went back to Atlanta University as a teacher, where his friend, John Hope, had in 1929 organized the Atlanta University System. In this period Du Bois wrote his Marxist study of Reconstruction,[22] and in 1936 he published a small study entitled "The Negro and the New Deal." For this work he wrote a statement and credo of the Negro which read, in part, "We believe in the ultimate triumph of some form of socialism the world over; that is common ownership and control of the means of production and equality of income." [23] This credo was rejected by the publishers.

In 1931 the Phelps-Stokes Fund called a committee to prepare and publish an encyclopedia of the Negro. Du Bois was made chairman of the editorial board. A scholarship award in 1936 made it possible for him to go back to Germany to study conditions there. From there he took a world tour. In 1938 he got permission from his publisher to rewrite his book entitled *The Negro* which had appeared in 1915 in the Home Library Series. The result was his *Black Folks Then and Now,* published in 1939.

Although retired from classroom teaching, after 1939

the activities of Du Bois were many and varied. In 1940 appeared his autobiography, *Dusk of Dawn,* and in 1945 the preparatory volume of the Encyclopedia of the Negro. No subsequent volumes of this endeavor were published, although such a work was long on the agenda of the Association for the Study of Negro Life and History. Appearing that year was his *Color and Democracy.* After 1939 he also was engaged in writing works of fiction, as well as history, and launching and editing the Atlanta University review of race and culture, *Phylon.* He also was a leader of the short-lived Progressive Party and ran unsuccessfully for the United States Senate on the New York Labor Party ticket in 1950. In 1951 he was tried and acquitted on a charge of serving as a representative of a foreign country without registering. This charge grew out of his prominent role in circulating the so-called Stockholm Peace Appeal in this country. Subsequently he moved to Ghana where that country's then political leader, Kwame Nkrumah, assisted him in efforts to produce an encyclopedia of the black man. He died in Ghana and was buried in Accra, the capital city.

In many ways the life of Du Bois was a mirror of his time. He received his training when the new "Scientific History" was just beginning to make its imprint on historical writing. Yet it is also true that the latter half of the nineteenth century saw the racial views of Count Gobineau and Houston Chamberlain passing as scientific sociology. This also is the period in which Radical Reconstruction made its brief appearance, only to be overthrown before the turn of the twentieth century. Antebellum teachings of the slaveholding South as to the nature, character and destined position of the Negro in society seemed to many to be vindicated. Caught up in the emotional heat engendered by these pseudo-scientific doctrines, Du Bois forged his excellent training and organizational and literary genius into a weapon of propaganda. Industrialism, colonialism, and modern warfare also played their part in shaping the life and changing outlook of this scholar. Ultimately his mind came to rest on socialism as the solution to not only the race problem, but to most of the ills which beset the modern world. Highly opinionated, and a man of action as well as of ideas, it seems that, while he began his career as a fighter against historical and sociological doctrines which he termed propaganda, he shifted to a position where he felt it advisable consciously to forge propaganda himself out of historical and sociological facts. He expressed criticism of the non-utilitarian nature of history as a science, and against its teachers. "It is perhaps the greatest indictment that can be brought against history as a science and against its teachers," he wrote, "that we are usually indisposed to refer to history for the settlement of pressing problems. We realize that history is too often what we want it to be and what we are determined men shall believe rather than a grim record of what has taken place in the past." [24]

It seems not inappropriate to end this discussion of the forces which molded Du Bois, and the forces which he molded, with another quotation concerning his personality and influence. In 1927 another writer, this time a woman, characterized him thusly:

Among the distinguished Negroes in America, none is so hated by the whites as Burghardt Du Bois. And for an excellent reason. He insists upon making them either angry or miserable. So great, moreover, is his genius, that it is impossible to read him and not be moved. Anger or misery, according to the disposition of the reader, comes from his merciless portrayal of the white man's injustice to the black. [25]

"There is a cruel look," continues this writer, "in Du Bois's sensitive, poet's face. It lurks somewhere about the mouth—a half sneer, a scorn." Yet she admits that "No man in this century has done more to secure the white man's reluctant gesture of respect for the Negro's attainments than Burghardt Du Bois." [26]

THE SUPPRESSION OF THE AFRICAN
SLAVE TRADE TO THE UNITED STATES
OF AMERICA, 1638–1870

Du Bois's dissertation was published in 1896 as Volume One in the Harvard Historical Studies.[27] In 1969 it was still considered an authoritative study of the suppression of the slave trade. Critics praise unstintingly the objectivity and thoroughness of research which characterize the volume. "The historical method employed is that of the strictest scholarship," states Loggins, "while the style is that of the scholar who is seeking the effect of accuracy and truth. . . . There is a certain charm in the sense of the logic with which the study is planned, in the discrimination with which the facts are grouped, and in the freedom from bias which we associate with all sound history."[28] On the significance of this volume in the history of black literature and scholarship, Loggins writes:

The Suppression of the African Slave Trade to the U.S. was by far the greatest intellectual achievement which had by 1900 come from any American Negro. It taught the colored man that if he were to be considered a historian he had to produce work which could meet the requirement of high standards. It prepared the way for a number of specialized historical studies of excellence which have come from American Negroes during the past thirty years.[29]

Even upon its appearance, observers saw that this initial volume was destined for permanence.[30]

Throughout his life, Dr. Du Bois viewed the question of slavery in the United States as essentially a moral problem. This viewpoint is typical of black historians in general, who have leaned heavily on the views of William Lloyd Garrison, Frederick Douglass, and other abolitionists. Thus, until recently, black historians have not given equal consideration to political, economic, constitutional, and psychological aspects of the slavery controversy.

In presenting this initial volume to the public, Du Bois wrote, "I . . . trust that I have succeeded in rendering this monograph a small contribution to the scientific study of slavery and the American Negro." Of the sources, scope, and limitations of the study, he explained:

This monograph was begun during my residence as Rogers Memorial Fellow at Harvard University, and is based mainly upon a study of the sources, i.e., national, State, and colonial statutes, Congressional documents, reports of societies, personal narratives, etc. The collection of laws available for this research was, I think, nearly complete; on the other hand, facts and statistics bearing on the economic side of the study have been difficult to find, and my conclusions are consequently liable to modification from this source.[31]

The first 197 pages of the volume are divided into twelve chapters. Appendices cover pages 201 to 325. The chapter titles are:

Introductory
The Planting Colonies
The Farming Colonies
The Trading Colonies
The Period of the Revolution, 1774–1787
The Federal Convention, 1787
Toussaint L'Ouverture and Anti-Slavery Effort, 1787–1807
The Period of Attempted Suppression, 1807–1825
The International Status of the Slave Trade, 1783–1862
The Rise of the Cotton Kingdom, 1820–1850
The Final Crisis, 1850–1870
The Essentials in the Struggle

The purpose of the monograph was "to set forth the efforts made in the United States of America, from early colonial times until the present, to limit and suppress the trade in slaves between Africa and these shores." [32] As expected of a doctoral dissertation, the volume is thoroughly documented.[33] Apart from the inadequate economic data which the author mentions, the volume does not give enough consideration to moral reasons for antislavery sentiment in the colonies and the young republic. Du Bois sums up the antislavery movement to 1774 as follows:

In the individual efforts of the various colonies to suppress the African slave-trade there may be traced certain general movements. First, from 1638–1664, there was a tendency to take a high moral stand against the traffic. This is illustrated in the laws of New England, in the plans for the settlement of Delaware and later, that of Georgia, and in the protest of the German Friends. The second period, from about 1664 to 1720, has no general unity, but is marked by statutes laying duties varying in design from encouragement to absolute prohibition, by some cases of moral opposition, and by the slow but steady growth of a spirit unfavorable to the long continuance of the trade. The last colonial period, from about 1760 to 1787, is one of pronounced effort to regulate, limit, or totally prohibit the traffic. Besides these general movements, there are many waves of legislation, easily distinguishable, which rolled over several or all of the colonies at various times, such as the series of high duties following the Asiento, and the acts inspired by various Negro "plots." [34]

For the period after 1820, he stated, "The history of slavery and the slave-trade . . . must be read in the light of the industrial revolution. . . ." [35] In assigning a cause for the disappearance of the slave-trade and slavery in the United States, Du Bois wrote that the cause was "a peculiar and almost fortuitous commingling of moral, political, and economic motives. . . ." [36]

This volume is, almost in its entirety, thoroughly objective, scholarly, temperate, and follows a broad interpretation. The only clear evidence of Du Bois's proclivity for, and almost irresistible tendency toward, proselytizing is found in the last topic of this volume. This topic is entitled "Lessons for Americans." "It may be doubted," he writes, "if ever before such political mistakes as the slavery compromises of the Constitutional Convention had such serious results, and yet, by a succession of unexpected accidents, still left a nation in position to work out its destiny." Du Bois fails to answer, or consider, the question of whether adoption of the Constitution could have been secured without these "slavery compromises." "We must face the fact," he continues, "that this problem arose principally from the cupidity and carelessness of our ancestors. It was the plain duty of the colonies to crush the trade and the system in its infancy: they preferred to enrich themselves on its profits. It was the plain duty of a Revolution based upon 'Liberty' to take steps toward the abolition of slavery: it preferred promises to straightforward action." [37]

THE PHILADELPHIA NEGRO

In 1899 *The Philadelphia Negro,* a sociological study, was published. It included a special report on domestic service by Isabel Eaton.[38] Two years previously, Du Bois had submitted to the American Academy of Political and Social Science a plan for the study of Negro problems. *The Philadelphia Negro* was "an essay along the lines there laid down, and . . . thus part of a larger design of observation and research into the history and social condition of the transplanted African." [39] "Until [the scholar] has prepared the ground by intelligent and discriminating research," Du Bois wrote, "the labors of philanthropist and statesman must continue to be, to a large extent, barren and unfruitful." [40] Du Bois hoped that similar studies would be made of Negro life in such cities as Boston in the East, Chicago and Kansas City in the West, and Atlanta, New Orleans and Galveston in the South. This would result, he felt, in "a trustworthy picture of Negro city life." [41] Almost two years of continuous research were spent in gathering data for *The Philadelphia Negro.* Du Bois contacted over 10,000 Philadelphians. The study had been made possible when Susan P. Wharton, a member of the Executive Committee of the Philadelphia College Settlement, asked the administration of the University of Pennsylvania to sponsor it as a philanthropic guide.

In this volume Du Bois censures the city of Philadelphia for not planning conditions so that a superior black citizenry would be developed by the local environment. The work carries statistics on crime, death rate, marriage status, occupation, and almost every conceivable aspect of life in the city. The last chapter is entitled "A Final Word," and is similar to the concluding portion of *Suppression of the African Slave-Trade*. The first topic under "A Final Word" is "The Meaning of all This." [42] This section tells the nation what it must do for blacks and tells the latter what they must do for themselves.

The Philadelphia Negro was one of the first scientific sociological treatises to come from the pen of an American. With this work, and the "Atlanta University Studies" which continued the pattern here outlined, Du Bois joined Carter G. Woodson in laying the foundation for subsequent scientific studies of the conditions of the race. Other university-trained Afro-Americans were soon to appear and advance the work inaugurated by these two men. The rise of graduate schools in the United States had much to do with the increase in the quantity and quality of scholarly productions by blacks after the first decade of the twentieth century. Still, "When Dr. Du Bois appeared he gave to his people a sense of pride. The race had had scholars before, but not one of such distinction and influence. To younger men accordingly he became an inspiration and a challenge." [43] The same can be said of his distinguished contemporary, Carter Godwin Woodson.

THE NEGRO IN THE SOUTH

In 1907 appeared a volume which Du Bois coauthored with Booker T. Washington. It bore the title *The Negro in the South,* and consisted of four essays, two by each of the authors.[44] In this volume, Du Bois states that the industrial revolution both fastened slavery on the South by creating markets for cotton, and doomed slavery at the same time by creating a free laboring class. "Such a system at such a time carried its own sentence of death," he wrote, "because it demanded extensive rather than intensive land culture, increased and made compulsory ignorance of the laboring class, and the rearing of a complete system of caste and aristocracy." Yet, he states, freedom meant for the freedmen only another type of bondage—industrial slavery.[45]

Like many intellectuals in all ages, Du Bois could never see any intelligence in, or much need for, war. He termed the American Civil War "that disgraceful episode of civil strife when, leaving the arguments of men, the nation appealed to the last resort of dogs, murdering and ravishing each other for four long shameful years." [46]

In this volume may be found the position on Afro-American participation in Radical Reconstruction which Du Bois was to amplify thirty years later in *Black Reconstruction*. "Although the new voters . . . introduced in the South were crude and ignorant, and in many ways ill-fitted to rule," he wrote, "nevertheless in the fundamental postulates of American freedom and democracy they were sane and sound. Some of them were silly, some were ignorant, and some were venal, but they were not as silly as those who had fostered slavery in the South, nor as ignorant as those who were determined to perpetuate it, and the black voters of South Carolina never stole half as much as the white voters of Pennsylvania are stealing today." [47] Du Bois then goes on to outline virtually all of the arguments which he later used in *Black Reconstruction*. Only the Marxist slant of the latter work, and its more thorough documentation, seem to be missing from *The Negro in the South*.

JOHN BROWN

In 1909 Du Bois published a biography of John Brown for the American Crisis Biographies series. This series was edited by E. P. Oberholtzer.[48] The author admitted that he had no new materials on Brown to bolster those already published in the biographies by Hinton, Connelly, and Redpath, or the autobiography of Brown edited by Sanborn. Du Bois gave his excuse for writing the volume as being to "lay new emphasis upon the material which they have so carefully collected, and to treat these facts from a different point of view." [49] Du Bois believes that John Brown "of all Americans has perhaps come nearest to touching the real souls of black folk." [50]

The volume is well written and ably documented. The tone is one of moderation, and the volume deserves, perhaps, greater acclaim among the works produced by Du Bois than it has received. Indeed, he himself seldom mentioned in later years that he had written this work.

In summing up the miscarried effort of John Brown, Du Bois reechoes the moral theme with which he concluded *Suppression of the African Slave-Trade* and *The Philadelphia Negro*. "Only in time is truth revealed," he writes. "Today at last we know, John Brown was right." [51] The "right" thing which John Brown taught posterity is that "the cheapest price to pay for liberty is its cost today." [52] Though he states in this volume that "John Brown was right," later he deprecates and disavows the use of violence and advocates a greater exercise of Christian principles.[53]

THE NEGRO

This volume was written for the "Home University Library of Modern Knowledge" for popular reading.[54] "In this little book," Du Bois writes, "we are studying the history of the darker part of the human family, which is separated from the rest of mankind by no absolute physical line, but which nevertheless forms, as a mass, a social group distinct in history, appearance, and to some extent in spiritual gift." [55]

Eight of the twelve chapters treat African history. The remaining four treat the slave trade, the Negro in the West Indies and Latin America, and in the United States. Du Bois here stated his belief that the Afro-American was a part of the world-mass of colored peoples who were being exploited by capitalistic Europe. He expressed the belief that there was coming a unity of working classes all over the world and that everywhere the color line would disappear.

THE GIFT OF BLACK FOLK

This volume appeared in 1924, bearing the subtitle *The Negroes in the Making of America*.[56] It was one of the Knights of Columbus racial series, and was for the author, "an attempt to set forth more clearly than has hitherto been done the effect which the Negro has had upon American life." The thesis of the volume was that "despite slavery, war and caste, and despite our present Negro problem, the American Negro is and has been a distinct asset to this country and has brought a contribution without which America could not have been; and that perhaps the essence of our so-called Negro problem is the failure to recognize this fact. . . ." [57] Here again is to be seen the persistent belief that miseducation or lack of education concerning the true nature of the achievements of the Negro constituted the primary basis of discrimination and prejudice against him.

The volume traces the aid given by blacks in the discovery of America and indicates the significant contribution of anonymous black labor to the founding of the nation. It also shows that black men served in all of the nation's wars and influenced the growth of a broader democracy through the humanitarian interest which was fanned by the issue of slavery. It shows that black persons contributed significantly to the body of American literature and art, and states that the race had played a "peculiar spiritual role" in American life.[58] The volume, like most of the writings of Du Bois, was received with mixed criticism, mostly favorable.[59]

BLACK RECONSTRUCTION

This volume was published in 1935.[60] In 1910 its author had read before the American Historical Association a paper entitled "Reconstruction and Its Benefits," "which greatly exercised Ulrich Phillips, protagonist of the slave South, but brought praise from Dunning of Columbia, Hart of Harvard and others." [61] *Black Reconstruction* was, in part, an enlargement of this paper. Du Bois began the larger study through a Rosenwald grant received while he was with the National Association for the Advancement of Colored People. After leaving this organization and returning to the classroom at Atlanta University, he completed it.

By this time, as stated earlier, Du Bois had become a Marxist. *Black Reconstruction* was the first of his writings in which he clearly revealed himself as an economic determinist. "It was not until I was long out of college," he wrote, "and had finished the first phase of my teaching career that I began to see clearly the connection of economics and politics; the fundamental influence of man's efforts to earn a living upon all his other efforts." [62] And again, "It was the Russian Revolution of 1917 I believe which first caused me to see clearly." [63]

The author states that *Black Reconstruction* was based "very largely upon secondary material; upon state histories of the Reconstruction, written in the main by those who were convinced before they began to write that the Negro was incapable of government, or of becoming a constituent part of a civilized state." [64] He also admitted that he had neither the time nor money to consult many important sources in the Library of Congress and the Widener Library, such as the papers of Johnson, Wells, Chase, McCulloch, McPherson, Sherman, Stevens, Schurz, Greeley, Sumner, and others. Had Du Bois been able to use these sources, he believes that his case would have been "vastly strengthened." [65]

The thesis of *Black Reconstruction* is that Radical Reconstruction was overthrown by northern and southern capitalists because of their fear that it represented a nascent form of proletarian rule. Du Bois regards it as the height of folly that southern poor whites did not see in the freedmen fellow members of the proletariat and form a continuing alliance with them against exploiting southern and northern capitalists.

The volume relies heavily on abolitionist arguments and quotes James Ford Rhodes frequently. Also, the author's case appears to be heavily bolstered because he frequently quotes from state histories which generally cast a bad light on Negro participation in government during Reconstruction.[66] Du Bois points out the constructive aspects of Radical Reconstruction, especially of the state constitutional conventions in which freedmen participated, and the work of the Freedmen's Bureau. Also characteristic of the general interpretation of this period by Afro-American historians, there is little but high praise for Thaddeus Stevens and Charles Sumner. Appended to the volume is a list of the main historians of the Reconstruction Period, grouped according to the degree in which Du Bois feels they are favorable or unfavorable to the participation of blacks in government.[67] At the end of almost every chapter, the author added eloquent "perorations" which together or singly reveal his literary genius and poetic nature, although perhaps such indulgences constitute a violation of "objective scholarship."

This volume contains chapters with such titles as "The Black Proletariat of South Carolina," and "The Black Proletariat of Mississippi." In Chapter IV, "The General Strike," it is asserted that though slaves did not stage a general revolt based on violence during the Civil War, they doomed the war effort by refusing to work and by absconding the moment northern armies reached their areas.

Black Reconstruction reveals Du Bois "as both the merciless critic and the constructive historian." Rayford W. Logan, in appraising this work, exaggerates the significance of its economic theory. "This fresh interpretation of the economic forces of our era of storm and stress is as significant," he writes, "as was Charles A. Beard's *Economic Interpretation of the Constitution of the United States* a quarter of a century ago." [68] However, studies of Reconstruction by other historians are far better at casting light on economic aspects of the period. The unique and valuable contribution of *Black Reconstruction* lies in the great emphasis which it placed on constructive aspects of the period. Again, Logan errs in his agreement with the Marxist theory which one finds in this book. "For the first time," Logan avers, "one clearly understands that America lost during Reconstruction her golden opportunity to found a political and industrial democracy." [69]

As previously stated, from this volume on, Du Bois ties the plight of "exploited" black labor in the United States with that of labor in the colonial world everywhere. He sees American Negro slavery as but one aspect of exploitation by industrialized Europe and America of colored peoples the world over. "It was thus the black worker," he states, "as founding stone of a new economic system in the nineteenth century and for the modern world, who brought the Civil War in America. He was its underlying cause, in spite of every effort to base the strife upon union and national power." [70]

Judging from the new position of Du Bois after the Russian Revolution, it seems difficult to believe that in his early years he had sided with the position of Booker T. Washington in the view that the Negro should compromise with the white South.[71] Henceforth, he was to attack not only the traditional attitude of the United States toward the black man, but the entire economic orientation of the United States and the Western world. In his youth, states this scholar, he saw only the "Negro problem" in the United States. "I did not," he wrote, "face the general plight and conditions of all humankind." [72] After this conversion, he repeatedly stated that "The history of our day . . . may be epitomized in one word—Empire; the domination of white Europe over black Africa and yellow Asia, through political power built on the economic control of labor, income and ideas. The echo of this industrial imperialism in America was the expulsion of black men from American democracy, their subjugation to caste control and wage slavery. This ideology was triumphant in 1910." [73] In his autobiography, as in *Black Reconstruction,* he reiterates his belief that with the end of Reconstruction there was an "expulsion of black men from American democracy."

Reviewers were almost unanimous in their praise of *Black Reconstruction* for giving a needed emphasis to the positive aspects of Reconstruction. They were almost equally unanimous in their denunciation of the bitterness of the author. On this latter point, Avery Craven wrote:

"By distorting facts and reviewing abolition propaganda in the name of history he has . . . probably done little toward averting the 'fire and blood' solution of the race question or securing that 'perfect and unlimited equality' with any white man he desires." [74] D. S. Muzzey, with the same general criticisms, praised "the beauty and brilliance of his style," while scoring "his bitterness and lack of judicial balance." [75] Crane Brinton did not feel that the book revealed any hatred on the part of the author, but that Du Bois "shares the desires for justice, for democracy, for free discussion, for gentlemanly competition among individuals, for dispassionate search for scientific truth which was the creed of nineteenth-century liberals like Mill." Du Bois will not, he wrote, "if he can help it, repay white scorn with Negro hatred. On the whole, he succeeds. The book is wistful rather than truculent." [76] S. D. Spero, reviewing the book for *The Nation,* stated that "Du Bois's old race consciousness and new Marxism do not allow him to remain content with the demonstration of this major thesis (to show that the Negro 'is an average and ordinary human being'); they lead him to transform the Negro plantation slaves into a revolutionary working class and make the Reconstruction legislatures into dictatorships of the proletariat." [77] A. A. Taylor correctly termed the book "the most comprehensive study of this period by a Negro author." [78]

BLACK FOLK THEN AND NOW

This volume first appeared in 1939,[79] bearing the subtitle *An Essay in the History and Sociology of the Negro Race.* Du Bois stated that it was an attempt to do "somewhat more thoroughly, the task which I attempted twenty-three years ago in a little volume . . . called *The Negro.*

This book incorporates some of that former essay, but for the most part is an entirely new production." [80]

The author early admitted some basic limitations. "This is not a work of exact scholarship; far too few studies in history are," he wrote. He continued: "The kernel of this work is, I believe, a body of fairly well-ascertained truth; but there are also areas here of conjecture and even of guesswork which under other circumstances I should have hesitated to publish." He excuses himself for writing the book, despite these limitations, because the black man has been so neglected in history, or misinterpreted, and because "millions of black and brown folk today, not to speak of most educated whites, have no conception of any role that black folk have played in history, or any hope in the past for present aspiration." [81]

The larger difficulties of the work Du Bois saw as "the breadth of the field which one mind can scarcely cover; the obstacles to securing data." He also admitted at the outset that his interpretation was probably biased because of his African descent and narrow group culture. "But there is little danger of long misleading here," he charged, "for the champions of white folk are legion. The Negro has long been the clown of history; the football of anthropology; and the slave of industry. I am trying to show here why these attitudes can no longer be maintained." Still, true to his training, Du Bois realized "that the truth of history lies not in the mouths of partisans but rather in the calm science that sits between." "Her cause I seek to serve," he continued, "and wherever I fail, I am at least paying truth the respect of earnest effort." [82]

The author states that he had acquired the urge to write on the past of blacks after hearing Franz Boas speak at Atlanta University in 1906 on the richness of the African past. Upon hearing these revealing facts, Du Bois states that he was "too astonished to speak," because all of this he had never heard. It is then that he first began to realize "how the silence and neglect of science can let truth utterly disappear or even be consciously distorted." [83]

In attempting to define "race," he concludes, "No scientific definition of race is possible. . . . In this book then we are studying the history of the darker part of the human family, which is separated from the rest of mankind by no absolute physical line and no definite mental characteristics, but which nevertheless forms, as a mass, a series of social groups more or less distinct in history, appearance, and in cultural gift and accomplishment." [84] Throughout the volume the tone is temperate. "What the facts concerning the culture of Africa begin to tell us," he concludes, "is simply that here we have a normal human stock whose development has been conditioned by certain physical and social factors." Du Bois had already stated that "It is . . . easy to exaggerate the cultural gifts of any particular people," and he steers clear of this pitfall. [85]

There are not many footnotes in the volume. The author used standard sources, mostly monographs in English, although a few in French and German are cited. Among the standard works are those of Lugard, Frobenius, Chamberlain, and Martineau. Du Bois repeated his oft-stated assertion that "black slavery gave birth" to the industrial revolution. [86] In one place he states, "England stopped the slave trade in order to defeat Napoleon," yet on the next page he admits that profits from slavery were declining. [87] In another instance, Du Bois states categorically, "There is no doubt that the thirst of the black men for knowledge . . . gave birth to the public school system of the South." [88]

About one-third of the volume deals with the African background. The interpretation given to such topics as the partition of Africa, the slave trade, and the American Civil War is largely that of the economic determinist. Yet, apart from faulty generalization and interpretation in some places, this volume is a mine of facts. The final chapter is entitled, "Future of World Democracy." Here the author reiterates his faith in socialism as the to-be-desired economic order, scores again racist explanations for the differences among individuals, disclaims any faith in violent revolution, and pleads for a greater practice of Christian virtues. Thus, it seems that, in this volume, he retreated somewhat from the type of faith in Marxism which he had manifested earlier. "It seems clear today," he wrote, "that the masses of men within and without civilization are depressed, ignorant and poor chiefly because they have never had a chance. . . . For centuries the world has sought to rationalize this condition and pretend that civilized nations and cultured classes are the result of inherent and hereditary gifts rather than climate, geography and happy accident. This explanation . . . is today, because of the decline and fall of [European] hegemony, less widely believed." Mankind, he states, can go on to far greater achievements "if mere political democracy is allowed to widen into industrial democracy and the democracy of culture and art. The possibility of this has long been foreseen and emphasized by the socialists, culminating in the magnificent and apostolic fervor of Karl Marx and the Communists." Although Du Bois here sees the same solution for the world's ills as Marx saw, he advocates not "violence and revolution, which is only the outward distortion of an inner fact, but . . . the ancient cardinal virtues: individual prudence, courage, temperance and justice, and the more modern faith, hope and love." [89]

By this time an internationalist outlook on race, together with his Marxist leanings, caused him to write of "the proletariat of the world," which he says, "consists not simply of white European and American workers but overwhelmingly of the darker workers of Asia, Africa, the islands of the sea, and South and Central America. These are the ones who are supporting a superstructure of wealth, luxury and extravagance. It is the rise of these people that is the rise of the world. The problem of the twentieth century is the problem of the color line." [90] Nowhere in this volume does he give credit to these exploiters of colored peoples for anything but "wealth, luxury and extravagance."

The book was generally well received by critics. Carter Woodson regretted the omission of certain secondary works, and stated that "the chapters devoted . . . to African kingdoms do not show much relief." [91] Woodson also held that Du Bois omitted the names and exploits of many Africans whom Woodson considered too significant to be overlooked. M. J. Herskovits praised the manner in which Du Bois viewed the race problem as a world problem.[92] Like Woodson, H. J. Seligman criticized the brief allotment of space for the African background. Yet he admitted that "No one can leave [the book] without a deepened sense of the part the Negro peoples have played and must play in world history." [93]

Du Bois later admitted that by the time he wrote *Black Folk Then and Now* his thinking on the race problem had undergone a change. In his autobiography he states that he felt, at first, that a quick revolutionary assault could end the problem. World War I caused him to see, he states, that violence plus the economic bases of race prejudice made "not sudden assault but long siege . . . indicated; careful planning and subtle campaign with the education of growing generations and propaganda." [94] Still, considering the generally restrained and temperate tone of *Black Folk Then and Now,* one might not guess that the work was written, as was *Dusk of Dawn,* "in tears and blood." [95]

COLOR AND DEMOCRACY: COLONIES AND PEACE

In 1945 *Color and Democracy: Colonies and Peace*[96] was published. This volume, like Logan's *What the Negro Wants,* was designed to help world leaders fashion the new order after World War II. Here the author called for the granting of democracy to all peoples, especially those long subjected to European colonialism. As already seen, Du Bois was convinced that the world could rise above the wars and depressions which had racked the twentieth century only by allowing the subjected colored masses to escape from their bondage. This, he felt, was the key to future peace. Such is the thesis of *Color and Democracy,* in which he "sought to say that insofar as . . . efforts [at peace] leave practically untouched the present imperial ownership of disfranchised colonies, and in this and other ways proceed as if the majority of men can be regarded mainly as sources of profit for Europe and North America, in just so far we are planning not for peace but war, not democracy but the continued oligarchical control of civilization by the white race." [97]

Topics treated are:

Dumbarton Oaks   Peace and Colonies
The Disfranchised Colonies   The Riddle of Russia
The Unfree Peoples   Missions and Mandates
Democracy and Color

Du Bois echoes his oft-stated position that World War I was caused by colonial rivalry. Colonies, he states, must be taken from European powers or there will be "recurring wars of envy and greed because of the present inequitable distribution of colonial gain among civilized nations." [98] He also repeats his conviction that the world's poverty, ignorance and disease are caused by "monopoly." "The possibility of producing wealth in our age," he avers, "has repeatedly been estimated to be great enough to furnish all the peoples of the world with the necessities of life and some of the comforts . . ." but monopoly prevents this being attained.[99] Nowhere does the author consider adequately that many of Europe's wars have been expansionist wars—that even in the absence of overseas colonies European states would probably have been fighting over one another's landholdings in continental Europe.[100]

This historian is to be commended for his cosmopolitan conception of race and for his world humanitarianism. This high position led Du Bois to an elevated conception of democracy, which he defined as "not simply the self-defense of the competent; it is the unloosing of the energies and the capabilities of the depressed." Again, he states his conviction that this is precisely the type of democracy which the Soviet Union is accomplishing.[101]

There is little in *Color and Democracy* which Du Bois had not already repeated many times in other of his writings. The volume ends on a note of optimism. The author felt that the rise of a new liberalism was pointing in the direction which he desired.

A reviewer for *Foreign Affairs* stated, "His survey of the whole question of dependent peoples . . . is so brief and episodic that his book constitutes little more than an anti-imperialist—especially an anti-British—tract." [102] Another reviewer called the work "Sound, challenging, thought-provoking." [103] H. A. Overstreet wrote: "This book . . . is a small volume of 143 pages; but it contains enough dynamite to blow up the whole vicious system whereby we have comforted our white souls and lined the pockets of generations of free-booting capitalists. Its chief value lies in what it reveals to us of conditions that hitherto we have merely taken for granted. . . . It is reading that is utterly essential if we want to understand the fullness of the world job that is ahead of us." [104] Vandenbosch called it "a tract for the times, and as such [of] considerable value; but

. . . not a scientific analysis of the large and difficult problem with which it deals." [105]

THE WORLD AND AFRICA

Also out of his new attitude toward the "race issue," Du Bois wrote and published in 1947 *The World and Africa*.[106] This volume bore the subtitle *An Inquiry into the Part which Africa Has Played in World History.* Like *Color and Democracy, The Gift of Black Folk,* and his autobiography, *Dusk of Dawn, The World and Africa* played up the theme that European colonialism was the fountainhead of modern industrialism and civilization, with the concomitant chronic warfare and depression. These volumes also sought generally to reveal what Carter G. Woodson had been attempting to show for almost three decades, that the Afro-American has a rich past and has made contributions to civilization which deserve high praise.

With *The World and Africa,* Du Bois was seeking "to remind readers of the crisis of civilization, of how critical a part Africa has played in human history, past and present, and how impossible it is to forget this and rightly explain the present plight of mankind." Already he had made two attempts to write the history of Africa. His first, *The Negro,* which had appeared in 1915, he now called a "condensed and not altogether logical narrative." He stated that *Black Folk Then and Now* was an enlargement upon *The Negro,* which he felt was necessary after World War I because he thought that period represented the "beginning of . . . a new era." He states that he decided to write *The World and Africa* and reinterpret these earlier works because the period after World War I actually was "the end of an age which marked the final catastrophe of the old era of European world dominance rather than [being] at the threshold of a change of which he had dreamed in 1935." He referred to this latest effort as "not so much a history of the Negroid peoples as a statement of their integral role in human history from prehistoric to modern times." [107]

Again, as with *Black Folk Then and Now*, Du Bois admits at the outset the limitations to the task which he was essaying. "I still labor," he wrote, "under the difficulty of the persistent lack of interest in Africa so long characteristic of modern history and sociology. The careful detailed researches into the history of Negroid peoples have only begun, and the need for them is not yet clear to the thinking world." He continues: "I feel compelled nevertheless to go ahead with my interpretation, even though that interpretation has here and there but slender historical proof. I believe that in the main my story is true, despite the fact that so often between the American Civil War and World War I the weight of history and science supports me only in part and in some cases appears violently to contradict me." [108]

On the lack of documentation to support his statements, he wrote: "I am challenging authority—even Maspero, Sayce, Reisner, Breasted, and hundreds of other men of highest respectability, who did not attack but studiously ignored the Negro on the Nile and in the world and talked as though black folk were non-existent and unimportant." [109] He used mostly secondary works.[110] Of his research, he stated:

I have done in this book the sort of thing at which every scholar shudders. With meager preparation and all too general background of learning, I have essayed a task, which, to be adequate and complete, should be based upon the research of a lifetime; but I am faced with the dilemma, that either I do this now or leave it for others. If out of my almost inevitable mistakes and inaccuracies and false conclusions, I shall have at least clearly stated my main issue—that black Africans are men in the same sense as white European and yellow Asiatics, and that history can easily prove this—then I shall rest satisfied even under the stigma of an incomplete and, to many, inconclusive work.[111]

Here one finds this author's often-stated positions on the slave trade, slavery, colonialism, and the two world wars. True to his moralistic proclivities, after flaying European exploitation of colonies, Du Bois writes of the "moral plight of present European culture and what capitalistic investment and imperialism have done to it." In seeking an explanation for this moral plight, he finds an answer in the subject matter of his doctoral dissertation. "I believe that the trade in human beings between Africa and America," he wrote, "which flourished between the Renaissance and American Civil War, is the prime and effective cause of the contradictions in European civilization and the illogic in modern thought and the collapse of human culture." [112]

In *The World and Africa,* this historian shows the very keen and admirable sympathy and feeling for the underdog and weak which is so characteristic of his life and writings. He depicts a touching scene from the killing of an elephant for the ivory trade and piano keys and billiard balls. "Neither for the keys nor the music," he writes, "was the death of the elephant actually necessary." [113] Topics covered in the volume are:

The Collapse of Europe	Atlantis
The White Masters of the World	Central Africa and the March of the Bantu
The Rape of Africa	Asia in Africa
The Peopling of Africa	The Black Sudan
Egypt	Andromeda
The Land of the Burnt Faces	The Message

The volume is lightly documented, and one reviewer called the book "timely," but criticized it for being "admittedly based on the work of other writers rather than research." [114] Another reviewer, while praising the volume for the attention which it focuses on a neglected field, criticized the "extensive excursions into classical mythology, Biblical literature, and Oriental legend . . . open to challenge for their validity." This reviewer also criticized some of the sources as being unreliable, and stated that "much of what Du Bois poses here has been substantiated, but its comprehensive treatment is the task of anthropologists and historians of the future." [115] Another reviewer scored the bitterness in the volume. Linton Wells believed that *The World and Africa* "would have been more convincing and would have better served his cause had Dr. Du Bois been less bitter. Imbued with such hate, no one can deal adequately or rationally with his subject," he stated.[116] "Though Dr. Du Bois is a distinguished scholar and his book is based on extensive research," comments another reviewer, "the result is not sober anthropology and history, but poetry and legend. It is full of corroded passion, of anger opening into illumination, of logic dwindling into nostalgia. It moves proudly, like a pageant. This is history as Herodotus understood it. It is also special pleading which will antagonize as much as it convinces." [117]

OTHER WORKS

In 1945 the preparatory volume of the *Encyclopedia of the Negro* appeared, edited by Du Bois, L. D. Reddick, G. B. Johnson, and Rayford Logan.[118] Carter Woodson, who certainly knew the difficulties of such a task, stated then that the editors should have waited until the entire work was ready for publication before issuing a part of it. He criticized the plan of the work as "inadequate" and expressed doubts that the editors would ever finish such a stupendous task.[119] He was right. Reviewers also criticized the work for "seeming capriciousness in the selection of subjects" and for poor listing of references.[120]

Du Bois wrote five novels. In 1911 he penned *The Quest of the Silver Fleece*,[121] in 1929, *Dark Princess: Romance*,[122] and in 1957, *The Ordeal of Mansart,* the first book of a trilogy called *The Black Flame*. The other books in the trilogy are *Mansart Builds a School* and *Worlds of Color*. What one reviewer said of *Dark Princess* is perhaps characteristic of much of his writing. This work was aptly described as "a piece of symbolic social literature and propaganda, written with fine nervous ardor and scorn for injustice." [123] Two other of his nonhistorical works were highly similar in content and form. In 1903 he had published his *The Souls of Black Folk: Essays and Sketches*. This book was very widely read, going through sixteen editions by 1928 and on to its twenty-first in 1937, and is still in print. It early revealed, even more clearly than his *Suppression of the African Slave-Trade* or *The Philadelphia Negro* had done, the keen sensitivity of Du Bois to the racial discrimination and oppression to which his race was subjected, and the very eloquent form which his protest could take. "Herein lie buried many things," he wrote, "which if read with patience may show the strange meaning of being black here at the dawning of the twentieth century." [124] Some of the essays in this volume had appeared previously in *The Atlantic Monthly, The World's Work, The Dial, The New World,* and *Annals*. By 1969 *The Souls of Black Folk* had won a place among the classics of American literature.

In *Darkwater* Du Bois had written that he has been "in the world but not of it." "I have seen the human tragedy," he continued, "from a veiled corner." [125] This work also carried a Credo in which he said he believed in God; the Negro race; Service, the Devil, the Prince of Peace; Liberty for all men; the training of children; and Patience.[126] Like *The Souls of Black Folk,* this publication is a collection of essays, stories, parables and poetry.

The following criticism of *Darkwater* might also have been made about many of the writings of this scholar, historical or otherwise. "There is a certain weakness in Prof. Du Bois's reasoning," comments this reviewer, "which is that his intense concentration on one subject leads him to turn general universal wrongs into special Negro wrongs. The error runs all through his book and disfigures it." The praise which this reviewer has for the volume might also be given to any of his works. "If we disagree with much in this beautiful book," continues this critic, "it is not possible to withhold the heartiest praise for the power of its statement, the force and passion that inspire it, and the entrancing style in which it is written." [127] In a review of this book, Oswald Garrison Villard called the ability of Du Bois "to suffer and to feel the wrongs of his race as deeply . . . at once his strength, the reason for his leadership, and also his chief weakness," because it carried with it "a note of bitterness, tinctured with hate, and the teaching of violence which often defeats his own purpose." He stated further: "Doubtless, few of us with sympathies so keen, with nerves so rasped, with wounds as raw, would do better. But still, some suppression of the ego, a lesser self-consciousness, and the omission of personal bitterness at all times would carry Mr. Du Bois and his cause much further."

In the *Sturm und Drang* of the first third of the twentieth century many persons lost faith in classical Liberalism. Total warfare and total depression came to convince many people that the decision of most pressing moment had come to be an unequivocal choice between security and liberty. Mussolini, Hitler, Stalin and their supporters typify those who, in the post-World War I period, abandoned liberty as an ideal in the interests of supposed security. The United States, faced with similar peril in this period, found a new balance between security and freedom. Du Bois, like some other liberals of his day, came to feel that only in a thorough abandonment of the old ideals and ways lay a permanent solution to the world's ills. True to his economic determinism, he felt too that the capitalistic system, which helped to give rise to classical Liberalism, must be abandoned.

Du Bois made the jump from being a historian of the black man, to being a champion of the entire underprivileged population of the earth. He made this jump because he believed that to work further to improve the lot of the black man in American society is only to lop off the branches of a tree which must be killed from its roots. After the 1930s, it was not against racial segregation and discrimination that he directed his blows, but against what he felt produced segregation, discrimination, and exploitation—the capitalistic system.[128]

Du Bois reached his zenith as a scholar—in the traditional sense—at the outset of his career. *The Suppression of the African Slave-Trade to the United States;* his sociological study, *The Philadelphia Negro,* and the Atlanta University Studies represent his most thorough and objective products. More and more, as he drifted deeper into causes centering around the "race issue," the character of his scholarly productivity changed. Still, perhaps as much because of his "bad" as well as good qualities as a scholar, he gave a great impetus to interest in the black race and to the scientific study of its history and culture. The body of writings which he contributed to black studies helped mightily to attract attention to the field of black history. While he antagonized, he also aroused attention, interest, sympathy and respect—not only for the race, but for black history. His *Black Reconstruction,* by focusing attention on the neglected aspects of that period, contributed greatly to bringing about a reinterpretation of the period. Because of this, *Black Reconstruction* and his doctoral dissertation must be ranked as outstanding products of American historiography. Du Bois must be ranked as an outstanding American historian.

CARTER G. WOODSON
The Father of Negro History

Carter Godwin Woodson (1875–1950), one of nine children, was born of ex-slave parentage in Virginia. He moved with his family to Huntington, West Virginia, where, forsaking a formal education, he worked in the coal mines and was a young man of twenty when he entered Douglass High School in Huntington, having mastered the fundamentals of common school subjects largely from self-instruction. The first two years after graduating from high school he taught in the public schools of West Virginia, and was given the honor of serving as principal of the high school from which he had graduated. Keenly ambitious, Woodson studied at Berea College in Kentucky and several summers at the University of Chicago. In 1907 he received the bachelor's degree from the latter institution.[1]

After travel in Asia and Europe, during which time he spent one semester at the Sorbonne in Paris where he learned French, he returned home and received his M.A. degree from the University of Chicago in 1908. The next year found Woodson working on a doctorate at Harvard, where he studied under such outstanding teachers as W. B. Munro and Edward Channing.

In order to do research on his dissertation, "The Disruption of Virginia," at the Library of Congress, Woodson took a job teaching Romance languages in a Washington high school. His dissertation completed, he received his Ph.D. from Harvard in 1912—only the second Negro ever to receive a doctorate in history from that institution. Woodson's dissertation was never published, however, probably because Charles W. Ambler had already brought out his book *Sectionalism in Virginia, 1776–1861*.[2]

The years 1919–1920 found Woodson serving as Dean of the Howard University School of Liberal Arts. He resigned after only one year because he disagreed with the educational policies of the school. From 1920 to 1922 he was a dean of West Virginia Institute (later West Virginia State College). Apparently for the same reason that he resigned from Howard University, and because he desired to live in Washington in order to continue his researches, he resigned from West Virginia Institute and gave up classroom teaching as a major interest. His dominant purpose, according to Kelly Miller, was to "turn his historical training and preparation to the best racial account."[3] Thus Woodson turned to what was to become his life's work.

THE ASSOCIATION FOR THE STUDY OF NEGRO LIFE AND HISTORY

On September 9, 1915, Woodson organized the Association for the Study of Negro Life and History at a meeting in Chicago. It was the "first systematic effort of the Negro to treat the records of the race scientifically and to publish the findings to the world."[4] The next year he brought out, on January 1, the first issue of the Association's quarterly, the *Journal of Negro History*. For this initial issue, he used largely his own funds, and published it without consulting the Executive Council. One member of the Council resigned in anger and disgust. Modeled after the *American Historical Review*, the purposes of the *Journal of Negro History* were "the collection of sociological and historical data on the Negro, the study of peoples of African blood, the publishing of books in this field, and the promotion of harmony between the races by acquainting the one with the other." [5]

Despite the fact that during its first three years annual deficits had to be made up from Dr. Woodson's small salary as a teacher at the Armstrong High School in Washington, D.C., in 1969 the *Journal* had never missed an issue. It soon became practically self-supporting. Included among the scholars who praised the appearance and quality of this new organ, and wished it well, were A. H. Buffington, Charles H. Haskins, A. C. McLaughlin, Ferdinand Schevill, and Frederick Jackson Turner.[6] Professor Buffington wrote: "The more I think of the matter, the more I do believe there is a place for such a publication. The history of the Negro in Africa, in the West Indies, in Spanish America and in the United States offers a large field in which little appears to have been done."

Woodson remained editor of the *Journal* throughout his life and wrote many of the articles which appeared in it. He was the largest single contributor of book reviews to this publication. The Association hired many young historians to work with him on topics in which the editor was interested. Money received from this work was of importance to some of the young scholars in enabling them to complete their doctoral studies. Among these investigators were Drs. Alrutheus A. Taylor, Lorenzo J. Greene, Rayford Logan, and Florence Beatty Brown, all of whom came to rank among the best of black historians and teachers.

Upon the inception of the *Journal of Negro History*, Frederick L. Hoffman, statistician of the Prudential Life

Insurance Company, "likened the movement unto the important work started by John R. Green, in popularizing the history of England." According to Woodson, the public immediately began to see that "the need of the hour was not to write books from the scant materials available, but to collect and preserve sufficient data of all sorts on the Negro to enable scientifically trained men to produce treatises based upon the whole truth." [7] Ferdinand Schevill stated that the first issue of the *Journal* bore "every evidence of a scientific disposition on the part of the editor and his board." [8]

The first substantial financial support for the *Journal of Negro History* came from Julius Rosenwald, who for years gave $100 a quarter for the support of the Association and its publication. It was not until after 1919 that this publication was self-supporting. However, rising costs of printing changed this favorable situation the very next year. The financial worries of this organization and its journal ended temporarily when the Carnegie Corporation, in 1921, appropriated $25,000 to the Association. This amount was to be paid at the rate of $5,000.00 per year. It is at this point that Woodson was able to give up teaching school and become full-time director of the Association. [9]

Also in 1921 the Laura Spelman Rockefeller Memorial appropriated a like sum of $25,000 to be paid to the Association in a similar manner. This fund was to be used for studying "the free Negro prior to the Civil War," and "the Negro in the Reconstruction of the Southern States." [10] In addition to Dr. Woodson, the Association was now able to hire other investigators to work in the United States and other parts of the world, collecting documents and facts on black people. Also, Woodson was then able to devote part of his time to field work with clubs and schools in his effort to popularize the teaching and studying of black history, and the Association was serving as a reference bureau for information respecting the black people.

Luther Porter Jackson pointed out in 1940 that the

early volumes of the *Journal of Negro History* "show a low standard of documentation," while the later volumes show "a high standard of documentation." This, he thinks, was due to the fact that few sources on the black man had been collected during the early years of the existence of the *Journal*. Of the documents which had been published in the *Journal* by 1968, almost all of them are found in volumes one through fourteen. Jackson attributes the failure of the Association to continue the publication of as many documents as were published during these early years to the lack of funds for the expensive task of locating them. He also points out that the first twelve volumes of the *Journal* carried sixteen book reviews each. Volume twenty jumped to twenty-six reviews, and volume twenty-two carried fifty-one.[11] The growing number of reviews reveals, perhaps, the growing interest in Afro-American history, as well as the growing number of Afro-American and other scholars who could be called on to prepare reviews.

Shortly after founding the Association for the Study of Negro Life and History, Dr. Woodson organized the Associated Publishers to handle both the publication and sale of books. This was a private corporation, in which he held over ninety percent of the stock, organized because he felt that white publishers were not interested in bringing out scholarly works by black scholars—a charge we frequently hear today. In addition to publishing Woodson's own volumes, the Association sponsored and published the researches of other scholars. On this point Woodson wrote:

The Negro faces another stone wall when he presents . . . scientific productions to the publishing houses. They may not be prejudiced, but they are not interested in the Negro. We understand that the more serious the work is the less chance it has for reaching a large reading public. Yet scholarship must be advanced by these strictly scientific works. This represents a very dark prospect for the rapidly increasing number of young men and women who are prepared for creative work but receive no encouragement whatever. In this way the cause of Negro scholarship has dreadfully suffered in spite of the one-sided method of the foundations in trying to broaden the minds of Negroes teaching in their own schools. What is the use of knowing things if they cannot be published to the world? If the Negro is to settle down to publishing merely what others permit him to bring out, the world will never know what the race has thought and felt and attempted and accomplished and the story of the Negro will perish with him.[12]

At the end of the Associated Publishers' first ten years, Woodson had published ten monographs, and "stimulated and trained young men with the capacity for research according to the methods of modern historiography." He regarded as the crowning achievement of this first decade of the Association's existence, that it had "made the world see the Negro as a participant rather than as a lay figure in history." By this time the *Journal* was a great success, circulating among libraries and scholars all over the world. This scholar always emphasized that his work was the beginning of a crusading movement to establish Afro-American history as a recognized and respected field. This attitude caused him to make repeated mention of the stimulation and training of "young men with the capacity for research according to the methods of modern historiography." [13] And near the conclusion of his life's work, he stated, "The stimulation and training of young men for historical research may be regarded as the outstanding achievement of the Association." [14]

By 1930 the contributions to the Association by wealthy white Americans and foundations had begun to fall off. Woodson always believed that this was due to people growing dissatisfied with his attacks on the "white supremacy" doctrine—his policy of "telling the whole truth and nothing but the truth regardless of whom it affected." He continued to organize the black population of the United States, hoping to obtain the needed support from them. By 1940 the income of the Association had risen to about two-thirds of what it was during its most prosperous years.[15]

In its first twenty-five years of existence, the Association received and spent $337,926.24, and published over thirty volumes. By 1940 the Association was publishing not only its own organs but directing studies and Afro-American history in clubs and schools, promoting the home study of the race by mail, producing textbooks, collecting and preserving documents, and subsidizing young scholars in their historical studies. It had sent investigators to work in the Archives of the West Indies, in Seville, Spain, the British Museum and the Public Record Office of London, and had sent one person to study folklore in Haiti. In addition, by this date the Association had purchased the A. A. Schomburg Collection of 4,000 books and presented this collection to the New York Public Library. Funds for this latter purchase were granted by the Carnegie Corporation.[16]

By 1935 at least 350 articles and series of documents had appeared in the *Journal of Negro History*, of which 241 were devoted either wholly or primarily to the Afro-American in the United States. Thus, about one-third of the material had dealt with the race outside the United States of America. Of this one-third, the greatest number had dealt with Africa, an almost equal number with Great Britain and Europe, and the remainder with Latin America, Canada, the West Indies other than Haiti and Cuba, and an almost negligible number with the Pacific Area and Near East.[17] Of these articles Rayford W. Logan wrote:

Some of the articles have been excellent, a few mediocre, but the general average has been entirely creditable. A large number of these articles utilized primary sources not only in English, but in French, German and Spanish. It is gratifying to find a growing number of Negro scholars able to read easily French. All too small a number, however, have mastered German. Some have used the rich store of Spanish resources. But the great mine of Brazilian sources in the Portuguese language has been left almost totally unexplored.[18]

Dr. Logan failed to mention the great neglect by Afro-American scholars of the ancient and medieval periods. Few have chosen these areas, and the American Negro researcher has made almost no contribution to them. Almost all have received their formal training with a concentration in American history. Thus, almost completely, they have failed to develop facility in some languages, such as Greek, Latin, Arabic, Spanish, and Portuguese, which is necessary for complete coverage of the field of Afro-American studies. (A notable exception to this is Frank M. Snowden, Jr., whose book *Blacks in Antiquity* is currently available.) Especially are the first three languages necessary for study of some important segments of the African background of the Afro-American. Dr. Logan ended his summation with an interesting prediction. "When the *Journal* has had an existence as long as has the *American Historical Review,* it is confidently expected that the *Journal* will not suffer by comparison with the best in the world." [19]

The Journal of Negro History gave tremendous impetus to scholarship in history by black scholars. It provided them with a journal which they felt would receive their articles with fairness, and gave them a living example of the level of scholarship that could be reached within the field of black history. Among early subscribers to the *Journal* were Oswald Garrison Villard, Helen Keller, J. E. Spingarn, Julius Rosenwald, Edward Channing. Among the early contributors of articles and reviews were Marcus W. Jernegan, Jerome Dowd, W. E. B. Du Bois, A. E. Jenks, J. S. Bassett, A. B. Hart, and other top scholars. During its first year, the *Journal* was circulated on all five continents and it began its second year with a circulation of 4,000.[20]

NEGRO HISTORY WEEK

THE NEGRO HISTORY BULLETIN

Negro History Week grew out of an effort to celebrate annually the literary achievements of black people begun by the Omega Psi Phi Fraternity.[21] Carter G. Woodson, an honorary member of this fraternity, convinced its leaders that he could make the celebration more effective by sponsoring it as an activity of the Association for the Study of Negro Life and History. Thus, in 1926, Woodson took over the celebration and gave it the name of Negro History Week. The celebration immediately became a national success. This annual event, said Woodson, "taught Negroes not to play up their grievances but to demonstrate what Negroes have actually achieved in spite of their handicaps," and "stimulated other efforts of the Association and of other organizations for the improvement of Negroes." [22] Again, calling the observance of Negro History Week one of the "most fortunate steps ever taken by the Association," Woodson pointed out that this event, "easily understood, . . . was readily taken up by ministers, teachers, social workers, and businessmen and several state departments of education," which rallied to the support of the movement.[23]

Woodson states that the success of Negro History Week led to a demand for a simplified organ which would regularly publish the many little-known facts such as those which he had sent to schools as a part of the annual celebration of Negro History Week. The result was the *Negro History Bulletin,* first published in October, 1937. The *Bulletin,* a monthly publication, appears only during the nine months of the regular school year, and is especially aimed at meeting the needs which grade-school teachers and pupils, and the general public, have for heavily illustrated literature and little-known facts about black people. By 1940 the circulation of the *Bulletin* was 5,000 and it was increasing annually.[24]

EDUCATION OF THE NEGRO
PRIOR TO 1861

This work appeared in 1915,[25] bearing the subtitle, *A History of the Education of the Colored People of the United States from the Beginning of Slavery to the Civil War*. Woodson had begun the research for this volume with the idea of writing a complete coverage of the field of Negro education up to 1915. He believed that there would be so little material on the antebellum period that the bulk of his volume would concern itself with post-Civil War events. However, he was surprised to find a great amount of material on the earlier period, and decided to cover only prewar years, since it would make "a much more interesting book." "In fact," he stated, "the accounts of the successful strivings of Negroes for enlightenment under most adverse circumstances reads like beautiful romances of a people in an heroic age." [26]

The author divided the history of Negro education before the Civil War into two periods. The first division ends with the year 1835. During this period, he found that many slaves were given education on the plantations. During the years from 1836 to 1861 he found that this patriarchal education disappeared, due largely to fear of insurrection which was aroused by such rebellions as those of Denmark Vesey and Nat Turner. During these latter years, the slave received only an industrial-type education.

Woodson found agreement on the high degree of interest which this topic would arouse. Reviewing the volume for the *American Journal of Sociology,* R. E. Park wrote: "Aside from the light which this book throws upon the rather obscure subjects, there is something at once touching and romantic in the story which its record of fact reveals." [27] The book was praised for the high standard of scholarship which it met. One reviewer, calling it "a model of scholarship," added, "Every available fact has been garnered and is made accessible to the reader by a painstaking index, while a scholarly bibliography gives the original sources. A valuable set of documents is appended, including many not hitherto laid open to the general public." [28] Another reviewer wrote, "The author has taken pains to substantiate every fact that he presents. . . . This is a work of profound historical research, full of interesting data on a most important phase of race life which has hitherto remained unexplored and neglected." [29] Woodson did not usually take the trouble to document so thoroughly in most of his future writings. Like his distinguished contemporary, Du Bois, his first two serious works were his most scholarly from the standpoint of documentation and general objectivity.

THE NEGRO IN OUR HISTORY

This scholar's textbook for the upper grades of high school and the general reader, *The Negro in Our History,*[30] went through nineteen editions during Woodson's lifetime. First published in 1922, the work was in its fourth edition by 1927. Until his death, it was constantly revised and enlarged to keep it up to date, and was unquestionably the best textbook on the subject until the appearance in 1947 of John Hope Franklin's *From Slavery to Freedom.*[31] Since Dr. Woodson's death his volume has been revised by Charles H. Wesley.

Woodson's textbook was designed "to present to the average reader in succinct form a history of the United States as it has been influenced by the presence of the Negro in this country." [32] It became the standard text for courses in Afro-American history throughout the United States. One reviewer stated that it bore "the brunt of the movement for the popularization of Negro history," and that "it has actually remolded the attitude of the popular mind, especially among Negroes, as to the place and importance of the Negro in American history." This same reviewer criticized the work for being "essentially a compendium of facts," although he admitted that the great influence of the volume might be due to its lack of interpretation. He stated, however, that for the university level a more interpretative text was needed. He concluded that this volume "belongs to that select class of books that have brought about a revolution of mind." [33] Beyond doubt, this book deserves a high place among the forces and events which have won general acceptance for the field of Negro history.

In *The Negro in Our History,* Woodson is especially temperate and objective. He was probably aware that, had he given the book an obviously biased nature, it would not have been widely used. While most black historians severely criticize President Andrew Johnson for opposing Radical Reconstruction, and present the character and personality of Johnson in an unfavorable light, Woodson steers clear of any characterization of this President. Throughout the volume one can observe a similar caution.

The volume gives a brief survey of early black civilizations in Africa, then discusses the enslavement of Africans, early efforts toward emancipation and colonization, the abolition movement, Civil War and Reconstruction, and the freedman's efforts at social justice. Profusely illustrated, the volume was finished five years before it was published. As World War I was then going on, and the cost of publishing was high, publication was delayed.[34] The fifth edition carried 651 pages and 350 illustrations. By then the volume was getting too bulky. Hubert Harrison, reviewing the book for the *New York Tribune,* called this a "primal defect." [35]

In 1928 Woodson adapted *The Negro in Our History* for the elementary school level. This adaptation was titled *Negro Makers of History.*[36] In 1935 he also published a shortened version for high school students, under the title *The Story of the Negro Retold.*[37] Both works were favorably received by critics. Also in 1928, he published *African Myths, Together with Proverbs,*[38] as a supplementary reader composed of folk tales from various parts of Africa. This volume was intended for children in the public schools.

A CENTURY OF NEGRO MIGRATION

In 1918 *A Century of Negro Migration* was published.[39] This volume reviews movements of Afro-Americans from the South to the North and West. It considers the causes and results of the migrations. The chapter on the Civil War period describes the breaking up of northern black communities when many persons followed the Union Army southward to resettle. Migration westward is also given close attention. The last chapter deals with the exodus during the First World War, which was the greatest voluntary movement of Negroes in the United States to that date. In a lengthy review, the *Times Literary Supplement* said of the volume: "There is no exuberance of statement, no fervid inaccuracy, no frothy declamation." [40]

THE HISTORY OF THE NEGRO CHURCH

This volume was published in 1921 and dealt with the evolution of the Negro Church "from the earliest period to the present time." Woodson admitted that the final product did not represent what he desired to make it. This was because, "many facts of the past could not be obtained for the reason that several denominations have failed to keep records and facts known to persons now active in the church could not be collected because of indifference or the failure to understand the motives of the author." [41]

The History of the Negro Church is one of this historian's most important productions. The work is important and is almost straight narrative. However, a critical reader would probably regret that it is almost completely devoid of documentation, and that there is no bibliography or bibliographical notes. Also, Woodson probably generalizes too much concerning what black church leaders have believed about certain political and economic questions during various periods.

In this volume, the church leaders are praised because they have been conservative on racial matters. He praises the traditional conservatism of the church as "fortunate." The statement seems somewhat contradictory to the arguments which Woodson directs at the church leaders in his *Mis-Education of the Negro*. This volume further reveals Woodson as an intellectual with a nineteenth-century faith in education. He felt that *the* way to improve race relations was through education of both American whites and blacks. His patience with racial advance probably sprang, in part, from a realization that education is necessarily a slow process.

EARLY NEGRO EDUCATION IN
WEST VIRGINIA

FIFTY YEARS OF NEGRO CITIZENSHIP
AS QUALIFIED BY THE
U.S. SUPREME COURT

In December, 1921, Woodson published a small booklet entitled *Early Negro Education in West Virginia*.[42] In the same year "Fifty Years of Negro Citizenship as Qualified by the United States Supreme Court" was published in the *Journal of Negro History* as an article, and in 1924 in booklet form.[43] In the latter work, the author began with the assertion: "The citizenship of the Negro in this country is a fiction. The Constitution of the United States guarantees to him every right vouchsafed to any individual by the most liberal democracy on the face of the earth, but despite the powers of the Federal Government this agent of the body politic has studiously evaded the duty of safeguarding the rights of the Negro." [44] Although it is a good objective study of Constitutional history of the United States as it affected the freedmen in the period under question, the work fails to give a balanced picture of the reasons why the Supreme Court discriminated against the race in its ruling. By failing to mention that the Court may not have been far behind American public opinion, Woodson makes the Court the villain.

THE MIS-EDUCATION OF THE NEGRO

Woodson's *The Mis-Education of the Negro* was published in 1923. In this work the author states that the Afro-American has been mis-educated because he has not been taught to value himself at his proper worth.[45] Topics handled in this volume are: "Negroes—Education," "Negroes—Moral and Social Conditions," "Negroes—Employment."

Woodson advocated a special type of education for the black American. The lack of sufficient race pride on the part of the Afro-American was a matter of serious concern to this scholar. Indeed, it was an obsession which helped move and direct the course of his life. An anonymous reviewer in *Commonweal* reported:

This is a challenging book. It throws down the gauntlet to those who have had anything to do with Negro education, whether of white or black race, and it bids the Negro to come forward in pride of race and heritage and standing on the basis of his own racial personality, demand an education that will develop that personality and its gifts rather than seek merely to imitate the white man.[46]

In *Mis-Education of the Negro,* Woodson is severe in his criticism of Negro educators. "The only question which concerns us here," he wrote, "is whether these 'educated' persons are actually equipped to face the ordeal before them or unconsciously contribute to their own undoing by perpetuating the regime of the oppressor." He believed that the reason black Americans "accepted" their inferior status was that, for years, they were "daily educated in the tenets of the status quo." [47] Continuing in this same vein, he stated: "The 'educated Negroes' have the attitude of contempt toward their own people because in their own as well as in their mixed schools they are taught to admire the Hebrew, the Greek, the Latin and the Teuton and to despise the African." [48]

Like Du Bois, Woodson had a peculiar faith in the need for scientifically studying the black race. In this same volume, Woodson wrote:

We must bear in mind that the Negro has never been educated. He has merely been informed about other things which he has not been permitted to do. . . . The program for the uplift of the Negro in this country must be based upon a scientific study of the Negro from within to develop in him the power to do for himself what his oppressors will never do to elevate him to the level of others. . . . But can you expect teachers to revolutionize the social order for the good of the community? Indeed we must expect this very thing. The educational system of a country is worthless unless it accomplishes this task. Men of scholarship, and consequently of prophetic insight, must show us the right way and lead us into the light which shines brighter and brighter.[49]

Here Woodson illustrates the manner in which he would reconstruct the curriculum for Negro schools.[50] As one would expect, black history and special problems peculiar to black people are given great prominence in this reconstruction.

FREE NEGRO OWNERS OF SLAVES

FREE NEGRO HEADS OF FAMILIES

These two works were published in 1924[51] and 1925[52] respectively. The first was a brief work, which also gave data on absentee ownership of slaves in the United States in 1830. Almost all of the data for both works came from the census reports for 1830. A grant given by the Laura Spelman Rockefeller Memorial in 1921 had made the studies possible, and much of the research had been carried out by employees of the Association. Woodson acted primarily as an editor. The aim of both publications was "to promote the further study of a neglected aspect of our history," [53] and both works were largely statistical compilations.

THE MIND OF THE NEGRO AS REFLECTED IN LETTERS WRITTEN DURING THE CRISIS

A work on source readings which Woodson compiled was *Negro Orators and Their Orations*.[54] This work was published as a companion volume to another production of source readings entitled *The Mind of the Negro Reflected in Letters Written During the Crisis, 1800–1860*.[55] In *Negro Orators* Woodson found that the "Negro spokesmen were in no sense different from the orators of other groups, although they were not usually so well educated." He concluded that the black orators should be judged, therefore, not on style, but on the effect which they produced in the listeners.[56] In the volume, each speech is prefaced by a brief biographical sketch of the life of the speaker.

The Mind of the Negro, The New York Times stated, "presents such an insight into the mentality of the Negro during the period of slavery as can hardly be found anywhere else."[57] The *Catholic World* indicated that the greatest value of such a publication would be for students, to whom it is a "mine of information."[58] Many of the letters included in this volume had already appeared serially in the *Journal of Negro History*. The first section of the volume contains letters to the American Colonization Society regarding the project of emigration to Liberia, and the second contains correspondence on the subject of the antislavery movement. The two small concluding sections contain personal, private, and miscellaneous correspondence.

THE NEGRO AS A BUSINESSMAN

THE NEGRO WAGE EARNER

THE RURAL NEGRO

In 1929, a work which Woodson coauthored with John H. Harmon, Jr. and Arnett C. Lindsay, entitled *The Negro as a Businessman*,[59] was published. The next year saw another collaborative effort, this one coauthored with Lorenzo J. Greene, a young Ph.D. in history just out of Columbia University. This volume was entitled *The Negro Wage Earner*,[60] and was the result of a survey conducted by Dr. Greene which considered such topics as occupations engaged in by Negroes, limitations of job opportunities for them, and the increasing proportion of jobs requiring skill. The book began with the jobs handled by blacks during the period of slavery and showed how members of the race had continued, to a large extent, in these same occupations. The volume is replete with tables and statistical accounts. The authors concluded that it was not until after World War I that more equal distribution of black labor occurred. This important change, wrought by the needs of American factories in the North and East, introduced black Americans to new sections of the nation and served, according to the authors, to improve race relations in the South.[61]

The Negro Wage Earner, together with *Free Negro Owners of Slaves*, *Free Negro Heads of Families*, and *The Rural Negro*[62] were all results of a three-year survey of Negro life in America undertaken by the Association beginning in 1926. Woodson's *The Rural Negro* was a treatment of rural persons of the South as to conditions of health, farming, tenancy, peonage, industry, trade, religion, education and recreation. It was well received. One reviewer called it "A first-hand piece of research, well-documented and intimately interpreted." [63] Another criticized Woodson for making the volume, at times, a tract against certain forms of exploitation of the rural black.[64] This reviewer also criticized the book because of its scanty documentation. The monograph was compiled largely from facts in United States census reports and questionnaires which were sent to rural families.

THE NEGRO PROFESSIONAL MAN AND THE COMMUNITY

In this volume Woodson gave special emphasis to the professions of medicine and law.[65] Topics treated were: "Negroes—Employment," "Negroes—Moral and Social Conditions," "Negro Physicians," and "Negro Lawyers." The survey on which the volume was based covered almost the whole of the South, and most of the large cities, with considerable coverage of populations outside of the South. For this survey, as with the other topics treated in this series of studies launched in 1926, Woodson had a staff of collaborators who did the bulk of the research, while he served as coordinator, editor, and interpreter. *The Negro Professional Man and the Community* possesses almost no documentation. This volume was a companion one to *The Negro Wage Earner*. The entire series of studies was designed "to portray the social and economic conditions obtaining among Negroes since the Civil War." [66]

The Harvard Law Review praised *The Negro Professional Man and the Community* as being "invaluable and indicating that the colored professional man has the ability to progress if given the opportunity," but added that the abundance of statistical material "may make its reading difficult save to the sociologically-minded reader." [67] *The New York Times* praised the scientific spirit in which the data were collected and the fair-minded manner in which the material was discussed. This review also stated that the study constituted "a valuable sociological contribution to knowledge of the present status of the Negro in the United States." [68]

THE AFRICAN BACKGROUND OUTLINED

This excellent volume is a syllabus for the study of Afro-American history.[69] It is misnamed since over one-half of its contents treats the development of the black man in America.[70] In this work, Woodson stated that the history of the black man shows that the race has achieved much in various fields, and "to know the possibilities of the race a scientific appraisal of its past is necessary." He went on, "The author considers the Negro as human—responding very much as others do to the same stimuli, advancing when free to go forward and lagging behind when hindered by obstacles not encountered by others." [71]

This syllabus readily won high praise as "one of the most useful and scholarly works" produced by Woodson. One reviewer felt that the syllabus should "definitely dispel the doubt still held in some quarters whether there is such a thing as Negro history." [72] A unique contribution of the syllabus was the section on Europe-in-Africa, in which Woodson drew on his life-long researches as well as three summers of special research in European libraries and book stores.

AFRICAN HEROES AND HEROINES

Woodson published this volume as a biographical account of various Africans who had risen to prominence.[73]

It was intended primarily for junior and senior high school students. As usual with him when writing on this aspect of African history, this scholar stressed especially the militant resistance of the African nations and tribes to both Arabic and European invaders. Also included in the volume are a brief survey of the geography and peoples of Africa and the black states which existed there. A reviewer writing for the *Boston Transcript* criticized the volume for its "strong note of militant vindication that rather mars the strictly expository portions of the book." On a whole, the volume, like most of Woodson's writings, was well received. Even the above reviewer admitted that it filled "a gap in our fund of information." [74] The volume carried a comprehensive bibliography. Of *African Heroes and Heroines,* the author concluded that these "leaders of a despised people measure up to the full stature of the heroic in the histories of other nations." [75] Of the general history of Africa, he wrote:

The Africans, we ignorantly say, left no history of their entire continent, but no nation has recorded a history of the whole natural division of the universe in which it developed. The ancient history of certain parts of Europe is as obscure as that of areas in Africa, and the past of Asia is scarcely better known than that of Africa. Much more of the history of Africa is known . . . than we appreciate.[76]

Woodson, as we see, was prolific. He edited *The Works of Francis J. Grimke* in four volumes[77] and was constantly writing articles.[78]

He entered the field of black history for essentially the same reason as did Du Bois. They were both attacking the neglect of the black man in the social science volumes most used in the late nineteenth and early twentieth centuries. Charles Wesley states that

Woodson did not set out deliberately to become a scholar. He seems to have been almost pressed into scholarship by . . . strivings for explanation in society. . . . He had seen that scholars had selected the facts which they desired to include in their published works and had neglected others.

As a result of the omissions and neglect of others, he then became a rebel against the learning of the scholars in the universities, after having tested this knowledge against fundamentally valid truths discovered through his own life experience. . . .

Woodson insisted upon the discovery of the complete truth, and when he came upon partial truth, he did not hesitate to abandon the false.[79]

As indicated, Woodson believed that a great history would stimulate achievement in the black race. "If a race has no history," he wrote, ". . . it becomes a negligible factor in the thought of the world, and it stands in danger of being exterminated." [80]

Woodson also believed that race prejudice was the result of faulty education, and that if American whites and blacks were told the truth about achievements of the black man in history, race prejudice would disappear. On this point, he wrote:

Race prejudice . . . is not something inherent in human nature. It is merely the logical result of tradition, the inevitable outcome of thorough instruction to the effect that the Negro has never contributed anything to progress of mankind.

Just as thorough education in the belief in the inequality of races brought the world to the cat-and-dog stage of religious and racial strife, so may thorough instruction in the equality of races bring about a reign of brotherhood through an appreciation of the virtues of all races, creeds and colors. In such a millennium the achievements of the Negro properly set forth will crown him as a factor in early human progress and a maker of modern civilization.[81]

Woodson was a strong believer in cultural history. No doubt he was influenced in this belief by the New History movement led by James Harvey Robinson, which was tending in this general direction. But it is highly probable that his desire for a greater consideration of the Negro underprivileged minority was a considerable factor in causing him to champion a history which included the story of the masses. On this point, he wrote that history should be broad, social and cultural. He complained that most written history was "that sort . . . which is merely the record of the successes and disappointments, the vices, the follies, and the quarrels of those who engage in the contention for power." [82] "The real makers of history," he wrote, have been "those servants of the truth who have labored to enlighten humanity, to lift it out of drudgery into comfort, out of darkness into light, and out of selfishness into altruism." [83] Du Bois also very frequently stated that most history was little short of "propaganda."

Though the purpose in writing his widely used *The Negro in Our History* was "to present to the average reader in succinct form the history of the United States as it has been influenced by the presence of the Negro in this country," there is in the volume an almost total omission of such bad features as high crime rates, slums, disease, and other undesirable phenomena which "the presence of the Negro in this country" has sometimes meant. When Woodson adapted his *The Negro in Our History* to the capacity of children in the elementary schools, he wrote that "The aim here is to facilitate the teacher's task of preparing children to play their part creditably in this new age. The teacher must hold up before them the examples of their own people, who have done things worth while. Those who have no record of what their forbears have accomplished lose the inspiration which comes from the teaching of biography and history." [84] Dr. Woodson felt keenly that the Afro-American must be reeducated to a greater appreciation of the race's past. He utilized almost every conceivable opportunity for reaching not only scholarly persons, but the elementary and high school populations, teachers of all levels, as well as the laity.

Woodson felt that the historian should strive for maximum objectivity and should be scrupulously exact and honest in presenting facts. He generally succeeded in keeping his history correct, and his writings are usually dispassionate. Unlike George Washington Williams, William Wells Brown, Du Bois and some others, Woodson's writings seldom read like orations and sermons. He lacks the prolific use of adjectives and elegant phrases which was until recently characteristic of much black historiography.

Woodson not infrequently interrupts his historical narrative or criticism to moralize. While this tendency is to be noted in many historians, ancient or modern, and is perhaps forgivable when kept to a minimum, this scholar took excessive liberties with the privilege. Still, he does not go to the extent in this regard to which many of his predecessors did. This tendency on the part of Woodson and others shows that they have sought to utilize historical writings as a weapon in the race "cause." Woodson's greatest fear for the black race was that "awful fate of becoming a negligible factor in the thought of the world." [85]

One writer referred to Woodson's style as "cramped and slovenly." [86] It is highly probable that some of the faults of his style are attributable to the speed with which he wrote. Along with Du Bois, he was by far the most prolific black historian which this country has produced. At his death in 1950, he was endeavoring to write a six-volume comprehensive history of the race. This, and an encyclopedia of the black race, he hoped to make the crowning achievements of his life.[87] Neither was finished. Woodson constantly mentioned the need for an Encyclopedia Africana. His greatest contribution to historiography lies not so much in his writings, as effective as they were, but in the fact that he launched and popularized a successful movement. He had great organizational abilities and an eye for the future. Thus he founded the Association for the Study of Negro Life and History, the *Journal,* the *Bulletin,* the Associated Publishers, launched Negro History Week, and interested promising young historians in his cause and aided them in their training. On this aspect of Woodson's life, Wesley writes:

His successful organization of membership campaigns, and the financial appeals, mark him as more than the scholar of the ivory tower. He collected disciples, young men and women who were invited to his meetings and who loved the cause even more than the master, but at the same time they admired him and his abilities. Many became of themselves pioneers in selected areas of Negro scholarship in the social sciences. He gave his movement a philosophy and built an organization for it.[88]

Woodson's pioneer efforts in studying the history of the race contributed tremendously to the coming into being of a new area for historical research and study which, stated M. J. Herskovits in 1951, "did not exist in recognizable form as recently as twenty years ago." [89] "Dr. Woodson," states another writer, "has probably done more than any single person to rescue Negro history from oblivion." [90] It is a judgment no one can disagree with.

PIONEERS IN BLACK STUDIES

CHARLES H. WESLEY

Charles H. Wesley is placed with the Middle Group of black historians because of his prominent role in establishing the field of Afro-American studies, and because his general attitude toward the place and importance of black history coincides with that of Woodson and Du Bois.

Wesley received the bachelor's degree from Fisk University, the M.A. from Yale, and the Ph.D. from Harvard, using as a dissertation topic "Negro Labor in the United States, 1850–1925." After getting his doctorate he immediately joined in the crusade which Du Bois and Woodson already had well under way. But Wesley did not confine his activities to historical research and writing as exclusively as did Carter Woodson. Indeed, no Negro scholar has. However, his emphases were generally identical with those of Woodson and Du Bois, and his writing, although usually restrained and scholarly, is to a considerable extent a protest against unfavorable racial doctrines.

Wesley's books are: *Negro Labor in the United States, 1850–1925*[1]; *Richard Allen, Apostle of Freedom*[2]; *The Collapse of the Confederacy*[3]; *The History of Alpha Phi Alpha*,[4] and *A History of the I.B.P.O.E.*[5] He also has written several brief monographs and numerous articles, most of which have appeared in the *Journal of Negro History*.[6]

His pioneer study of Negro labor in the United States was a significant contribution in this area and of excellent quality. All of the major factors which have affected the general labor movement in this country are applied to the evolution of Negro labor. Wesley blamed the shortcomings of black workers largely on racial prejudice. Considering the high quality of this work, it may be regretted that this scholar did not claim the overall labor movement in the United States as a specialty. There have been no specialists in the labor movement among Negro historians. Indeed a general criticism which may be levelled at black historical scholars is their failure to develop and stick to specialties.

In 1935 Wesley published what has been termed a definitive biography of Richard Allen, founder of the African Methodist Episcopal Church. In 1929 his *History of Alpha Phi Alpha, A Development in Negro College Life* appeared. This work is the standard history of this organization and is of considerable value in depicting an aspect of the social history of the Negro.

Wesley's *Collapse of the Confederacy* is an effort to interpret the causes for the defeat of the South in the Civil War. He had written an essay on this topic while a student of Professor Edward Channing at Harvard University, and this volume was the result of a revision and expansion of that essay.[7] Wesley comes to the somewhat novel conclusion that the South lost the war, not because of economic or military reasons, but due to poor morale. "The collapse of the South," he writes, "was due . . . more directly to the absence of a wholehearted and sustained resistance." [8] Since the morale of the North was even worse than that of the South for much of the war, it is highly probable that Wesley's conclusion lacks substance. It is more probable that declining morale in 1864–65 was due to the fact that many Southerners realized that the war was already lost. At the time this volume was published, Dr. Wesley was Professor of History at Howard University.

Like Woodson, with whom he worked intimately, Wesley believes that there should be no such thing as race history. Yet, he too feels that American history is incompletely written unless the story of the Negro is made an integral part of it. Wesley has labored unceasingly, through pen and forum, to bring about such a revision of American history and to attain recognition for the general area of Afro-American studies.

Pleading in 1935 for a reconstruction of history, this scholar stated: "History is not the story of men and women of one race or color and the neglect and omission of the men and women of another race or color. It is neither the glorification of white people nor black people, but it is the story of the people irrespective of race or color. It should deal with people in all times and places and should present the contribution of all the people to civilization." Laying down the lines along which the history of the United States and the Western world should be rendered, Wesley declared that (1) "History should be reconstructed so that Africa . . . shall have its proper place"; (2) "History should be reconstructed so that Negroes shall be known on a higher level than that of jokes and minstrels"; (3) "History should be reconstructed so that Negroes shall appear not only as the recipients of liberty, but as the winners of it, not only for themselves, but also for others"; and (4) "History should be reconstructed so that Negroes shall be regarded as Americans and not simply as slaves or as an alien part of the population." [9]

Also like Woodson, Wesley feels that Negro history should be a prime concern of all historians. Scoring the concept of the inferiority of the Negro, he wrote in 1940: "Here then is the challenge to American scholars, Negro and White, for the days of race propaganda continue. . . . It is imperative that we study again the capacity of races. Historians of the Negro people should direct attention to Africa and the Africans. These African peoples should be rescued from oblivion and from the belief in their savagery, barbarism and inferiority." [10]

MONROE NATHAN WORK

Monroe Nathan Work (1866–1945) was a pioneer in establishing the field of Afro-American studies. He would deserve mention in any discussion of Negro historiography if he had produced only one of his several writings. That volume is his *Bibliography of the Negro in Africa and America*.[11]

He was born of slave parents in Iredell County, North Carolina, and educated in the public schools of Kansas and at the University of Chicago. From the latter, he received the Bachelor of Philosophy degree in 1902 and an M.A. in Sociology and Psychology in 1903. From 1903 to 1908 Work taught History and Education at the Georgia State Industrial College.[12]

While at the University of Chicago, states one observer, Work decided to "dedicate his life to the gathering of information and the compiling of exact knowledge concerning the Negro." [13] He began his study and collection of titles on Africa in 1904 while a teacher of history at the Georgia State Industrial College in Savannah.

At the invitation of Booker T. Washington, Work went to Tuskegee in 1908 where he was Director of Records and Research for almost a generation. Every few years, with the Director as editor, this organization issued the *Negro Year Book*. This publication first appeared in 1912. Each issue carried a select bibliography of the Negro and a thorough coverage of recent activities concerning the Negro.

Readers of the *Negro Year Book* constantly requested more bibliographical information on the Negro than it regularly published. In 1921 a Carnegie grant to the Department of Records and Research at Tuskegee enabled Work to devote a major portion of his time to compiling a comprehensive bibliography in this area. Between 1921 and 1925 he collected over 30,000 references, from which 10,000 were chosen for publication in a special bibliography. New demands from persons interested in studying the history of the Negro caused Work to add over 7,000 more titles to the selected 10,000. By 1927 he had decided to enlarge the title from the first projected *The Negro in the United States* to *The Negro in Africa and America*. A Phelps-Stokes Fund grant made it possible for him to go to England, France, Germany, and other centers in Europe in his search for titles.[14]

The *Bibliography* was published as "an effort to furnish extended and comprehensive references to sources of information relating to all phases of the present day life of the Negro, to the conditions affecting this life and also to the anthropological and historical background of the same." [15] Over twenty years of research and study went into the making of this production. The volume was very well received upon its publication and has been ever since the best single work on the topic. It has not yet been superseded and is badly in need of being brought up to date. In the introduction, Anson Phelps Stokes states: "Someone was sure to undertake the task of meeting the need for this comprehensive bibliography. I, for one, am extremely glad that an American Negro . . . had the imagination to conceive of the work on broad lines, the scholarly mind to follow the best bibliographic standard in its preparation, and the persistence to carry it through effectively in spite of the enormous labor and difficulties involved. It is a monument of which any race may well feel proud." [16]

Work died May 2, 1945, but not before he had also published many articles on Negro life and history and edited nine editions of the *Negro Year Book*. In 1913, he published the first of the famed annual Tuskegee Reports on lynching in the United States. His purpose in publishing this information was "to change the South's attitude toward lynching." [17] He also gave extensive aid to Booker T. Washington in the writing of Washington's *Story of the Negro*,[18] and built at Tuskegee a "priceless collection of information on Negro life and achievement that cannot be duplicated." [19] His many scholarly articles about the race appeared in the leading publications in the United States. These articles, as well as the *Bibliography of the Negro in Africa and America,* and editions of the *Negro Year Book* give him rank among the top Negro historians produced in this country. His efforts, like those of Woodson, Du Bois, and Wesley, contributed greatly to establishing Negro history as a recognized and respectable field of study.[20]

MERL R. EPPSE

Merl R. Eppse (1900–1967), long-time Chairman of the Department of History and Geography, Tennessee State University, Nashville, holds the A.B. from Drake University, M.A. from Columbia University, and LL.D. from Wilberforce University. Together with Woodson, Du Bois, Wesley, and Work, Dr. Eppse shares the honor of being one of the founders of the field of Afro-American studies. Also with these men, he has had great faith in the ability of instruction in Negro history to effect a positive change in race relations. With this end in mind, he produced, for grade-school children, a textbook in American history which included "the contributions of the Negro race." [21] This work was coauthored with the Recording Secretary of the Tennessee Historical Society, and introduced as "an attempt to help America solve one of her most complex problems—the relation between the white race and the Negro race." [22] Dr. Eppse is also the author of a general history of the American Negro in which he attempted to tell the story of the Afro-American as a part of the national scene.[23] His syllabus on Negro history is one of the best ever produced,[24] and, like Woodson, he successfully organized his own publishing company. His writing style is simple and straightforward.

THE BLACK HISTORIAN:
The Layman as a Writer of History

7

HISTORIANS WITHOUT PORTFOLIO

It has already been indicated that a few of the works produced by the earlier writers were published by "Associations of Colored Men" specifically organized to encourage research and publication in the nascent field of Negro history. The works of Robert Benjamin Lewis and James Theodore Holly were placed before the public in this manner.

Little is known about these early groups, but during the last quarter of the nineteenth century, well-organized Negro historical societies were created. As the efforts of Du Bois and Woodson attracted national attention, many such societies came into existence.[1] Negroes in all walks of life had been made conscious of the fact that they had a past in which they had been something more than "hewers of wood and drawers of water." Their interest in this past produced what might be termed a third school of historians, the modern layman.

Due to the inadequacy of available records, some of these historical societies must remain anonymous. During

the last quarter of the nineteenth century, the Bethel
Literary and Historical Association was founded in Washington. Daniel A. Payne, prominent Negro church historian, was a leading figure in the organization of this group.
In 1911 Arthur A. Schomburg founded the Negro Society
for Historical Research, which issued a series of studies on
Negro themes as "Occasional Papers." [2] Booker Washington was prominently associated with this organization.
There was also a Massachusetts Historical Society of the
same nature.[3] Perhaps, next to Woodson's own Association
for the Study of Negro Life and History, the most prominent organization fostering Negro history was the American Negro Academy of Washington, D. C., which published
several volumes, many articles, and small monographs as
occasional papers, and worked intimately with Woodson.
Founded March 5, 1897, under the leadership of Alexander
Crummell, this organization had among its members such
scholars as John W. Cromwell, William Henry Crogman,
Kelly Miller, J. E. Moorland, and Archibald H. Grimke.

Judged by the nature and quality of their writings, the
members of the Modern Laymen's School generally should
be placed between the earlier writers and those associated
with Woodson and Du Bois. Yet, in point of time, the
laymen were contemporaries of the latter group and share
the honor of establishing Negro history as a respectable
field of study.[4]

The lay Negro historians of this period represent that
group of non-professional persons, in all periods, who have
a fondness for the discipline of history, feeling that their
life experiences peculiarly fit them for chronicling some
historical events. The following persons are outstanding
laymen of Negro history.

ARTHUR ALPHONSO SCHOMBURG

Arthur Alphonso Schomburg (1874–1938) was born in San Juan, Puerto Rico. After attending elementary and high school there, he read law for five years and served for five years as Secretary of the Las Dos Antillas Cuban Revolutionary Party. Schomburg came to the United States in 1891. Here he served for five years (1891–1896) as a member of the New York Puerto Rico Revolutionary Party. He also taught Spanish in New York and served as a journalist and editor. He was a member of the Negro Academy of Washington, D. C., as well as Secretary-Treasurer for the Negro Society for Historical Research, Yonkers, New York, which he founded.[5] He is, and will be, best remembered as a very active bibliophile. At his death in 1938, *Crisis* observed that he was "one of the leaders in that band of historians, literateurs and researchers who are contributing to the enlightenment of all people on the history of Negroes."[6]

A significant aspect of this period, which Schomburg typifies, is the great interest in collecting and preserving documents and other sources on the history of the Negro. Libraries at Negro colleges, such as Fisk University, Atlanta University, Tuskegee Institute, Hampton Institute, and Howard University, all evidenced their growing interest in the history of the race by beginning Negro collections. Schomburg sold his collection to the New York Public Library, and it has been substantially increased since it was first opened to the public. By 1940 Professor Merl Eppse of Nashville, Edward T. Garrett of New York, E. K. "Duke" Ellington, and a number of other Afro-Americans possessed private libraries on the Negro, each of which numbered over a thousand volumes. Upon the opening of the Schomburg Library to students in 1926, *Opportunity* summarized this contribution as follows:

The New York Public Library receives the Schomburg Collection of several thousand books, . . . autographs and manuscripts on the Negro, as the result of the purchase by Carnegie Foundation of New York City of this matchless collection from Mr. Schomburg. The sum of $10,000 was sought and obtained for this purpose by the National Urban League. . . .

Mr. Schomburg's desire to have this collection available in a strategic center for students of Negro life, and his wish to stimulate the aspirations of young Negro literary talent were largely responsible for the good fortune which has come to the Library and to these students. . . . In the Collection are . . . practically every important book written by or about the Negro in America and an astonishing revelation of books on the subject in French, Latin and Spanish.[7]

JOHN WESLEY CROMWELL

John Wesley Cromwell (1846–1927), historian, lawyer, teacher, was born in Portsmouth, Virginia, of slave parentage. After obtaining his freedom, he moved to Philadelphia where he received his education. He taught school in Virginia, then studied for and in 1874 received the law degree at Howard University. He practiced law in Washington, D. C., until 1892, and earned an M.A. degree from Wilberforce University in 1914. Closely associated with the Negro Academy of Washington, D. C., Cromwell had his volume *The Negro in American History* published by that organization in 1914.[8]

When this volume appeared, Cromwell was Secretary for the Academy. The work was subtitled *Men and Women Eminent in the Evolution of the American of African Descent.* Unlike most histories, this volume carries no section on the African background of Negro history. After devoting seventy-six pages to the story of the development of the race, Cromwell exhausts the remainder of the volume with the biographical sketches of outstanding Negroes. The work contains 267 pages divided into thirty-five chapters.

JOHN R. LYNCH

John R. Lynch (1847–1939) was a congressional representative from Mississippi during Reconstruction. After his term in office he wrote two volumes on the Reconstruction, the most outstanding being *The Facts of Reconstruction*. The appearance of this book was part of efforts and activities which properly may be labeled "Black Progressive Movement." *The Facts of Reconstruction* vigorously challenged the then-hardened view advanced by many white historians that newly enfranchised blacks—supposedly in control of southern states—and cynically selfish scalawags and carpetbaggers were responsible for just about all of the evils of a nightmarish Reconstruction era. This racist, conservative, propagandistic view of the Reconstruction era was used to justify driving blacks out of office and away from the polls. Disenfranchisement, armed attacks by whites on black communities, and the frequent lynchings of blacks were major factors behind the public efforts of Lynch and other black muckrakers.

The Facts of Reconstruction is scholarly in tone—"accurate and trustworthy information," Lynch termed it—and shows that the author possessed keen insight into the forces that were at work locally and nationally during this period. Since he held high public offices in the state of Mississippi, Lynch was a participant in many of the developments which he relates. Later, writing in 1917 in the *Journal of Negro History* on "Some Historical Errors of James Ford Rhodes," Lynch attacked this scholar for presenting the propagandistic view of the Reconstruction era. Still later,

Lynch vigorously dissented from the same basic interpretation of the period which had recently appeared in Claude G. Bowers' book, *The Tragic Era.*

Although Lynch was largely self-educated, he had a keen appreciation for constitutional and legal matters. As the slow recognition given W. E. B. Du Bois's book, *Black Reconstruction,* published two decades later, shows, for both the white American scholarly and lay publics, *The Facts of Reconstruction* was a book ahead of its times. The other volume was similar in subject matter and material. He was constantly in close correspondence with Woodson and gave him many facts concerning the events of the Reconstruction period.[9]

HENRY A. WALLACE

Henry A. Wallace was born in Columbia, South Carolina, in 1856 of a free Negro family which later migrated to Canada. In 1870 he returned to South Carolina and served as a Page of the State Legislature, thus getting to know very well most of the Reconstruction politicians. After Reconstruction, Wallace moved to Washington, D. C., where he worked for the federal government. He later moved to New York City, and spent the last two years of his life in West Chester, Pennsylvania. He died in 1923. His literary activities paralleled those of John R. Lynch; letters in the Woodson Collection reveal that he too gave Woodson many facts concerning the Reconstruction Period. Wallace was greatly interested in keeping the historical record straight on the true facts of Reconstruction. His interest in this connection caused him to correspond with D. S. Muzzey, James Ford Rhodes, Henry Cabot Lodge, John W. Burgess, and other persons interested in history. Though his formal education extended only through grade school, his letters reveal him to have been a keen student of American history.[10]

JOHN EDWARD BRUCE

John Edward Bruce used the nom de plume "Bruce Grit." He came into close contact with Woodson while in Government service in Washington, D. C. Later Bruce moved to New York City which became the center of his activity. A newspaperman of great intelligence and ability, Bruce did wide researches into history and was the founder of the Negro Historical Society of New York. He was one of the most outstanding and active of the laymen who stayed in close contact with Woodson and the Negro history movement during its earliest days.[11]

EDWARD AUSTIN JOHNSON

Edward Austin Johnson (1860–1944), historian, lawyer, and teacher, published two major works in history. After teaching school and practicing law in Raleigh, North Carolina, he moved to New York where he continued his law practice and served for a time in the State Legislature. In 1891 his *School History of the Negro Race in America from 1619 to 1890* appeared.[12]

This textbook on black history had the format of most public school textbooks and contained much well-presented information. When the revised edition appeared in 1896, he was principal of the Washington School, Raleigh, North Carolina. He dedicated the book to "the many thousand colored teachers" in the nation. In the preface he stated that during an eleven-year career as a teacher, he often had felt that black children needed to learn something about the "many brave deeds and noble characters of their own race." He criticized white authors for their "sin of omission and commission" where the subject of blacks in history is concerned, and said that most white authors "studiously left out the many creditable deeds of the Negro." Although "the general tone of most of the histories taught in our schools has been that of the inferiority of the Negro," Johnson continued, "true historical records prove him to have been among the most patriotic of patriots, among the bravest of soldiers, and constantly a God-fearing, faithful producer of the nation's wealth." On the subject of the negative treatment constantly meted out to blacks, Johnson declared, "patriotism and valor under such circumstances possess a peculiar merit and beauty." The work carried an extended account of the role of Negro soldiers in the Spanish-American War as well as a sketch of the history of Liberia. Johnson was a "pioneer in adapting Negro history to the capacity of children." [13] He also published a *History of Negro Soldiers in the Spanish American War*.[14]

LAURA ELIZA WILKES

Another historian of this school was Laura Eliza Wilkes. Born in 1871, Miss Wilkes served for years as a teacher in the public schools of Washington, D. C., and was a life-long student of Negro history. In 1898 her *Story of Frederick Douglass* appeared, and in 1919 she published a study entitled *Missing Pages in American History, revealing the Services of Negroes in the Early Wars of America*.[15] She complained bitterly to Woodson because he had not seen fit to review her efforts in the *Journal of Negro History*.[16]

THEOPHILUS GOULD STEWARD

The Reverend Theophilus Gould Steward (1843–1924) was for many years a professor at Wilberforce University, Wilberforce, Ohio. Having travelled widely, he was a keen student of Negro history and a prolific writer. Among his many writings—mostly religious—are *The Colored Regulars in the U. S. Army* and works on Haiti and the siege of Savannah.[17]

WILLIAM HENRY CROGMAN, SR.

Like Schomburg, Crogman (1841–1931) was born in the West Indies. Having earned the master's degree, Crogman became a Professor of Classics at his alma mater, Atlanta University. He also served as President from 1903 to 1910. He is coauthor of *The Colored American from Slavery to Honorable Citizenship*,[18] and *Progress of a Race*.[19] These works fit the general pattern of the Laymen's School, pointing up their general lack of formal training in historical methodology. One statement in *Progress of a Race* does reveal how far, in many respects, the lay Negro historians writing in the twentieth century had advanced beyond those who wrote in the nineteenth. While mentioning the origins of the black man and the idea gleaned by some people from the Bible that the African had been cursed by God, Crogman writes: "We have neither inclination nor time to spend on extended argument against this theory so contradictory to all facts revealed by the light of true history and now no longer a question of debate." The beginning writers frequently had gone to great pains to refute this idea.

KELLY MILLER

Another member of the Negro Academy was Kelly Miller (1863–1939). He was born in South Carolina and graduated from Howard University. In 1901 he received the M.A. degree and later did postgraduate work in mathematics and physics at Johns Hopkins University. He taught mathematics in the public schools of Washington, D. C., after which, beginning in 1890, he was a faculty member at Howard University. He also served this institution as Dean of the College of Arts and Sciences.

Though Miller's historical writings were among the crudest produced by any member of this Laymen's School, his great popularity and widespread activities helped greatly to popularize Negro history. One of his largest works bore the title *Kelly Miller's History of the World War for Human Rights,* and was subtitled: "An Intensely Human and Brilliant Account of the World War . . . and a Thrilling Account of the Important Part Taken by the Negro in the Tragic Defeat of Germany." [20]

J. A. ROGERS

Born in Jamaica, British West Indies, J. A. Rogers (1880–1966) became a naturalized citizen of the United States in 1917. His efforts in history were largely in the direction of discovering and publicizing facts which illustrated the contributions of Negroes to civilization. Like most black historians, Rogers crusaded against the idea that some races are biologically superior to others. He is the author of ten volumes and numerous articles.

A prodigious researcher and writer, Rogers has done much to help establish the field of Afro-American studies. "No man living," wrote W. E. B. Du Bois, "has revealed

so many important facts about the Negro as Rogers." [21]
Others have said much the same thing. Though lacking the
university training which has been characteristic of Negro
historians in the twentieth century, Rogers's contribution
is no less significant. For years his illustrated feature, "Your
History," appeared in the Pittsburgh Courier, a leading
weekly newspaper. This feature is designed to acquaint
black people with their history. In this same paper, he
also had a column entitled "Rogers Says."

Another outstanding member of this school was Helen
Adele Whiting, whose contributions have been of great significance.[22] James S. Allen, a white historian who has been
mistaken for a black one, has contributed a significant volume on Reconstruction.[23]

8

CHURCH HISTORIANS

American Negroes have produced a considerable body of church history. In the main, these writings have been race-centered and by persons trained for the ministry.[1] Of course this training was sometimes more informal than formal. This section is an attempt to trace the evolution of this particular aspect of historical writings by American Negroes. While not every volume produced in this area is mentioned here, most of those works which are readily to be found in public libraries are included. In truth, some writings of considerable merit in this area have never been published.[2] Doubtless, some have been privately published and are not readily accessible.

Because of the importance of the Negro church in the life and culture of the race and of this country, this history is an important area of Negro literature. It had its beginnings as early as 1843. In the antebellum period the names of Christopher Rush,[3] William Catto,[4] and William Douglass[5] stand out. Vernon Loggins, historian of

Negro literature, is high in his praise of the writings of these men. Catto and Douglass, states Loggins, were "far better equipped for historical research than either William Wells Brown or William C. Nell," and had the commendable advantage of being "concerned with relating actual facts rather than with producing anti-slavery propaganda." [6] Both Catto and Douglass were well educated.

In the post-war period, one encounters the names of B. T. Tanner, L. M. Hagood, P. H. Thompson, C. H. Phillips, Lewis G. Jordan, Daniel Alexander Payne, R. R. Wright, and Miles Mark Fisher. While this body of literature shows evolution in quality, after surveying the church history produced to 1900, John Hope Franklin concluded that it is "more important as source materials than as authoritative studies." [7] In fairness to the church history written in this period, one must add that a similar observation is appropriate for the general body of Negro historiography produced to that date. Like the other works of history written by American Negroes, the church history utilizes a biographical approach to a large extent. The major denominations written about were the African Methodist Episcopal (AME); the African Methodist Episcopal Zion (AMEZ); the Colored Methodist Episcopal (CME); and various Baptist groups.

B. T. TANNER

In 1884, B. T. Tanner (1835–1923), a bishop of the church, published *An Outline of Our History and Government*,[8] for African Methodist churchmen, both ministerial and lay. Catechetical in form, the volume carries 206 pages. This was not orthodox history at all. Still, Bishop Tanner displayed a keen interest in the past of his race. He had previously published works entitled *Apology for African*

Methodism, Is the Negro Cursed?, The Negro's Origin,
and *The Negro: African and American.*

L. M. HAGOOD

In 1890, L. M. Hagood wrote *The Colored Man in
the Methodist Episcopal Church.*[9] The author wrote this
book "because some wrong impressions may be righted
by the collation of facts that lay bare the glaring inaccuracies . . . concerning the imposition of the white
members of the Church upon the colored." [10] Hagood
states that the history of the black man in the Methodist
Episcopal Church reveals the Negro in a light of which
anyone may be proud.[11] The book carries no documentation. Chapters are fairly well proportioned. There are
numerous direct quotations and, throughout the work,
Hagood stops his chronicle periodically to elaborate on
various points of doctrine.

WESLEY J. GAINES

Bishop Wesley J. Gaines's *African Methodism in the
South, or Twenty-five Years of Freedom* was published
in 1890.[12] This story is concerned almost exclusively with
the development of the denomination in Georgia and
Alabama; the author states that such was his limited
aim.[13] Divided into twenty-nine chapters, this work carries
very little documentation. It is, however, well proportioned
and well written. The author expressed the hope that
other writers would prepare the history of this denomination for their states.[14]

J. W. HOOD

Five years later, in 1895, Bishop J. W. Hood published *One Hundred Years of the AMEZ Church, or The Centennial of African Methodism*.[15] This was a poorly organized work, which was "not put forward as anything like a complete history." Bishop Hood stated that he was limited in securing materials. "He has not," the author states, "been able to get those interested who might have furnished him very interesting and important matter," thus "what [he] has given is very largely what has come within his own knowledge." Indulging his interest in general history, Bishop Hood points out that: "A little outside matter is thrown in to heighten the interest," of the work. Chapter Two is thus made a brief sketch "of the origin and greatness of the ancient ancestors of the Afro-American race." [16] There are many biographical sketches of bishops and preachers of the church. The denomination is treated by conferences all over the United States. The volume contains no chapter or any other type of division.

DANIEL ALEXANDER PAYNE

Payne was born in Charleston, South Carolina, February 24, 1811. A free Negro, he launched his own school for educating black people in that city in 1829. Slave revolts and rising abolitionist activity in the North later caused the South Carolina legislature to close all such schools in the state.[17] Torn from his chosen profession, Payne moved North, first to New York, then to Gettysburg, Pennsylvania, where he enrolled in a Lutheran school to improve his own education. He became a minister in the growing African Methodist Episcopal Church and quickly established a reputation as an able and progressive man.

In 1848 Payne was appointed to write a history of the African Methodist Episcopal Church. His many duties and the extensive research which the task necessitated caused this work to be forty-two years forthcoming; it appeared in 1891.[18] In the meantime, Payne had become a bishop of the church and President of Wilberforce University in Ohio. He served in the latter position from 1863 to 1876.[19]

In his *History of the AME Church,* Payne devotes several pages to a statement of his philosophy of history. He reveals an awareness of the need for acquiring all possible facts and for judiciously weighing and fitting them together in a true, coherent story. Yet he felt that it was the job of the historian to "teach mankind by living and striking examples that Righteousness exalteth a nation; but sin is a reproach to any people." Payne believed also that "the Great Teacher . . . is also the greatest factor of human history." He pleaded for better record-keeping on the part of the church so that its future historians would have an easier task than had been his lot. In enumerating the uses of history, Payne pointed out only such uses as that history could be made to prove God's existence, as well as the omnipotence of Right over Wrong. He asserted, "History is philosophy teaching by example." [20]

For this study, Payne visited churches throughout the United States and in Ontario, Canada. He relied heavily on church minutes and the letters and papers of Richard Allen, first bishop and founder of the church. The work contains 502 pages divided into thirty-seven chapters. The first part of the study traces the history of the Methodist Episcopal Church in America from 1784 to 1816, the date when black Methodists broke with the white body. Then the development of the separate and independent black branch of the church is treated. Included are biographical sketches of many of the leading ministers and bishops produced by the church, information on the outstanding organizations within the body, the general conferences, and the general contributions of the church to various aspects of American life and culture. The schools and colleges supported by this organization are given special attention. This is a thorough work of scholarship.

PATRICK H. THOMPSON

Another good study which appeared in the nineteenth century is *The History of Negro Baptists in Mississippi* by the Reverend Patrick H. Thompson.[21] Appearing in 1898, this book was five years in preparation. Indicating the scholarly detachment with which the volume was written, Thompson writes in the preface:

It has not been the object of the author to deal with new views or to engage in discussing controverted points of church polity and religion; but to compile a history of facts, and not to philosophize upon the principles which the facts dealt with may involve.

Reverend Thompson produced this volume because there was no study existing which told of the development of Negro Baptists in Mississippi. The author had graduated from Jackson College, Jackson, Mississippi, in 1887 with highest honors. In 1892 he had received the Bachelor of Divinity degree from the Theological Seminary at Richmond, Virginia. From 1892 to 1898 he had served as a teacher at Jackson College, and he also served as a grade-school principal.[22]

Negro Baptists in Mississippi is divided into seven lengthy chapters. The first part gives historical sketches of various Baptist churches in the state. The next part, chapters three and four, gives historical sketches of the Baptist Associations and Conventions which had met in the state. The last chapter presents a series of biographical sketches of outstanding members of the denomination. The work carries no footnotes, but the text frequently refers to sources. The book was written primarily from official church records. A serious fault of this history is that there is too much stringing together of direct quotations from resolutions, minutes, and other official records.

JAMES A. HANDY

Around 1900, Reverend James A. Handy published a small volume entitled *Scraps of African Methodist Episcopal History*.[23] The work is not dated, but it treats events to 1900. The author states in the preface that with this volume, he "makes no attempt to collect all the Scraps, or say the last word but simply presents . . . a few facts that have attracted his attention." He excuses his failure to prepare a more detailed and comprehensive history with the statement that "Bishops Payne, Arnett and others to come, will write the Church history." [24] Poorly written and not at all well organized, its chief value is as source material.

N. H. PIUS

Reverend N. H. Pius published *An Outline of Baptist History* in 1911.[25] This volume bore the subtitle *A Splendid Reference Work for Busy Workers, A Record of the Struggles and Triumphs of Baptist Pioneers and Builders*. It was not intended as a complete history of the denomination. The suppression of black history by white authors was a motivating factor with Reverend Pius.[26] Well written, this book contains twelve balanced chapters. There are no footnotes.

CHARLES SPENCER SMITH

Reverend Charles Spencer Smith has written *A History of the AME Church*.[27] Intended as a supplement to Daniel A. Payne's outstanding history of this denomination, the study appeared in 1922. Smith's work concentrates on the period from 1856 to 1922, but the first two chapters take the development of the church prior to 1856. The entire study is divided into twenty-three well-balanced chapters. A lengthy appendix swells the volume to 557 pages. There are far too many lengthy direct quotations from conference minutes and other similar sources.

LEWIS G. JORDAN

In the 1930s, the Reverend Lewis G. Jordan published a volume entitled *Negro Baptist History, U.S.A., 1750–1930*.[28] The author had attended the Roger Williams Institute, Nashville, Tennessee, in the 1880s and was appointed historiographer of the National Baptist Convention.

When *Negro Baptist History* appeared, Reverend Jordan had pastored churches in Mississippi, Texas, and Pennsylvania. For almost a generation he served as Recording Secretary of the Baptist Foreign Mission Board.[29]

The Introduction, written by Wesley F. Graham, mentions the difficulties which such a task involved. "The task of the collector of information relative to Negro Baptists," he writes, "is not easy. Men who founded the denomination have passed. Those who stood colossus-like over the gulf that divided slavery from emancipation are passing. They have left little to writing. They had not time to write, although many of them were good scholars." [30]

Negro Baptist History carries no chapter or other divisions. Biblical authority is cited very frequently, and without criticism. "In preparing this book," comments Jordan on his method, "I have had occasion to look up the method used by more than a dozen historians." [31] He engages in considerable proselytizing for the doctrinal viewpoints of his denomination. The book carries numerous biographical sketches and quotations from Conference minutes. There is no documentation. Despite the author's having looked up the method used by more than a dozen historians, this work is poorly written when judged by acceptable standards. (A work appearing earlier than Jordan's *Negro Baptist History,* but similar in organization, content, and quality, is Charles H. Brooks's *Official History of the First American Baptist Church, Philadelphia, Pa.*[32])

CHARLES HENRY PHILLIPS

In 1925 the third edition of the history of another Negro denomination appeared. This was Reverend Charles Henry Phillips's *The History of the CME Church in America.* Originally published in 1898, this was the first full-volume history of this denomination.[33] Well written in a reportorial style, it represents creditable scholarship. The primary sources used were Conference minutes and the official organ of this church, the *Christian Index.*[34] The quality of this history reflects the fact that by the 1920s church historians were more than likely to be persons with some training in the methods of research.

MILES MARK FISHER

Miles Mark Fisher, long pastor of White Rock Baptist Church, Durham, North Carolina, and sometime Professor of Church History at Shaw University, Raleigh, North Carolina, is an outstanding representative of the more recent school of church historians. Born October 29, 1899, he holds an A.B. from Morehouse College, a B.D. from the Northern Baptist Theological Seminary, and a Ph.D. in Religious History from the University of Chicago; the latter degree was conferred in 1949. Dr. Fisher's reworked doctoral dissertation, *Negro Slave Songs,* was published in 1953 by the American Historical Association.[35]

In *Negro Slave Songs* Dr. Fisher attempted to determine the historical events or situations which gave rise to specific Afro-American folk songs before the Civil War. Numerous songs about ships and the sea—such as "The Old Ship of Zion"—he believes were "composed" because slaves became excited about the "possibility" that, through the work of the American Colonization Society, they would be freed and sent "back to Africa." "Caution Songs"—such as "You Better Mind"—were first sung after unsuccessful slave plots or rebellions. Dr. Fisher presents essentially a secular interpretation of the Spirituals, and he stresses what he denotes as a primary African or "Oriental" strain in the Negro mind which is revealed in slave songs. He is also the author of several other monographs and scholarly articles.[36]

BENJAMIN E. MAYS

Benjamin E. Mays, President Emeritus of Morehouse College, holds a doctorate from the University of Chicago. His published dissertation carries the title *The Negro's God.*[37] Among his subsequent productions is a volume which he coauthored with Joseph W. Nicholson, entitled *The Negro's Church.*[38] This study was made under the auspices of the Institute of Social and Religious Research as "an attempt to give an accurate description of the Negro church . . . in the United States." The work was based on first-hand study of 609 urban and 185 rural churches. Despite the fact that Woodson's volume on the Negro church had already appeared, the authors termed this the "first comprehensive contemporary study of the Negro church." [39]

CHARLES H. WESLEY

In 1935 Charles H. Wesley published what has been termed a definitive biography of Richard Allen, founder of the African Methodist Episcopal Church. Using pamphlets, periodicals, newspapers, Conference minutes, antislavery literature, and similar materials, Wesley made a significant contribution with this volume.[40] "The dominant theme of the volume," states the author in the preface, "is the rise of organized independence and self-expression in the economic and social life of Negroes in America under the leadership of Richard Allen and his associates." Included also is the story of the rise of the African Methodist Episcopal Church. The study is divided into twelve chapters and carries a total of 286 pages. Although very little documentation is used, it is well written, and based on considerable research done in numerous public and private libraries. Wesley concludes that Richard Allen was "the first of the organizers of Negro unity and race solidarity in the United States." [41] Wesley himself is numbered among the outstanding makers of Negro historiography.[42]

R. R. WRIGHT

R. R. Wright, Bishop and historian of the African Methodist Episcopal Church, included among his writings an encyclopedia of his church.[43] Born April 16, 1878,

Bishop Wright held an A.B. from the Georgia State College, Savannah, Georgia; a B.D. from the University of Chicago; an M.A. from the same school, and a Ph.D. from the University of Pennsylvania (1911). Bishop Wright has also studied at the Universities of Berlin and Leipzig. In addition to serving as a minister, he was a college teacher. His encyclopedia of his church is largely biographical in approach and is a valuable source on the church history of the Negro in the United States. Wright also wrote *The Negro in Pennsylvania: A Study in Economic History* (Philadelphia: A.M.E. Book Concern, 1912, 250 pp.).

Church history written by Afro-Americans, like other history produced by this group, shows steady improvement in quality. This is true of the calibre of both the research and presentation. Still, it would seem that this area has been too much neglected by the trained historian. While for at least the past quarter-century denominations have sought as official historians persons whose training fits them for scholarly research and writing, only now and then have ministerial personnel with graduate training in history been available for the task at hand. It would seem that here is an area in which denominations might employ historians who are not necessarily ministers. Individual Negro churches with a rich past might do likewise. The quality of the finished products might more than justify the expense involved.[44]

THE BLACK
HISTORIAN:
The New School,
1930–1960

Introduction

As with the Beginning and Middle Schools, members of this group show many divergencies in the style, interests, quantity, and quality of their writings. Yet, I feel that their similarities greatly outweigh their dissimilarities. The justifications for grouping them together are:

1. They began their professional careers after 1930.
2. They are considerably less concerned with refuting the racist arguments of the nineteenth century than their predecessors.
3. They document their writings more thoroughly, and generally show evidence of a better grasp of the social sciences, than did either of the two preceding schools.
4. They are less concerned with the "black theme." With the members of this school, black historians, for the first time, express a resentment at the exclusive preoccupations with the racial theme which had been characteristic to their day.
5. They show less tendency to crusade or to use history as propaganda.

6. They are not prolific. This is perhaps because: (a) They do not feel the urge to crusade for any cause; (b) they feel—wrongly, I think—that the "slavery theme" has been exhausted; and (c) they realize the need for more thoroughgoing research and careful writing, and do not rush their works to the press.

With the New School, black historiography reached its majority. Helen Boardman states in the *Negro History Bulletin*, April, 1945, that "The combatting of anti-Negro propaganda has ceased to be a primary purpose of Negro historians," but she admits that the many books on Negro history recently written especially for black children were conceived as one way to combat this propaganda. In the twenties and thirties, the Negro history movement, launched by Carter Woodson in 1915, became a broad movement, at least among black intellectuals. It found expression in such forms as novels, poems, high school and college courses, plays, the very popular Negro History Week, and the beginning of private and public manuscript and book collections of Afro-Americana. It is impossible to determine the degree to which the Negro history movement either influenced or was influenced by other notable events of the twenties. Yet there can be little doubt that it was closely intertwined with the urban trek which saw great centers of Negro life arise in New York, Chicago, Memphis, and other cities; the rise of literacy and resurgence of the Negro voter; growth of black businesses and wealth; the pugilistic successes of Jack Johnson; and the Harlem literary and artistic renaissance. The latter featured everything from literary criticism, novels, poetry, and drama to the tantalizing rhythms of blues and jazz.

Finally, the connection between the black history movement and the upheaval caused by the master-propagandist Marcus Garvey is impossible to assess. I suspect that the two movements were in some fashion related. While back-to-Africa schemes have never had great appeal to the majority of Afro-Americans, Garvey's glorification of things black won surprising response and revealed that the defensive psychology so long characteristic of much Negro thought and action was being displaced by a new aggressiveness and self-confidence, at least in Northern cities.

In some respects the 1900–1930 period was the most significant epoch of organizing which the Afro-American has had. Not only did Woodson launch his successful movement in this period, but scores of new businesses, newspapers, churches, schools, the Urban League, and NAACP attest to this fact. In these formative years, individual leaders stood out as giants. Their efforts and utterances indicate that they shared not only the uncertainty but the heady optimism of the Progressive Movement and the roaring twenties. The Great Depression and World War II dimmed this optimism, and by and large the giant leaders were fast disappearing. The formative years were largely over, and henceforth most leaders were to be lost in the anonymity of organization. Just as there were to be no more Booker Washingtons in education, Frederick Douglasses in politics (save perhaps for the South), or A. F. Herndons or M. L. or S. B. Walkers in business, so perhaps would Negro historiography never again be dominated by figures who loomed as large as Woodson and Du Bois. There were plenty of topics and sources which needed exploration, but the organization had been formed, an audience and scholars aroused, and a point of view articulated. Though much remained and still remains to be done in Afro-American historiography, by 1930, when the whole of American literature entered a new phase in terms of quality and themes, this historiography had more in common with the larger body of national literature than ever before. In his presidential address before the April, 1969, annual session of the Organization of American Historians, entitled "Clio with Soul," C. Vann Woodward paid homage to the contributions of black historians and recognized the growth and importance of the field of Afro-American history.

BLACK SCHOLARS

RAYFORD W. LOGAN

Rayford Whittingham Logan, longtime Chairman of the Department of History at Howard University and onetime editor of the *Journal of Negro History,* is one of the few black historians who has specialized in the area of international relations. He received his A.B. from Williams College, and both the master's and doctor's degrees from Harvard University, the latter degree being awarded in 1936. His dissertation was "Diplomatic Relations between the United States and Haiti, 1776–1891." A member of Phi Beta Kappa, Dr. Logan is the author of several books, and numerous articles and book reviews. Among his books are *The Attitude of the Southern White Press Toward Negro Suffrage, 1932–1940;*[1] *What the Negro Wants;*[2] *Diplomatic Relations between the United States and Haiti, 1776–1891;*[3] *The Senate and the Versailles Mandate System;*[4] *The Negro and the Post-War World: A*

Primer;[5] *African Mandates in World Politics,*[6] and *The Operation of the Mandate System in Africa.*[7] He is also co-author of the introductory volume of *The Encyclopedia of the Negro,*[8] and author of *The Negro in American Life and Thought: The Nadir, 1877–1901.*[9]

Dr. Logan's dissertation was published in 1941, bearing its original title. With this work, he established his reputation as a scholar in the field of diplomatic history. For this study, which covers the long period from the year of the Declaration of Independence to the Mole St. Nicholas Affair, Dr. Logan used material from British and French archives as well as official papers of the United States government. He also used private papers of various statesmen. This volume has been called the "most authoritative and complete study of the diplomacy of the place and period" [10] by a critic who praised the "detachment and balanced judgment." The thirty-six-page bibliography which is appended to the study has been called the "most extensive and up-to-date list of materials concerning an insular American republic that has yet been made available to scholars." [11]

Few of the other productions of Dr. Logan measure up to his dissertation in thoroughness, objectivity, or documentation. His *Attitude of the Southern White Press Toward Negro Suffrage* was a study of limited scope which covered only eight years. The work is a collection of excerpts from southern newspapers which relate to Negro suffrage.[12] Dr. Logan's excellent study *The Senate and the Versailles Mandate System* fits into the pattern of the general outlook of Negro historians on the treatments of colonial peoples in the modern world. In this volume, Dr. Logan scores the great gap which existed between the Wilsonian idealism which permeated the founding of the mandate system and the actual treatment which colonial peoples received under this system. He also criticizes the attitude which southern Congressmen had toward this particular aspect of President Wilson's idealism, and blames the unfriendly attitude to nonwhite people on the prevailing pattern of race relations in the American Southland.

Dr. Logan's *The Negro and the Post-War World: a Primer* is a brief study of only ninety-five pages which is highly reminiscent of W. E. B. Du Bois's *Color and Democracy*. Both works were pleas for a more liberal treatment of the world's colored peoples than had been meted out after World War I. Both indicate the conviction that the old colonialism did not work, and that it was the principal cause of World War I and helped to bring about World War II.[13]

The Negro in American Life and Thought is mainly an examination of white racist thoughts and acts, as reflected in northern newspapers and magazines, the national Congress, political party platforms, and statements by Presidential candidates during the 1877–1901 period. Such phenomena as racist propaganda and lynchings of blacks during these years support Dr. Logan's conclusion that, in many ways, these years mark the nadir in race relations.

WILLIAM SHERMAN SAVAGE

Longtime Professor of History at Lincoln University, Jefferson City, Missouri, William Sherman Savage received his doctorate in history from Ohio State University in 1934. His dissertation topic was "The Controversy over the Distribution of Abolition Literature." [14]

Dr. Savage's dissertation has been published bearing its original title.[15] He also has completed a *History of Lincoln University*.[16] Dr. Savage is the only Negro historian to specialize in the history of the West. A prolific writer of scholarly articles, the productions of Dr. Savage, like those of almost all historians of the New School, are temperate and restrained in tone. His works are objective and ably documented.[17]

LORENZO JOHNSTON GREENE

Dr. Greene received his A.B. degree from Howard University, Washington, D. C., and his M.A. and Ph.D. in history from Columbia University. His dissertation topic was "The Negro in Colonial New England." Dr. Greene has continued his researches into this topic and area, and he is the author of several books and scholarly articles. His books are *The Negro Wage Earner* (coauthored with Carter G. Woodson),[18] *The Negro in Colonial New England, 1620–1776,*[19] and *The Employment of Negroes in the District of Columbia,* which was coauthored with Myra Colson Callis.[20]

Greene's *Negro in Colonial New England* discusses the New England slave-trade and markets, and the effects of slavery and the slave-trade on the political, social, economic and religious life of New England. He throws a vivid light on this dark chapter of American history. The slave regime in New England is usually slighted by most historians. Greene shows that the slave-trade was at the core of the economic life of New England, even on the eve of the American Revolution.[21] He concluded that it was primarily the slave-trade which caused New England's opposition to the Sugar Act of 1764. This, he thinks, was because rum was the medium of exchange in Africa for slaves.[22]

The Negro in Colonial New England was generally well received by critics. "The only important weakness," wrote Oscar Handlin of the book, "is a lack of familiarity with some phases of Puritan ideas that sometimes leads to serious misinterpretation." [23]

The Negro Wage Earner resulted from a general project of the Association for the Study of Negro Life and History to study the position of this minority in American society. Although Dr. Woodson aided in outlining the study, Dr. Greene did almost all of the research. The work begins with the division of labor among Negroes as slaves and traces the manner in which these initial occupations were continued after emancipation. The volume is replete with tables and statistical facts, and holds that only with the mass migrations of this people to northern industrial centers did the early pattern of Negro occupations begin to change significantly. While not a comprehensive history of the Negro labor movement, as a compendium on the occupational status of Afro-Americans the work is a distinct contribution.

LUTHER PORTER JACKSON

Another historian of the New School was the late Luther Porter Jackson. Much of his career as a teacher and scholar was spent at Virginia State College for Negroes, Ettrick, Virginia. Like Wesley, Du Bois, John Hope Franklin, and several other top-ranking Negro historians, Jackson received his undergraduate training at Fisk University. His M.A. degree was conferred by Columbia University and the doctorate in history by the University of Chicago in 1937. His dissertation topic was "Free Negro Labor and Property Holding in Virginia, 1830–1860." Like most other Negro historians who rose to prominence in the twenties and thirties, Jackson was a close acquaintance of Carter G. Woodson, and worked with him in fostering the field of Afro-American research and study. Again, like the other disciples of Woodson and Du Bois, he was more restrained in tone, objective, and less bitter than either Du Bois or Woodson. The generally high literary qualities of the writings produced by members of the New School are perhaps due in part to the fact that these men write less and are engaged in fewer activities of a broad time-consuming nature than were either Du Bois or Woodson. In 1937, Jackson published a small study entitled *A*

History of the Virginia State Teachers Association.[24]
Jackson's *Free Negro Labor and Property Holding in Virginia* was published under the auspices of the American Historical Association.[25] This work, ably documented and written in a thoroughly scholarly and restrained style, was well received by critics.[26]

ALRUTHEUS AMBUSH TAYLOR

Professor Alrutheus Ambush Taylor (1892–1950), a dean and teacher of history at Fisk University, received the A.B. degree from the University of Michigan, and the M.A. and Ph.D. from Harvard, using as a dissertation topic, "The Negro in the Reconstruction of Virginia." [27] He has subsequently published *The Negro in Tennessee, 1865–1880*,[28] *The Negro in South Carolina during the Reconstruction*,[29] and *A Study of the Community Life of the Negro Youth,* a work which he coauthored.[30] He is also author of a number of articles which appeared in historical and educational journals.

A. A. Taylor's scholarly productions are all of the commendable quality which is characteristic of the writers of the New School. While his writings come to the defense of the Negro as a participant in history, they are restrained, indulge in no lengthy sermonizing, and are ably documented. While earlier black historians were frequently short on facts and long on argument and interpretation, writers of the New School generally tend to reverse this situation. This school seems to have a reluctance to interpret boldly, and their works are sometimes made less readable on this account. A competent critic, reviewing Taylor's *The Negro in Tennessee,* criticized the paucity of interpretation. "The facts so systematically and methodically assembled," observed this reviewer, "have a much broader historical message which finer interpretation would bring." [31]

This same reviewer praised Taylor's "objectivity and detachment while studying a complicated problem." [32]

BENJAMIN QUARLES

Benjamin Quarles, Professor of History at Morgan College, Baltimore, Maryland, has written what is perhaps a definitive study of Frederick Douglass.[33]

Upon the appearance of *Frederick Douglass,* W. M. Brewer wrote: "The work is indispensable for study and research on the period of crisis from 1830–60 as well as the Reconstruction. Frederick Douglass lives again as a result of the painstaking researches and interpretations of this author who merits the deepest gratitude and highest praise." [34] A reviewer for the *Springfield Republican* stated that the volume was "worthy of nomination for a Pulitzer award." [35] Representing years of study of the life of Douglass, the work was praised for its very readable style, as well as organization, thoroughness of research, and accurate interpretation.[36] Dr. Quarles is also the author of several scholarly articles.[37] In 1954 Prentice Hall published his book, *The Negro in the Civil War.* This was an effort to bring together data gathered since the appearance of George W. Williams's *Negro Troops in The War of the Rebellion.* Although it contained some new information and is a stylistic improvement over Williams's work, few critics seemed to think that *The Negro in the Civil War* is a definitive work.

In 1961 Professor Quarles's book, *The Negro in the American Revolution,* was published by the University of North Carolina Press. This excellent and scholarly treatment completed a task which William C. Nell envisioned, but was not trained to perform in the most acceptable way. Doubtless, this book by Quarles will stand for a long time as the best treatment of this subject.

One year after the appearance of Professor Quarles's study of blacks and the Revolutionary War, Oxford University Press published his *Lincoln and the Negro*. Interest in this book was heightened by the fact that the nation then was involved with the Civil War Centennial celebration.

Professor Quarles expanded the scope of his study of the life of Frederick Douglass and, in 1969, his volume *Black Abolitionists* was published by Oxford University Press. Here, again, this scholar has produced a volume which probably will rank for years as an excellent study of the subject. Also, the Collier Book edition of his brief textbook for black history, entitled *The Negro in the Making of America* (first published in 1964), is very widely used by students enrolled in black history courses.

JOHN HOPE FRANKLIN

Dr. Franklin, author of what is probably the best college textbook on Negro history,[38] received his bachelor's degree from Fisk University, and his M.A. and Ph.D. from Harvard University. Receiving the latter degree in 1941, he used as dissertation topic, "The Free Negro in North Carolina, 1790–1860." A tireless researcher and writer, he is the recipient of several scholarships and research grants, and has served as visiting lecturer at the University of Wisconsin, at Harvard, and at universities in England and Germany.

Dr. Franklin's *Free Negro in North Carolina* is a definitive treatment of this subject, although Woodson regretted that the author did not say more about Negro-Indian relations and the antislavery movement in that state.[39]

In 1947 Franklin's *From Slavery to Freedom* was published. Written to serve largely as a textbook, the volume follows the conventional pattern of histories of the race and relies heavily on the researches of such earlier writers as George W. Williams, W. E. B. Du Bois, and Carter G. Woodson. There is little that is new in the volume, either by way of facts or interpretation. Still, the objectivity of the author, his temperateness in tone, thorough grasp of his materials, and scholarly presentation make the work a significant contribution.

From Slavery to Freedom was variously received. Most reviewers were favorable in their comments. Most severe was Roi Ottley, who reviewed the production for the *New York Times*. Ottley concluded that the "discussion of the Negro in Canada is fresh and informative, if somewhat sketchy. . . . Beyond these few pages, 'From Slavery to Freedom' is a bulky, unwieldy, conventional history, with the studied scholarship of a doctoral thesis." [40] One other reviewer joined Ottley in this severe criticism,[41] but Alain Locke felt that "it will be a long while until another book in this field supersedes it." [42] Franklin has also published one work which he edited,[43] and many articles.[44] In 1956 Harvard University published his study, *The Militant South*. This was only the second manuscript by a black author to be accepted for publication in the Harvard Historical Series.

In 1961, as a part of the Chicago University History of American Civilization series, Professor Franklin's book, *Reconstruction: After the Civil War,* was published. The tone and general conclusions for this able study had been set in 1935 in *Black Reconstruction* by W. E. B. Du Bois.

During the nation's celebration of the Civil War Centennial, Professor Franklin's excellent little volume, *The Emancipation Proclamation,* was published (Doubleday, 1963).

LAWRENCE D. REDDICK

Lawrence Dunbar Reddick, graduating from Fisk in 1932 with highest honors, went on to earn the M.A. and Ph.D. from the University of Chicago. He was awarded the latter degree in 1939. From that date until 1948, Reddick was curator of the Schomburg Collection of Negro literature. During much of this period, he also served as a lecturer in history for New York's City College.[45] Also he has been associated with Atlanta University and Alabama State College.

Dr. Reddick was coeditor of the already mentioned introductory volume of the *Encyclopedia of the Negro* and is the author of several scholarly articles.[46] He coauthored a juvenile book, *Worth Fighting For*. This book was published in 1968 as a part of Doubleday's Zenith series.

WILLIAM M. BREWER

A very active contributor of high-quality reviews to the *Journal of Negro History* is William M. Brewer. For several years a teacher of history at Miner Teachers College in Washington, D. C., Mr. Brewer, a Harvard graduate, worked closely with Carter Woodson and the Association for the Study of Negro Life and History. He is currently serving as Editor of the *Journal of Negro History*. His reviews reveal thoroughness in reading, a keen grasp of the essential facts in American history and historical literature, and impartial judgment.[47]

CLINTON EVERETT KNOX

Clinton Everett Knox, Professor of History at Morgan State College, is one of the few Afro-Americans to take a doctorate in European history. Professor Knox received the A.B. from Williams College, the M.A. from Brown University, and the Ph.D. from Harvard University in 1940. He used as his dissertation topic, "French Interests and Policy in the Empire, 1887–1905." [48]

There are probably two major reasons why Negro historians have not specialized more in European history. The first is that their intense concern with the history of their own race has turned them to Afro-American studies. The second is that the predominantly Negro colleges, where most Negro historians were, have taught almost exclusively survey courses in American history, and only recently, the history of Western Civilization. A third factor is the absence of university level training in history at these colleges. Indeed, correction of the third factor would automatically eliminate the first two, since university level training would compel these schools to broaden their course offerings. These conditions have created a situation wherein the few Afro-Americans who have received the bulk of their training in European history generally have not followed this interest to the point of producing scholarly articles or monographs beyond their dissertations. Recently Dr. Paul McStallworth of Wilberforce, Ohio, has done excellent work in the field of European colonialism in Africa, while Dr. Matthew Crawford of Virginia State College has cultivated English history as his major field.

ERIC E. WILLIAMS

Eric Eustace Williams holds a doctorate in European history and has followed up his study in this area, especially of European policies in the Caribbean. Williams received the Ph.D. in History from Oxford University, England, in 1938 using as a dissertation topic, "The Economic Aspect of the Abolition of the British West Indian Slave Trade and Slavery." Among his other works are: *Capitalism and Slavery*;[49] *The Negro in the Caribbean*;[50] and *Education in the British West Indies*.[51]

The thesis of *Capitalism and Slavery* is that the two were inextricably intertwined—that the latter made possible the former, although the evolutionary growth of capitalism doomed slavery. "This book," states one reviewer, "marks the beginning of the scientific study of slavery from the international point of view." [52] For this study, Williams used documents relating to slavery from virtually all parts of the British Empire. Writing on the dominant ideas during the eras of commercial and industrial capitalism, Williams stated: "Political and moral ideas of the age are to be examined in relation to economic development. . . . Politics and morals in the abstract make no sense." [53]

Four Negro women who have received doctorates in history are Lula M. Johnson, Helen G. Edmonds, Merze Tate and Elsie Lewis. Dr. Johnson received all three of her degrees from Iowa State University. Her Ph.D. was awarded in 1941. Dr. Edmonds received the bachelor's degree from Morgan State College, Baltimore, and the master's and doctor's degrees from Ohio State University. She received the latter degree in 1946, using as a dissertation topic, "The Negro and Fusion Politics in North Carolina, 1894–1901." Her reworked dissertation was published under this title in 1951.[54] Written in the restrained, scholarly, well-documented manner which is generally characteristic of the New School, this work was well received.[55] Dr. Merze Tate received the A.B. from Western Michigan College, the M.A. from Columbia University, and the Ph.D. from Radcliffe College, the latter degree in 1941. Her dissertation topic was "The Disarmament Illusion." This production was published in 1942 under the auspices of the Bureau of International Research of Harvard University and Radcliffe College. Carter Woodson stated that this book was "eloquent evidence that Dr. Tate deserves rank among the historians of our time." [56] In 1948 Dr. Tate published another volume in this field.[57] Dr. Elsie M. Lewis received the A.B. from Fisk University, the M.A. from the University of Southern California, and the Ph.D. from the University of Chicago.

Professor Herman Dreer, sometime teacher of English and History at Stowe Teachers College, St. Louis, Missouri, has been a warm supporter of the work of the Association for the Study of Negro Life and History. He is the author of two books and several scholarly articles.[58]

Dr. Joseph H. Taylor, long-time Chairman of the Department of Social Sciences at North Carolina College at Durham, and Professor of History at that institution received the doctorate in history from the University of California in 1936. His master's degree was awarded by the University of Michigan. His unpublished dissertation was entitled "The Restriction of European Immigration, 1890–1924." He is also the author of several scholarly articles.[59]

Dr. Horace Mann Bond, long-time President of Lincoln University in Pennsylvania and presently a member of the faculty at Atlanta University, holds the Ph.D. in History from the University of Chicago (1936), and is the author of *Education of the Negro in the American Social Order* (1934); *Education in Alabama: A Study in Cotton and Steel* (1934); *Education for Production* (1944); author of the sections on Negro Education in *The Modern Encyclopedia of Education* and *The Encyclopedia of Educational Research*; as well as numerous articles.[60]

Williston H. Lofton has made several scholarly contributions to the growing body of literature on the Negro.[61] Joseph C. Carroll, long-time high school teacher in Indianapolis, Indiana, received the doctorate in history from

Ohio State University in 1937. Rufus E. Clement, long-time President of Atlanta University, received the doctorate in history from Northwestern University in 1930. Edward M. Coleman, Professor of History at Morgan College, Baltimore, received the doctorate from the University of Southern California in 1940. Robert L. Gill received the doctorate from the University of Michigan in 1942. James H. Johnston and Prince Wilson were awarded this degree by the University of Chicago. Lewis C. McMillan, some-time Professor of History, Philosophy and German at Wilberforce University, received the doctorate from the University of Bonn, Germany, in 1933, while Susie Owen Lee received the degree in 1943 from New York University. George William Brown, businessman of Cleveland, Ohio, received the doctorate in 1938 from the London School of Economics and Political Science, University of London, using as a dissertation topic, "The Economic History of Liberia." This work was published by the Associated Publishers in 1942. Leo Hansberry, Professor of History at Howard University, was perhaps one of the leading students of African history in the United States. Holder of an M.A. degree from Harvard University, Professor Hansberry also has studied African culture and history in England. After years of careful research, he is preparing a history of Africa.[62] Another scholar who has specialized in African history is Professor Caulbert Jones of the North Carolina Central University. Finally, it may be noted that several scholars have found state history an interesting and fruitful field of endeavor. In addition to studies already mentioned, significant work has been done on the Negro in Georgia by Dr. Alonzo T. Stephens and Dr. Clarence Bacote, the latter of Atlanta University; Alabama by Drs. Robert D. Reid and Henry E. Cobb and Mr. Norman Walton; West Virginia by Dr. J. Reuben Sheeler; Pennsylvania by Dr. James Brewer; Louisiana by Mr. Charles Rousseve; Maryland by Dr. Augustus Low; and Tennessee by Dr. Raleigh Wilson.

The fact that one could list, together with brief biographical sketches, *all* Afro-Americans who have received the doctorate in history on eight or nine pages of a book as Professor Greene does in his *Negro Holders of the Doctorate,* is proof of the youthfulness of trained scholarship in this field. With the growth of colleges and universities that have predominately Negro student bodies,[63] it is perhaps not too much to expect that the necessary improvements in faculty, library facilities, and broadened course offerings in history will have a stimulating effect on scholarship among American Negro historians. Also working in the same direction is the recent tendency of white northern universities to employ black historians, either as full-time teachers, or visiting professors. There can be little doubt that today the thoughts and interests of Afro-Americans, both scholarly and lay, are less race-centered than in the first fifty years of their post-bondage existence. This is a welcome sign. It will be a welcome day also when there will be black scholars of national and international repute, in all of the major areas for historical research and study —ancient, medieval and modern. Until such a day arrives, the black American historian, by chronicling and interpreting the story of his race's development, will probably continue to make a contribution of no small proportions to the historical literature and understanding of the United States and the world.

In fact, the youngest group of historians (a group not properly considered here) have shown great promise during the 1960s. Most, but not all of them, are university-trained professional historians. Prominent among those not university-trained are Lerone Bennett, Jr., and John Henrik Clarke. Clarke is an able writer and lecturer on both African and Afro-American history.

Lerone Bennett, Jr., came to historical research and writing from the field of journalism. From newspaper work in his native Mississippi, he moved to the *Atlanta Daily World* and then *Ebony* magazine. By 1970 his historical works included *Before the Mayflower: A History of the Negro in*

America, 1619–1964; *Black Power U.S.A.: The Human Side of Reconstruction, 1867–1877*, first published by Johnson Publications, 1967, and *What Manner of Man: A Biography of Martin Luther King, Jr.* (1964). Other books by Bennett by 1970 were *The Negro Mood* (1964) and *Confrontation: Black and White* (1965). Bennett's style has the power and force of the historical writings of W. E. B. Du Bois, and reveals the same passionate attack on white racism and the same dedication to human dignity and freedom.

A writer whose scholarship, style, and dedication are highly similar to Lerone Bennett, Jr., is the University of Chicago Ph.D. holder, Vincent Harding. A frequent contributor to books and scholarly journals, Dr. Harding has served as chairman of the Department of History at Spelman College and as Director of the Martin Luther King, Jr., Memorial Center in Atlanta.

The Mind of the Negro: An Intellectual History of Afro-Americans (1961), by Earl E. Thorpe, was an effort to fill the void caused by the absence of a general history of Afro-American thought. In their volumes on intellectual history, such scholars as Vernon L. Parrington, Merl Curti, Henry S. Commager, and Stow Persons had said practically nothing on Afro-American thought.

During the 1960s Edgar Toppin continued his high level of scholarly productivity. Two works which he coauthored were *Pioneers and Patriots: The Lives of Six Negroes of The Revolutionary Era* (New York: Doubleday, 1965, with Lavinia G. Dobler) and *The Unfinished March* (New York: Doubleday, 1967, with Carol F. Drisko). Among other Afro-American scholars who achieved notably in the field of black history were Sterling Stuckey, James Turner, and William Strickland.

BLACK HISTORY:
Substance and Shadow

SUBSTANCE AND SHADOW

Because black historians have depicted the sufferings of black people in America, it is easy to conclude that their view of history conforms with Gibbon's observation that history is "little more than the register of the crimes, follies, and misfortunes of mankind." But such an observation would not be correct. Negro history is largely social history. And running throughout the gloomy picture which it usually depicts is a small note of optimism, of faith in a new day.

George Washington Williams performed the researches for his *magnum opus* with tears pouring from his eyes because of the sufferings of his race.[1] Du Bois composed two of his works in "blood and tears,"[2] and Carter Woodson, while composing a history, frequently stopped to devote several paragraphs or pages to point out some particular "lesson of history."

Most of American history (white) has had as its theme national progress. It has played up the achievements of a people living under the conditions of "freedom and democracy." For the nation and its historians, the story of "that triumphant advance had to be recorded, for the edification of Europe, for the gratification of posterity." [3] A graphic description of the spirit in which the bulk of American historical literature has been conceived is given by Professor Commager in his *The American Mind*. He writes:

A people so aware that they were making history were conscious of their duty to record it. A people sure that they were beating out paths for other nations to follow were sensible of the obligation to mark those paths well. A people whose institutions were continually under scrutiny were zealous to explain and defend them. A people so proud of their achievements and so uncontaminated by modesty were eager to celebrate their triumphs. A people made up of such conglomerate elements and with so little racial or religious or even geographical unity were at pains to emphasize their common historical experience and validate their historical unity. A people whose collective memory was so short were inclined to cherish what they remembered and romanticize it. [4]

Only a casual acquaintance with Negro historical literature reveals that many of the above generalizations do not apply to it. Not that Negro historians have not been aware of the above forces and impressions, for they have. But often they have felt, with justification, that they were not accepted and respected members of the American community. In the words of Du Bois, the black historian felt that he was "in the world but not of it." [5] Thus, when he has pointed to the magnificent achievements of Americans under "democracy and freedom," it has been in order to show that the treatment to which his race has been subjected is a violation of this record.

Still, American Negro historical literature fits, in many ways, into the general pattern of historiography in the United States. New England, and especially Harvard College and University, produced Bancroft, Prescott, Irving, Motley, Parkman, Hildreth, and other top-ranking historians of the nineteenth and twentieth centuries. Though beginning their work later, many of the best black historians were Harvard-trained. W. E. B. Du Bois, Carter G. Woodson, Charles Wesley, William M. Brewer, Rayford Logan, Leo Hansberry, John Hope Franklin, Merze Tate, and Clinton E. Knox are all Harvard graduates.

Also, black historians have been affected by the many new theories and movements which have swept the Western world, although not to the same extent as historians of the majority group. Like so many other intellectuals prior to the 1930s, and perhaps indeed more than most, they have shown strong romanticist leanings. This tendency is perhaps best evidenced in the profound faith in education which has been so characteristic of these scholars. Yet, this faith undoubtedly also has roots in the race's actual benighted condition, which was characteristic for so many years after emancipation. Though most of these historians have denied that there was anything unique or peculiar about the black man and have insisted that he is "just like any other average human being," much about their statements and program for the uplift of the race indicates that they sometimes have been touched with J. G. Herder's conception of the *Volksgeist*.

Marxism had its strongest impact on W. E. B. Du Bois. Apart from the contention that the race is inherently the equal of any group, black historians generally have not adhered to rigid schools of thought. Where their interpretations have been broad they were generally eclectic. Few besides Du Bois have followed any varieties of Marxism or Socialism. This historiography has been to a large extent defensive.

Again the Negro historian was of his age when, in the twentieth century, he gave less emphasis to personalities than had been the case in the nineteenth century. For as Professor Commager observes, "the historians of the new century . . . concerned themselves more largely with forces than with persons." [6]

Unlike scholars in the majority group, among Negroes

there have been no revisionist historians save on the issues centering around slavery, the Civil War, and Reconstruction. This is perhaps because black historians have not taken strong and elaborately stated positions on such matters as the cause of the Revolutionary War, the War of 1812, significance of the frontier, or the War of 1898. As to the two recent World Wars, Negro writers have generally adhered to the belief that both were caused by European competition for colonies, just as they contend that the Civil War was caused primarily by slavery. Perhaps again the sociological term "ethnocentrism" explains these interpretations.

The black historian has not joined in the twentieth-century search for historical laws which has been characteristic of historians of the majority group.[7] The one law of history which may be evidenced as a part of the historical apparatus of this scholar, until very recently, has been a faith in the moral law that "righteousness exalteth a nation or a people, while sin abaseth a nation." Carter Woodson is one of the few who, before 1930, does not persistently hold up the workings of the moral law in the explanation for most historical phenomena.

No black historian has counseled violence as a means of raising the status of his group. Nor has any advocated any other economic or political system as a salvation for his group, with the exception of Du Bois. These scholars have accepted and upheld liberalism, democracy, tolerance, majority rule, republicanism, and other traditional ideals of American society, despite the fact that it is frequently the majority-rule principle which deprives them of first-class citizenship. While L. D. Reddick has deplored some aspects of this traditionalism and conservatism in the thought of Negro historians, he offers no real substitute. The faith of the black man in his future is due in large part to his faith in the nation and its ideals.

Negro historians have been ardent lovers of liberty "for all peoples."[8] Yet it was not until World War I aroused an internationalist outlook in many Americans that they reveal any considerable interest in the problems of colonial peoples over the world. Du Bois achieved what is probably the highest degree of catholicity and humanitarianism. Like Tom Paine's, his "world-citizenship" not infrequently caused him to subordinate what some would call the immediate interests and safety of his own country to larger, perhaps more remote ends.[9]

Because these scholars have been such persistent seekers of democracy, hence its champions themselves, there have been no Negro historians espousing elitist ideology. There have been many white scholars who have advocated that some small elite should rule in society. Too, Negro historians have been opponents of militarism. They have not been able to identify the objectives of modern wars with the interests of any group. This is due, perhaps, to the general lack of concern which they have shown for political science at any level. Most Negro history is social and cultural, and, as stated, Afro-American scholars generally have limited causality in history to economic or moral considerations.

Despite their basic conservatism, these scholars have not been willing to compromise on the objectives which were being sought by most Negro people. When in 1944 a group of black historians and other leaders asserted that "nothing less than complete equality is what the Negro wants and intends to achieve," they were introducing no novel pattern or action.[10]

The Negro historian has produced no multi-volume work, individually or cooperatively. With the exception of the two-volume histories by George Washington Williams, Booker T. Washington, and Daniel A. Payne, it is difficult to find other Negro historians who have written works exceeding one volume. This situation is to be explained in part, perhaps, by the character of the audience for which the Negro scholar was writing. The lack of source materials is another possible explanation. Also, he has not had much time to devote to research and writing. In this connection, the holders of doctorates are frequently criticized for not being more prolific writers. However, when one considers that there was, until recently, no Negro college giving even the master's degree, it can be seen that the Negro Ph.D. has taught at the undergraduate level almost exclusively. Consequently his schools have lacked library facilities or time allotted for research, both of which are necessary for the production of scholarly treatises. And, whether real or imagined, fear of difficulties in getting the results of their researches published has, until recently, deterred Negro scholarship.[11]

Of the sixty-seven black Americans receiving doctorates in the social sciences to 1943, forty-nine wrote their dissertations on topics dealing with the Negro.[12] Many of the others treated related or similar problems. It is estimated that by 1945 Afro-American holders of doctorates in the social sciences had produced only eighty-two books.[13] That this level of production does not compare with that of white Americans goes without saying. However, in view of the obstacles which these persons have had to surmount, they deserve high praise for their achievement. Racial prejudice and discrimination have cost the nation dearly, in this and other regards. It is not impossible that there are many non-racial themes in American history which black historians might make a unique contribution in handling. It may be that their long tenure in a position of oppression may have given some of them an outlook which is particularly favorable for the interpretation of problems which they, in their race-centered outlook, have been overlooking.

Another interesting fact to be observed is that, while these scholars have been mainly preoccupied with the slavery theme, they have produced few of what might be termed definitive studies in this area. Exceptions are to be found in such works as Du Bois's *Suppression of the African Slave Trade to the United States*[14] and Lorenzo Greene's study of the Negro in colonial New England.

While many works produced by Negroes on such race topics as labor, the church, business, or Negro history in general represent the best available writings on these topics, it is still interesting to observe that the "definitive" study of slavery in the Caribbean is by a white author,[15] that Gunnar Myrdal's *An American Dilemma* is the most ambitious undertaking in the sociology of the race problem,[16] that to date, for the period he covers, Vernon Loggins's *The Negro Author* is the definitive study on literature, and that the writings of U. B. Phillips and Kenneth Stampp on slavery in the United States rank above all others in this area.[17] All of these men are Caucasians. Might it be that many black historians have not been proud enough of their ancestors who were slaves?

Considering their great importance to the emancipation of the race, it is somewhat surprising that Negro scholars have not written more on the abolitionist movement and the activities of the so-called Radical Republicans. While most Negro historians have little but praise for such men as Lundy, Garrison, Lovejoy, Stevens, or Sumner, they have failed almost completely to produce biographical studies of abolitionists or Radical Republicans. Du Bois did produce a creditable biography of John Brown, and there are a few other exceptions to this generalization. A classic indictment of some of the traditional pattern is to be seen in the already mentioned article by L. D. Reddick. He wrote in 1937:

The first indictment to be brought against this body of writing is that insofar as subject matter is concerned, the scope has been narrow, the treatment traditional. The notorious example of this is furnished in the preoccupation with the slavery theme. Let it be declared here and now that for the purposes of Negro history, barring the discovery of new materials, the topic of slavery in the United States has been virtually exhausted.[18]

The two aspects of this area which Reddick lists as exceptions are efforts of slaves to break the system by flight, suicide, and revolt, and the effort to get a picture of the institution as seen through the eyes of the slaves themselves.[19]

On the interpretation of history by Negro historians, Reddick states that:

The history of Negro historiography falls into two divisions, *before* Woodson and *after* Woodson. In this later span, remarkable improvement has been made in method and scholarship. But when it comes to the fundamental frame of reference, that is, the final interpretation of the philosophy, even this division may not be necessary. The whole group has written under the influence of the prevailing spirit permeating the American mind. This ideology . . . may be labelled "liberalism." [20]

Reddick believes the essential ingredients of this liberalism to be faith in the ideas of tolerance, faith in rationalism, laissez-faire and progress.[21] He finds no quarrel with this philosophy as far as it goes, but states that "it doesn't answer the questions *why* and under what circumstances things happened." [22]

Dr. Reddick then gives his own frame of reference for interpreting major events in American history which relate to the Negro. "It is about clear by this time," he writes, that: (1) the Abolitionist movement began in the colonial period because the supply of colonial staples came to exceed the world market, (2) the Civil War was basically a clash between "economic systems rather than a naturalistic geographic identification," (3) Reconstruction took the course that it did because the North saw in the Negro a tool "to consolidate the gains made through the Civil War," and dropped the Negro as soon as the South accepted this *fait accompli,* (4) American history since the Civil War has been the development of the industrial revolution.[23] Reddick states that failure to comprehend these "dynamic forces" explains "how it was that the social philosophy of the Negro historians . . . turned out to be the rather naive Emersonian gospel of self-reliance, simple op-

timism and patient regard for destiny." [24] Disregarding his
own too-narrow "dynamic forces," Reddick concludes:

If Negro history is to escape the provincial nature of its first
phases, it will surely *re-define the area of subject matter in
terms of a larger focus; recast its catalog of the determinative
influences affecting Negro life and re-examine the social
philosophy implicit throughout the work.*[25]

There is still a great need for an encyclopedia of the
Negro. Few subjects in Negro history have been treated
definitively, despite the fact that some persons may be tired
of the "slavery theme." The black historian has produced
(as indeed have few white historians) no novel thesis of
particular note, with the exception of the Marxist thesis
of Dr. Du Bois concerning the nature of the Reconstruction Period. Among these writers there have been almost
no outstanding specialists in any area other than American
history. Professor Leo Hansberry of Howard University
has done extensive researches into African history. Too,
despite the limited number of large Negro businesses, it
would seem that the history of business is an area which
has been almost completely overlooked.

Since the freedom of the Negro may be said to have been
born in civil war, it is somewhat surprising also that no
Afro-American has won recognition as a specialist in such
revolutionary periods as seventeenth-century England, the
French Revolution, the Napoleonic Era, or the Russian
Revolution. With the interest which the black man naturally has in the color problem, it is perhaps even less un-
derstandable that so few have sought to become specialists
in colonialism.

In view of the penchant which these scholars have shown
for emphasizing the creditable aspects of their past, it is
to be wondered at that they have not written more biography than has been the case. It is only recently that Benjamin Quarles wrote a good biography of Frederick Doug-

lass, although Booker T. Washington had made an earlier effort in this direction.[26] While Charles Wesley has written a biography of the founder of the African Methodist Episcopal Church, Du Bois a life of John Brown, and Archibald Grimke wrote several biographies, these efforts are exceptions rather than the rule. Here, despite the frequent paucity of sources, the black historian seems to be overlooking an interesting and possibly fruitful area. Shirley Graham, whose biographies are sometimes fictional, is perhaps the most prolific Negro writer of biography.[27] And many of today's prominent Afro-Americans have had their biographies written by white authors.[28] Yet, historians of the majority group also frequently have left biography to non-academic persons.[29]

In view of their great interest in reform, one might expect to find more black historians who have centered their focus on the labor movement, the agrarian crusades of the eighties and nineties, the Progressive Movement, or the New Deal. There are a few today who may claim the area of international relations as a specialty. Usually, however, the interest of these persons in international relations has been confined to African colonialism and the slave trade.

The New School is slowly filling in many of the gaps in Negro historiography. Members of this group are less obsessed with the "slavery theme." They document their works better and are not as interested in case-proving or cause-serving. And they write on a wider range of subjects. Yet, they seem to lack the inspiration which lifted such of their predecessors as George Washington Williams, W. E. B. Du Bois, and Carter Woodson so far above the heads and shoulders of their contemporaries. It is questionable whether historians produce better works in the calm atmosphere of dispassionate observation, or when fired by a zealous cause or crusade. German historical writing reached its greatest heights when caught up in the heated nineteenth-century issue of national unification. Though ultra-nationalistic and biased, this literature could boast of such luminous lights as Ranke and Treitschke. The historiography of our own Southland reached its greatest heights as a crusade against the biased nationalistic preachments of late nineteenth-century New England historians. Similarly, the historiography of our West reached its greatest heights following Frederick Jackson Turner in a crusade against the Eastern orientation of early American writing. It may be that before American Negro historiography can again produce men of the stature of Du Bois and Woodson, it will have to get caught up in another crusade.[30]

But what is to be the future of that species of knowledge which these scholars have cultivated with such assiduousness that a discussion of the men is a discussion of the area? This question calls forth a reference to the race-relations question which always has had a heavy hand on the nature and status of the historiography produced by Afro-Americans. Perhaps the dominant post-World War II words on this nation's race relations front have been Integration and Black Power. The old and traditional pattern of segregation and exclusiveness is dramatically giving way in sports, industry, education, and practically all areas of American life. The changes which are being made have occasioned a multitude of complex problems for both the majority and minority groups involved. Not the least of these problems is what is to be done with many heretofore all or predominantly Negro organizations, institutions, and activities; which ones are being made obsolescent, redundant, and unnecessary in a fast-growing racially integrated America.

In early post-World War II years it was practically impossible to attend any broad policy-forming meeting of Negro organizations where this problem did not come up. Such was the case with several annual meetings of the Association for the Study of Negro Life and History. A sizable number of well-intentioned persons had come to believe that continued effort to teach and popularize Negro History would be to further the idea of racial differentness and uniqueness, and to defeat the main objective of the race, which objective is that black Americans be accorded the same treatment and respect that is given all other Americans. These critics felt that Negro History should be taught only in general American History courses and co-incident thereto, and that the Association for the Study of Negro Life and History should close up shop and cease activity. These critics were wont to point out that, when Woodson launched Negro History Week and related activities, one of his main motives was to prove to a doubting world that Afro-Americans had thought worthwhile thoughts and committed commendable acts. This was justified because then the race had no Jack Johnson, Joe Louis, Jackie Robinson, "Duke" Ellington, Marian Anderson, or Ralph Bunche whose national and international recognition alone gave the lie to charges of racial inferiority. Furthermore, these critics say, many imperialistic politicians and erudite social scientists were then in league with those who most viciously preached doctrines of racial inferiority, but today all of this has changed. Now press, radio, and television daily trumpet outstanding achievements of Negroes, social scientists are practically unanimous in their frequent assertions that no race is inherently inferior to another, and the old Kipling-style imperialistic thinking is in its deaththroes.

Still, proponents of the Negro History Movement are wont to counter that the notion of racial inferiority is far from dead, that desegregation is not integration, and that it is unwise to let current achievements stand as the only justification for according a group its due respect. Too, the debate as to whether Negro History should be taught so as to instill race pride in Negro students was far from settled. At the 1957 annual convention of the Association Dr. Charles H. Wesley urged that the facts of this minority's past should be taught because they constitute a significant part of American History which has too long been too largely omitted. The teacher of Negro History, he declared, should do exactly what the teacher of any other fragment of American or civilizational history does, teach facts. The necessary race pride, he felt, would come as a by-product of the objective teaching of long-neglected facts.

As for the question of whether Negro History has a place in an integrated or integrating society, at the outset of this volume I indicated my belief that it does: that the proper justification for Negro History, as with any other work of scholarly endeavor, is that *it constitutes a contribution to the knowledge and understanding of mankind*. Race, national, sectional, or religious pride are not necessary inspirations for the scholar. The only inspiration which he really requires is that through researches, writings, and teaching he is giving to his generation and to posterity knowledge and understanding. Any other outlook is often detrimental to scholarship and truth.

Black History can be "pure" history, and as such is as justifiable as a separate entity as is state, regional, institutional, or national history. As Arnold Toynbee has shown, the history of this or any other nation is a hyphenated or fragmentized tale. Individual states are incomprehensible save in a civilizational framework, and civilizations are comprehensible only when viewed against the still vaster history of mankind, life, and the cosmos.

Those black Americans who are, may well stop being ashamed of predominantly "Negro newspapers," "Negro businesses," "Negro behavior," "Negro History," and everything else that is racial. This self-degradation heritage of slavery and second-class citizenship too often has obscured our view of many things good and desirable. Only by isolating the frontier and studying it as a separate entity did Frederick Jackson Turner come to evaluate fully its contribution to the national culture. The same is true of Walter P. Webb's epic study of the nation's plains region. While black history probably should not be a required course at any grade level, as an elective it should continue to have a place in curricula wherever and as long as there are interested and competent persons to teach it. For the prospective novelist, poet, dramatist, musician, theologian, social philosopher, or lay American, the unique history of this tenth of the American body politic always will be a mine of inexhaustible and variegated wealth.

NOTES

Part 1
BLACK HISTORY

CHAPTER 2
THE WHY AND WHAT OF BLACK HISTORY

1. J. H. Franklin, "George Washington Williams, Historian," *Journal of Negro History*, XXXI, January, 1946, p. 61; Vernon Loggins, *The Negro Author*, pp. 278–279; W. J. Simmons, *Men of Mark* (Cleveland, 1887), pp. 549–559.

2. *History of the Negro Race in America, 1619–1880* (New York: G. P. Putman's Sons, 1885), pp. v–vi.

3. *Ibid.*, pp. 551–552.

4. H. W. Greene, *Negro Holders of the Doctorate* (Boston: Meador-Publishing Company, 1946), p. 46.

5. See sketch of his life in Benjamin Brawley, *Negro Builders and Heroes* (Chapel Hill: University of North Carolina Press, 1937), pp. 186–190; and in Edwin R. Embree, *Thirteen Against the Odds* (New York: Viking Press, 1946); also, Chapter 3, this study.

6. L. D. Reddick, "A New Interpretation for Negro History," *Journal of Negro History*, XXII, January, 1937, p. 21; and Loggins, *op. cit.*, p. 283.

7. Du Bois, *Dusk of Dawn* (New York: Harcourt Brace, 1940), p. 58.

8. In Rayford W. Logan, ed., *What the Negro Wants* (Chapel Hill: University of North Carolina Press, 1944), p. 49.

9. These facts are taken from Woodson's "Ten Years of Collecting and Publishing the Records of the Negro," *Journal of Negro History*, X, October, 1925, pp. 598–606. Also see C. H. Wesley, "Carter G. Woodson as a Scholar," *loc. cit.*, XXXVI, January, 1951, pp. 12–24; J. G. Van Deusen, in *The Black Man in White America* (Washington, D.C., Associated Publishers, 1944), p. 284 says, "Dr. Woodson has probably done more than any single person to rescue Negro history from oblivion." Also see Chapter 5 of this study.

10. Woodson, *loc. cit.*, XI, April, 1926, p. 239.

11. *Ibid.*, p. 240.

12. Woodson, "Ten Years of Collecting and Publishing the Records of the Negro," *loc. cit.*, X, p. 600.

13. Woodson, *loc. cit.*, XI, April, 1926, p. 239.

14. Vernon Loggins believes that it is a racial trait of the Negro to strive for advancement. "There is something within him," he writes, "undoubtedly a racial inheritance, which stirs him to strive to get

on the mountain-top." With our American social organization such as it is, much is denied to him. But literature and the related arts are open freely to him. (Negro historians, at least, have not agreed with this statement.) It is in them that he has his best opportunity to rise and shine. P. 366 of *The Negro Author*.

15. Arnold J. Toynbee, *A Study of History*, IV, pp. 289–291.

16. The phrase is borrowed from Evarts B. Greene, speech before Sixteenth Annual Meeting of the Association for the Study of Negro Life and History, New York, published in *Journal of Negro History*, XVII, January, 1932, p. 9.

17. See related comments in R. R. Palmer, *History of the Modern World* (New York: Knopf Publishers, 1946), p. 821; Eric Fisher, *Passing of the European Age* (New York: Oxford Press, 1949); Lowell J. Ragatz, *March of Empire* (New York: H. L. Lindquist, 1948), p. 70.

18. L. D. Reddick, *op. cit.*, p. 20.

19. *Dusk of Dawn*, p. 217.

20. *Ibid.*, pp. 173–220. It should be noted that, despite this change, Du Bois never gave up entirely the educational aspect of his work.

21. In Logan, ed., *What the Negro Wants*, pp. 56–57.

22. Both studied such topics as the Rural Negro, the Negro Professional Man, the Negro in Business, the College-bred Negro, Negro Crime, the Negro Church, and the Negro Artisan.

23. Du Bois, *The Philadelphia Negro*, p. v. See also Logan, ed., *What the Negro Wants*, pp. 56–57. Since Du Bois had shown in all of his earlier writings a keen awareness of economic forces in history, it is highly probable that the manner in which the Bolshevik Revolution affected him was to make him very impatient with gradual progress in race relations. For the rest of his career he was to champion ideas and causes which promised a quick solution to the race problem and other social problems.

24. *Black Reconstruction*, p. 724.

25. Quoted in *Journal of Negro History*, I, April, 1916, p. 230, in reprint of comment from the *New York Evening Post*.

26. Evarts B. Greene, *loc. cit.*, p. 8. Other outstanding scholars in history indicated the value of Negro history upon the appearance of the *Journal of Negro History* in 1916. At that time A. H. Buffington wrote from Willliams College: "The more I think of the matter, the more I do believe there is a place for such a publication. The history of the Negro in Africa, in the West Indies, in Spanish America and in the United States offers a large field in which little appears to have been done." (p. 229). A. C. McLaughlin stated that after a few years it would have "considerable historical value." (p. 228). Charles H. Haskins wrote, "You have struck a good field of work." (p. 228). See also favorable comments by Edward Channing (p. 225), Ferdinand

Schevill (p. 227), and Frederick Jackson Turner (p. 228). All of these comments were taken from "How the Public Received the *Journal of Negro History*," in this organ, 1, April, 1916.

27. On the general development of Negro historiography, see also John Hope Franklin, "New Perspectives in American Negro History," in *Social Education*, XIV, No. 5, May, 1950; Helen Boardman, "The Rise of the Negro Historian," in *The Negro History Bulletin*, April, 1945, pp. 148–154; Carter G. Woodson, "Negro Historians of Our Time," in *Negro History Bulletin*, April, 1945, pp. 155–156. It is interesting that a contemporary Marxist and keen student of Negro history views it as a source of propaganda for a larger purpose than elevation of the Negro. (Cf. Herbert Aptheker, "Negro History: Arsenal for Liberation," *New Masses*, February 11, 1947, pp. 8–9. See also his "Distorting the Negro's History," *New Masses*, September 23, 1941, pp. 21–23; and his "Negro History—A Cause for Optimism," *Opportunity*, XIX, August, 1941, pp. 228–231.)

Part 2
INTRODUCTION

---

1. New York, Samuel Woods, 12 pp. For further biographical facts on Cuffee, see Dorothy Porter, *op. cit.*, p. 20; and H. N. Sherwood, "Paul Cuffee," *Journal of Negro History*, VIII, April, 1923, pp. 153–228. Cf. also, W. Simmons, *op. cit.*, pp. 336–339. See also Cuffee's *The History of Prince Lee Boo* (Dublin: J. Jones, 1822), 180 pp., to which is added an autobiographical sketch; his *Memoirs of Paul Cuffee* (York: W. Alexander), 32 pp., and his *Narrative of the Life and Adventures of Paul Cuffee* (Vernon: H. N. Bill, 1839), 21 pp.

2. Biographical facts on Saunders were taken from J. C. Wilson and John Fiske, eds., *Appleton's Cyclopedia of American Biography*, V, p. 404; and Dorothy E. Porter, *op. cit.*, p. 34.

3. Boston, C. Bingham and Co., 1818, 156 pp.

4. Porter, Dorothy E., *Early American Negro Writings: A Bibliographical Study* (Bibliography Society of America Pamphlet: No. 3).

5. Saunders, *Haitian Papers*, Preface.

CHAPTER 3
PIONEERS IN PROTEST

---

1 Robert Benjamin Lewis, *Light and Truth: Containing the Universal History of the Colored and Indian Race, from the Creation of the World to the Present Time* (Boston: Published by a Committee of Colored Gentlemen, 1844), 400 pp.

2. Vernon Loggins, *Negro Author: His Development to 1900* (New York: Columbia University Press, 1931), p. 93.

3. *Light and Truth,* Introduction.

4. James W. C. Pennington, *The Fugitive Blacksmith; or, Events in the Life of James W. C. Pennington* (3rd ed., London, C. Gilpin, 1850), 84 pp.

5. *Ibid.* Also, Loggins, *op. cit.,* pp. 191–197.

6. Pennington, *A Text Book of the Origin and History, &c. &c. of the Colored People* (Hartford, Conn.: 1841), 96 pp.

7. Pennington, *A Text Book,* p. 6.

8. James Theodore Holly, *A Vindication of the Capacity of the Negro Race for Self-Government, and Civilized Progress, as Demonstrated by Historical Events of the Haitian Revolution; and the Subsequent Acts of That People since Their National Independence* (New Haven: 1857), 48 pp.

9. Author's preface to William Cooper Nell, *The Colored Patriots of the American Revolution: With Sketches of Several Distinguished Colored Persons: to which Is Added a Brief Survey of the Condition and Prospects of Colored Americans* (Boston: R. F. Wallcut, 1855), 396 pp; Vernon Loggins, *op. cit.,* p. 177. Joseph Grimes contends that Nell was born a free Negro in Charleston, S.C., moving to Boston in 1812 (*op. cit.*). Helen Boardman calls Nell's *Colored Patriots* "the first full volume on the Negro in American history," and states that it represents "a careful investigation of the documents and records available." "The Rise of the Negro Historian," *Negro History Bulletin,* April, 1945.

10. Cf. also Nell's brief *Property Qualification or No Property Qualification;* subtitled, "A few facts from the Record of Patriotic Services of the Colored Men of New York, during the Wars of 1776–1812." (New York: T. Hamilton and W. H. Leonard, 1830), 24 pp. For another such work in the antebellum period, see Martin Robinson Delaney (1812–1885), *The Condition, Elevation, Emigration and Destiny of the Colored People of the U.S. Politically Considered* (published by the author, 1852), 215 pp.

11. Vernon Loggins, *op. cit.,* pp. 158–165; and the introduction to William Wells Brown, *The Black Man: His Antecedents, His Genius, and His Achievements* (New York: Thomas Hamilton, and Boston: R. F. Wallcut, 1863). Two editions in 1863, 288 pp. and 310 pp.

12. Biographical data on Brown obtained from his "Memoir of the Author," in his *Sketches of Places and Peoples Abroad* (New York: Jewett, Proctor and Worthington, 1852); Loggins, *op. cit.,* pp. 145–158; W. Edward Farrison, "William Wells Brown, America's First Negro Man of Letters," *Phylon,* IX, No. 1, pp. 13–24; William Wells Brown, *Narrative of William Wells Brown* (Boston Anti-Slavery Society, 1847); Edward M. Coleman, "William Wells Brown as an

Historian," *Journal of Negro History*, XXXI, No. 1, January, 1947, pp. 47–60; and *Dictionary of American Biography*, III, p. 161.

13. *The Rising Son; or, The Antecedents and Advancement of the Colored Race* (Boston: A. G. Brown and Company, 1874), 555 pp.

14. Edward M. Coleman, *loc. cit.*, p. 57.

15. Second edition, Cambridge, Massachusetts, 1863, Preface.

16. These reviews quoted in *The Black Man*, p. 312.

17. *Ibid.*, p. 311.

18. Vernon Loggins, *op. cit.*, p. 120.

19. Brown, *The Negro in the American Rebellion: His Heroism and His Fidelity* (Boston: Lee Shepard, 1867), 380 pp.

20. Loggins, *op. cit.*, p. 120.

21. W. E. Farrison, *William Wells Brown, Author and Reformer* (Chicago and London: University of Chicago Press, 1969), p. 445.

22. William Still, *The Underground Railroad. A Record of Facts, Authentic Narratives, Letters, &c., Narrating the Hardships, Hairbreath Escapes and Death Struggles of the Slaves in Their Efforts for Freedom, As Related by Themselves and Others, or Witnessed by the Author; Together with Sketches of Some of the Largest Stockholders, and Most Liberal Orders and Advisers of the Road*. (Philadelphia: Porter & Coates, 1872), 780 pp.

23. Joseph T. Wilson, *Emancipation: Its Course and Progress, from 1481 B.C. to A.D. 1875, with a Review of President Lincoln's Proclamation, the XIII Amendment, and the Progress of the Freed People since Emancipation; with a History of the Emancipation Monument*. (Hampton, Virginia: 1882), 242 pp. This work had appeared the previous year in only twenty-four pages.

24. Wilson, *The Black Phalanx: A History of the Negro Soldiers of the United States in the Wars of 1775–1812, 1861–'65* (Hartford, Conn.: American Publishing Company, 1888), 528 pp.

25. 1890 and 1897. For further biographical facts on Wilson see W. T. Andrews, *In Memoriam* (Washington, D.C.: Howard University Press, 1891), 12 pp. For another example of Wilson's work see his *Voice of a New Race*, a selection of poems and an oration (Hampton, Virginia: 1882), 43 pp.

26. This oration is reprinted in his *History of the Negro Race*, pp. 111–114. John Hope Franklin has written the best evaluation of Williams's work as an historian in his "George Washington Williams, Historian," *Journal of Negro History*, XXXI, No. 1, January, 1946, pp. 60–90; also see, especially for the early life of Williams, William J. Simmons, *Men of Mark*, pp. 549–559; *Dictionary of American Biography*, XX, pp. 263–264; *Encyclopedia Americana; Biographical Cyclopedia and Portrait Gallery of the State of Ohio*, III, 1884; *American Authors, 1600–1900*, edited by S. J. Kunitz and H. Haycroft, p. 819; J. Grimes, *op. cit.*, pp. 20–30.

27. George Washington Williams, *A History of the Negro Race in America from 1619 to 1880. Negroes as Slaves, as Soldiers, and as Citizens; together with a Preliminary Consideration of the Unity of the Human Family, an Historical Sketch of Africa, and an Account of the Negro Governments of Sierra Leone and Liberia.* In 2 volumes (New York: G. P. Putnam's Sons, 1883), 481 pp. and 611 pp.

28. *Ibid.*, p. v.

29. *Ibid.*, p. vi, ix–x.

30. *Ibid.*, p. vii.

31. *Ibid.*, p. x.

32. *Ibid.*, p. 108.

33. *Ibid.*, p. 109.

34. *Ibid.*, p. 110.

35. George Washington Williams, *op cit.*

36. *Ibid*, p. 364.

37. *Ibid.*, p. vii.

38. *Ibid.*, p. 377.

39. Franklin, *loc. cit.*, p. 72.

40. Vol. IX, April, 1883, pp. 299–300.

41. Vol. XIV, pp. 72–73.

42. Vol. LI, April, 1883.

43. Vol. XXXVI, April 12, 1883, pp. 325–326.

44. Quoted in Simmons, *Men of Mark*, p. 561. See also review quoted in Simmons, p. 561, from the *Westminister Review* for July, 1883.

45. Simmons, *op. cit.*, p. 562.

46. Williams, *A History of the Negro Troops in the War of the Rebellion, 1861–1865, preceded by a Review of the Military Services of Negroes in Ancient and Modern Times* (New York: Harper Brothers, 1888), 353 pp.

47. *Ibid.*, pp. x–xii.

48. *Ibid.*, p. xiv.

49. *Ibid.*, p. x.

50. *Ibid.*, p. xii.

51. *Ibid.*, pp. ix, xiii.

52. See review quoted here in *The Nation*, XXXXVI, March 1, 1888, p. 180; also, cf. *Literary World*, XIX, Feb. 18, 1888, p. 55.

53. Franklin, *loc. cit.*, pp. 70–71.

54. Vernon Loggins, *op. cit.*, p. 280.

55. Benjamin Brawley, *The Negro in Literature and Art* (New York: Duffield and Co., 1921), p. 70.

56. *History of the Negro Race in America*, II, p. 553. Herbert Aptheker also states that Williams accepted some of the "myths" about

the Negro which were currently in vogue. (Cf. Aptheker's *The Negro in the Civil War* [New York: International Publishers, 1938], p. 48.)

57. These biographical facts on Brawley are taken from *Who's Who in America*, XVIII, p. 379; *Who's Who in Colored America*, 1932; and Grimes, *op. cit.* See also the eulogistic article by John W. Parker, a former student of Brawley's, entitled "Benjamin Brawley—Teacher and Scholar," *Phylon*, 1st qtr., 1949, pp. 15–23. This article lists all of Brawley's many writings.

58. Brawley, *A Short History of the American Negro* (New York: Macmillan, 1913. Revised, 1919, 1921, 1926, 1939, and 1941).

59. Brawley, *A Social History of the American Negro: Being a History of the Negro Problem in the U.S., Including a History and Study of the Republic of Liberia* (New York: Macmillan, 1921).

60. *Ibid.*, p. ix.

61. *Journal of Negro History*, VII, No. 1, January, 1922, p. 114.

62. Brawley, *The Negro in Literature and Art* (New York: Duffield and Co., 1918).

63. See review by Carter Woodson, *Journal of Negro History*, III, 1918, p. 329.

64. *History of Morehouse College* (Atlanta, Georgia: Morehouse College, 1917), 218 pp.

65. Brawley, *Africa and the World War* (New York: Duffield and Co., 1918), 84 pp.

66. Brawley, *A Short History of the English Drama* (New York: Harcourt Brace and Co., 1921), 260 pp.

67. Brawley, *A History of the English Hymn* (New York: Abingdon Press, 1932), 256 pp.

68. Brawley, *Doctor Dillard of the Jeanes Fund* (New York: F. H. Revill Co., 1930), 151 pp.; and *Paul Laurence Dunbar* (Chapel Hill: University of North Carolina Press, 1936), 159 pp.

69. See his articles on James M. Bell, Lott Carey, Paul Cuffee, Martin Delaney, and Joseph Fortein in this work, II, p. 156; III, p. 155; IV, p. 385; V, p. 219, VI, p. 536, VIII, p. 564; IX, p. 156.

70. Brawley, *Social History of American Negro Women of Achievement* (Chicago: Woman's American Baptist Home Mission Society, 1919), 92 pp.

71. Brawley, *Negro Builders and Heroes* (Chapel Hill: University of North Carolina Press, 1937), 315 pp.

72. Brawley, *The Negro Genius* (New York: Dodd, Mead and Co., 1937), 366 pp.

73. Brawley, ed., *Early Negro American Writers* (Chapel Hill: University of North Carolina Press, 1935), 305 pp.

74. For a statement of his philosophy of history, see p. 389 of his *Social History of the American Negro*.

75. Facts on Washington's life are taken from his autobiography and his own subsequent writings, as well as Basil Matthews, *Booker T. Washington* (Cambridge: Harvard University Press, 1948); Loggins, *op. cit.*, pp. 280 ff.; Emmett J. Scott and Lyman Beecher Stowe, *Booker T. Washington* (New York: Doubleday, Page and Co., 1918); *Dictionary of American Biography*, XIX, pp. 506–508.

76. Washington, *Up From Slavery* (New York: A. L. Burt and Co., 1900), 330 pp.

77. Washington, *Working with the Hands* (New York: Doubleday, 1904), and *My Larger Education* (New York: Doubleday, 1911), 313 pp.

78. Washington, *Frederick Douglass* (Philadelphia: George W. Jacobs and Co., 1906), 355 pp.

79. Washington, *The Story of the Negro* (New York: Doubleday, Page and Co., 1909), I, 332 pp.; II, 437 pp.

80. Loggins, *op. cit.*, p. 281.

81. *The Story of the Negro*, I, p. 3.

82. *Ibid.*, Preface.

83. See review of 1940 reprint by Peter Smith and Co., New York, by Carter G. Woodson, *Journal of Negro History*, XXVI, No. 2, April, 1941, p. 266.

84. *Ibid.*

85. II, p. 399, 1909 edition by Doubleday and Company.

86. II, p. 400, 1940 edition by Peter Smith and Company.

Part 3
INTRODUCTION

---

1. Maurice R. Davis, *Negroes in American Society* (New York: McGraw-Hill Book Company, 1949), p. 168, and Harry W. Greene, *op. cit.*, Introduction.

2. Alain Locke, ed., *The New Negro* (New York: Albert and Charles Boni, 1925), p. 48. See also W. S. Braithwaite, "Alain Locke's Relationship to the Negro in American Literature," *Phylon*, XVIII, No. 2, second quarter, 1957.

3. Introduction by William Dean Howells to Dunbar's *Lyrics of Lowly Life* (New York: Dodd, Mead and Co., 1896).

4. On the influence of late nineteenth-century thinking on the New School, see Carter Woodson's "Negro Historians of Our Time," *Negro History Bulletin*, pp. 154–156. Here Woodson also gives insight into the differences between the Negro historiography of the nineteenth century and that of the twentieth century.

5. Cf. Introduction, *Dusk of Dawn*.

CHAPTER 4
W. E. B. DU BOIS
Writing with a Sword in His Hand

1. E. R. Embree, *Thirteen Against the Odds* (New York: The Viking Press, 1946), p. 153. See also F. L. Broderick, *William E. B. Du Bois: Negro Leader in a Time of Crisis* (Stanford: 1959), and E. M. Rudwick, *W. E. B. Du Bois: A Study in Minority Group Leadership* (Philadelphia, 1960).

2. W. E. B. Du Bois, *Dusk of Dawn: An Essay toward an Autobiography of a Race Concept* (New York: Harcourt Brace, 1940), pp. 11–13.

3. *Ibid.*, p. 14. Biographical facts on his life are also taken from *Who's Who in Colored America*, 1931, p. 717; *Who's Who in America*, 1934, XVIII, p. 753, and B. G. Brawley, *The Negro in Literature and Art*, pp. 50–55.

4. Du Bois, *Dusk of Dawn*, p. 14.

5. *Ibid.*, p. 34. See also Earl E. Thorpe, "Frederick Douglass, Booker T. Washington, and W. E. B. Du Bois," *Negro History Bulletin*, January, 1957.

6. *Dusk of Dawn*, pp. 139–140.

7. *Ibid.*, pp. 35, 36.

8. *Ibid.*, pp. 42–47.

9. *Ibid.*, p. 47.

10. *Ibid.*, pp. 56–57.

11. *Ibid.*, p. 51.

12. *Ibid.*, p. 28. (See also Earl E. Thorpe, "The Booker T. Washington–W. E. B. Du Bois Controversy," *Quarterly Review of Higher Education Among Negroes*, October, 1955.)

13. Mary W. Ovington, *Portraits in Color* (New York: Viking Press, 1927), p. 85; See also *Dusk of Dawn*, pp. 95–96.

14. *Ibid.*, p. 94. Du Bois gives a comprehensive account of his differences with Washington in his *The Souls of Black Folk: Essays and Sketches* (Chicago: A. C. McClurg and Co., 1903), 264 pp.

15. *Dusk of Dawn*, p. 96.

16. *Ibid.*

17. *Ibid.*, pp. 295–296.

18. *Ibid.*

19. *Ibid.*, pp. 286–287. (See also the excellent study by D. W. Wynn entitled *The NAACP Versus Revolutionary Protest* [New York: Exposition Press, 1955], esp. Ch. III.)

20. *Ibid.*, p. 304.

21. *Ibid.*, p. 314.

22. Du Bois, *Black Reconstruction* (New York: Harcourt Brace, 1935).

23. *Dusk of Dawn,* p. 321.

24. *Ibid.*

25. Mary W. Ovington, *op. cit.,* p. 78.

26. *Ibid.,* pp. 86, 91.

27. Du Bois, *The Suppression of the African Slave-Trade to the United States of America, 1638–1870* (New York: Longmans, Green and Co.), 335 pp.

28. Loggins, *The Negro Author,* p. 281.

29. Loggins, *op. cit.,* p. 282.

30. Anonymous reviewer, *The Nation,* LXIII, Dec. 31, 1896, pp. 498–500.

31. *Suppression of the African Slave-Trade,* p. v.

32. *Ibid.,* p. 1.

33. One of the few places where one might expect to find documentation, and does not, is the statement on page 15 that "As a whole, it may be said that whatever opposition to the slave-trade there was in the planting colonies was based principally on the political fear of insurrection."

34. *Ibid.,* p. 39.

35. *Ibid.,* p. 151.

36. *Ibid.,* p. 196.

37. *Ibid.,* pp. 197–198.

38. Du Bois, *The Philadelphia Negro: A Social Study* (Philadelphia: Published for the University of Pennsylvania, 1899), 520 pp. This volume was published as No. 14 in the University of Pennsylvania Series in Political Economy and Public Law.

39. *Ibid.,* Preface, p. iii.

40. *Ibid.,* p. v.

41. *Ibid.,* p. iv.

42. *Ibid.,* p. 385.

43. Benjamin Brawley, *Negro Builders and Heroes* (Chapel Hill: University of North Carolina Press, 1937), p. 190.

44. Du Bois and Booker T. Washington, *The Negro in the South* (Philadelphia: G. W. Jacobs and Co., 1907), 222 pp. The two chapters by Du Bois are entitled "The Economic Revolution in the South," pp. 77–122, and "Religion in the South," pp. 123–192.

45. *Ibid.,* pp. 81–83.

46. *Ibid.,* p. 85.

47. *Ibid.,* p. 90.

48. Du Bois, *John Brown* (Philadelphia: G. W. Jacobs and Co., 1909), 406 pp.

49. *Ibid.,* p. 2.

50. *Ibid.,* p. 8.

51. *Ibid.,* p. 338.

52. *Ibid.,* p. 395.

53. Cf. his *Color and Democracy,* p. 382.

54. Du Bois, *The Negro* (New York: Henry Holt and Co., 1915), 254 pp.

55. *Ibid.,* p. 16.

56. Du Bois, *The Gift of Black Folk: The Negroes in the Making of America* (Boston: The Stratford Co., 1924), 349 pp.

57. *Ibid.,* Foreword pp. ii–iii.

58. *Ibid.*

59. See for example, review by Walter White, in the New York *Tribune,* September 21, 1924, p. 12.

60. Du Bois, *Black Reconstruction* (Harcourt Brace, New York, 1935), 736 pp.

61. Du Bois, *Dusk of Dawn,* p. 318.

62. *Ibid.,* p. 41.

63. *Ibid.,* p. 284.

64. *Ibid.*

65. *Black Reconstruction,* p. 724.

66. In addition to Dunning's *Reconstruction, Political and Economic,* he used the following state histories: Simkins and Woody, *South Carolina During Reconstruction;* Garner, *Reconstruction in Mississippi;* Fleming, *Civil War and Reconstruction in Alabama;* Ramsdell, *Reconstruction in Texas;* Coulter, *The Civil War and Reconstruction in Kentucky.*

67. *Black Reconstruction,* pp. 731–736.

68. Review by Rayford W. Logan, *Journal of Negro History,* XXI, No. I, January, 1936, pp. 61–62.

69. *Ibid.*

70. *Black Reconstruction,* p. 15.

71. *Dusk of Dawn,* p. 55.

72. *Ibid.,* p. 26.

73. *Ibid.,* p. 96.

74. *American Journal of Sociology,* XXXXI, January, 1936, p. 535.

75. New York *Herald-Tribune Books,* June 23, 1935, p. 1.

76. *Christian Science Monitor,* August 7, 1935, p. 12.

77. 141: 108, July 24, 1935. For other reviews see: Lewis Gannett, in the New York *Herald-Tribune*, June 13, 1935, p. 17; John Chamberlain, in *Current History*, XIV, August, 1935, p. 42, and, Charles S. Johnson, in *Survey Graphic*, XXXXVIII, January, 1936, p. 25.

78. In his "Historians of the Reconstruction," *Journal of Negro History*, XXIII, No. 1, January, 1938, p. 32.

79. Du Bois, *Black Folk Then and Now: An Essay in the History and Sociology of the Negro Race* (New York: Henry Holt and Co., 1939), 401 pp.

80. *Ibid.*, Preface.

81. *Ibid.*, p. viii.

82. *Ibid.*, p. ix.

83. *Ibid.*, p. vii.

84. *Ibid.*, p. 1.

85. *Ibid.*, p. 92.

86. *Ibid.*, pp. 128–129.

87. *Ibid.*, pp. 177–178.

88. *Ibid.*, p. 210.

89. *Ibid.*, p. 383.

90. *Ibid.*

91. In *Journal of Negro History*, XXIV, No. 4, October, 1939, p. 461.

92. In *New Republic*, LV, August 16, 1939, p. 100.

93. In *Saturday Review of Literature*, XX, July 29, 1939, p. 18. Other reviews, mostly favorable, are: C. G. Stillman in New York *Herald-Tribune Books*, June 25, 1939, p. 12; W. S. Meacham in *New York Times*, July 2, 1939, p. 3.

94. *Dusk of Dawn*, p. 6.

95. *Ibid.*, p. viii.

96. Du Bois, *Color and Democracy: Colonies and Peace* (New York: Harcourt, Brace and Co., 1945), 143 pp.

97. *Ibid.*, Preface.

98. *Ibid.*, p. 57.

99. *Ibid.*, pp. 74–75.

100. See, for example, the statements by Dr. Walter Dorn on the expansionist tendencies of the European states system in his *Competition for Empire, 1740–1763* (New York: Harper and Bros., 1940), 426 pp.

101. *Color and Democracy*, p. 116.

102. October, 1949, XXIV, p. 159.

103. D. R. Homer, in *Library Journal*, LXX, May 15, 1955, p. 486.

104. In *Saturday Review of Literature*, XXVIII, June 23, 1945, p. 17.

105. In *Annals of the American Academy of Political and Social Science*, 242: 174 November, 1945. See also reviews by Alain Locke, in *Survey Graphic*, XXXIV, October, 1945, p. 415; Carter G. Woodson, *Journal of Negro History*, XXX, No. 2, July, 1945.

106. Du Bois, *The World and Africa: An Inquiry into the Part Which Africa Has Played in World History* (New York: The Viking Press, 1947), 276 pp.

107. *Ibid.*, pp. vii–viii.

108. *Ibid.*

109. *Ibid.*

110. Works which he used most include Robert Briffault's *The Decline and Fall of the British Empire*; George Padmore's *How Britain Rules Africa*; Eric Williams's *Capitalism and Slavery*; his own *Suppression of the African Slave Trade*; Rayford Logan's *The United States and Haiti*; Chapman Cohen's *Christianity, Slavery and Labor*; E. D. Moore's *Ivory: The Scourge of Africa*.

111. *The World and Africa*, pp. xi–xii.

112. *Ibid.*, p. 43.

113. *Ibid.*, p. 75.

114. In *Booklist*, XXXXIII, February 15, 1947, p. 182.

115. Review by W. M. Brewer, *Journal of Negro History*, 1948.

116. *Saturday Review of Literature*, XXX, March 29, 1947, p. 10.

117. Robert Peel, in *Christian Science Monitor*, February 10, 1947, p. 14.

118. Du Bois, L. D. Reddick, G. B. Johnson, and Rayford Logan, eds., *The Encyclopedia of the Negro*, vol. I (N.Y.: H. W. Wilson and Co., 1945), 207 pp.

119. In *Journal of Negro History*, XXX. No. 3, July, 1945, pp. 341–342.

120. See above review by Woodson, and *Subscription Books Bulletin*, XVI, July, 1945, p. 38.

121. Du Bois, *The Quest of the Silver Fleece* (Chicago: A. C. McClurg and Co., 1911), 434 pp.

122. Du Bois, *Dark Princess: A Romance* (New York: Harcourt, Brace and Co., 1928), 312 pp.

123. In *The World Tomorrow*, XI, November, 1928, p. 473.

124. *The Souls of Black Folk*, 21st ed., 1937, Foreword.

125. Du Bois, *Darkwater: Voices from Within the Vale* (New York: Harcourt, Brace and Howe, 1920), p. vii.

126. *Ibid.*, pp. 3–4.

127. In *The New York Times*, August 8, 1920, p. 19.

128. On the loss of the old ideals which succeeded World War I, see R. R. Palmer, *op. cit.*, chapter on "The Decline of Classical Liberal-

ism," or Crane Brinton, *op. cit.*, pp. 447–526. For other works by W. E. Du Bois, see the work which he edited entitled *From Servitude to Service* (Boston: American Unitarian Association, 1905), 232 pp.; his "The Enforcement of the Slave-trade Laws," *Annual Report of the American Historical Association* (Washington, D. C.: 1892), pp. 163–174; his *In Battle for Peace: the Story of My 83rd Birthday* (New York: Masses and Mainstream, 1952), 192 pp.

CARTER G. WOODSON
The Father of Negro History

1. Biographical facts are taken from the introduction written by Kelly Miller for Woodson's *The Negro in Our History* (Washington, D. C.: Associated Publishers, 1947, 9th ed.); Charles H. Wesley, "Carter G. Woodson—as a Scholar," *Journal of Negro History*, XXXVI, No. 1, January, 1951, pp. 13ff. For activities of Woodson after 1915, the *Journal of Negro History* is the best source. He founded and edited this work until his death in 1950, and each volume carries information on his activities.

2. Wesley, "Carter G. Woodson, as a Scholar," *loc. cit.*, p. 17.

3. Miller, *loc. cit.*, p. xxv.

4. C. G. Woodson, "An Accounting for Twenty-five Years," *Journal of Negro History*, XXV, No. 4, October, 1940, pp. 422–423.

5. Woodson, "Ten Years of Collecting and Publishing the Records of the Negro," *Journal of Negro History*, X, No. 4, October, 1925, pp. 598–600.

6. *Journal of Negro History*, I, No. 2, April, 1916, pp. 227–229 carries their comments in letters to the editor.

7. Woodson, "Ten Years . . . ," *loc. cit.*, p. 600.

8. Letter to Woodson, reprinted, *Journal of Negro History*, I, No. 2, April, 1916, p. 227.

9. Woodson, "Ten Years . . . ," *loc. cit.*, pp. 600–602. In 1920 Edward Channing wrote Woodson: "It would be a great misfortune for the cause of historical truth for you to be obliged to suspend publication." (Letter from Channing to Woodson, March 30, 1920, Harvard University, in Woodson Collection, Library of Congress.)

10. Woodson, "Ten Years . . . ," *loc. cit.*, pp. 602–603.

11. Luther Porter Jackson, "The First Twenty-Five Volumes of the *Journal of Negro History* Digested," *Journal of Negro History*, XXV, No. 4, October, 1940, p. 433–436.

12. Charles H. Wesley, "Carter G. Woodson—as a Scholar," *loc. cit.*, p. 20, quoting letter from Woodson to Wesley of June 19, 1937, Washington, D. C.

13. Woodson, "Ten Years . . . ," *loc. cit.,* p. 598.

14. Woodson had a voluminous correspondence with persons all over the United States of America and various other countries who became interested in fostering research in Negro history as a result of Woodson's work. Some of these persons founded organizations similar to Woodson's to foster the study of Negro history. Some of these letters gave him little-known facts about the race, while other letters corrected him on errors of fact which appeared in some of his books. (See, for example, letter from D. E. Carney, Freetown, Sierra Leone, West Africa, January 19, 1921; letter from Monroe Work, Tuskegee Institute, July 14, 1920; letter from Bishop B. G. Shaw, Birmingham, Alabama, February 2, 1926; letter from Prof. W. Westergaard, University of California at Los Angeles, October 27, 1925; letter from Prof. A. E. Jenks, University of Minnesota, January 13, 1921; letter from George Washington Cable, Lathen, Mass., November 7, 1916—all in Woodson Collection in Library of Congress.)

15. Woodson, "An Accounting . . . ," *loc. cit.,* pp. 425–426.

16. *Ibid.,* pp. 426–428. For a full list of the volumes published by the Association to 1940 see this article, pp. 426–427. Woodson asked colored persons from various countries to write articles for the *Journal* on various aspects of their history. (See, for example, letter to Woodson from the Secretary of the National Congress of British West Africa, the Gold Coast, February 7, 1921; and a similar letter from W. Esuman-Givira Seky, Cape Coast, Gold Coast, West Africa, October 14, 1920. These and similar letters are in the Woodson Collection, Library of Congress, Washington, D.C.

17. Rayford W. Logan, "An Evaluation of the First Twenty Volumes of the *Journal of Negro History,*" *Journal of Negro History,* XX, No. 4, October, 1935, p. 399.

18. *Ibid.,* p. 400.

19. *Ibid.,* p. 403. Also see L. P. Jackson, "The Work of the Association and the People," *ibid.,* pp. 385–396.

20. *Journal of Negro History,* II, 1917, Foreword.

21. See *The History of the Omega Psi Phi Fraternity,* by Herman Dreer (published by the Fraternity, Washington, D. C., 1940, 331 pp.).

22. C. G. Woodson, "An Accounting . . ."

23. C. G. Woodson, "Negro History Week," *Journal of Negro History,* II, No. 2, April, 1926, p. 238.

24. Negro History Week and other activities of the Association designed to popularize Afro-American history could not have met with the great success which they did without the cooperation of many persons in many locales. Though these persons were not always professional historians or writers, they made a significant contribution

to the effort to let the world know that Afro-Americans have been more than criminals or hewers of wood and drawers of water. Businessmen, ministers, housewives, lawyers, doctors, school presidents or principals or grade-school teachers, they came from all walks of life and made some aspects of the work of the Association a middle-class "mass movement." A few nonprofessional historians who played such a role are: Dr. H. Councill Trenholm, long-time president of Alabama State College; Mrs. Mary McCloud Bethune, late President of Bethune-Cookman College; Dr. Albert N. D. Brooks, long-time editor of *The Negro History Bulletin*; Mrs. Geneva C. Turner, Nerissa L. Milton, and Jessie H. Roy of Washington, D. C.; Jane Shackleford; Helen Adele Whiting, Atlanta, Georgia; Mrs. Irene M. Gaines, Chicago, Illinois; Mr. O. A. Jackson, Okmulgee, Oklahoma; Mr. Louis R. Mehlinger, Washington, D. C.; Mr. H. A. Tynes and Dr. Marguerite Cartwright of New York; Dr. Benjamin E. Mays, Atlanta, Georgia; Mrs. Jessie P. Guzman, Tuskegee, Alabama; Mrs. Vernell M. Oliver, Wilberforce, Ohio; Mr. Harvey C. Jackson, Detroit, Michigan; Mr. Arnett G. Lindsey, Washington, D. C.; Mr. J. Rupert Picott, Richmond, Virginia; Mrs. Irene M. Gaines and Messrs. John H. Johnson and James H. Jackson, Chicago, Illinois; and Mrs. Vassie D. Wright, Los Angeles, California.

Some of the professional historians, social scientists, and others who played important roles in getting Afro-American history established as an accepted area of specialization are: Herbert Aptheker, Clarence Bacote, William Brewer, Herman Dreer, Merl R. Eppse, Helen G. Edmonds, John Hope Franklin, Lorenzo Green, Joseph Grimes, Leo Hansberry, Melville J. Herskovits, Luther Porter Jackson, Caulbert A. Jones, Rayford W. Logan, Augustus Low, Dorothy Porter, Benjamin Quarles, Lawrence D. Reddick, James H. Brewer, J. Reuben Sheeler, J. A. Rogers, William T. Savage, A. A. Schomburg, Alrutheus A. Taylor, Joseph H. Taylor, Monroe Work, Charles Wesley, and Prince Wilson.

25. Woodson, *Education of the Negro Prior to 1861* (New York and London: G. P. Putnam's Sons, 1915), 454 pp. A second edition appeared four years later.

26. *Ibid.*, Preface.

27. XXI, July, 1915, p. 119.

28. J. F. Gould, *Survey*, XXXV, January 29, 1916, p. 521.

29. Mary C. Terrell, *Journal of Negro History*, I, No. 1, January, 1916, pp. 96–97.

30. Woodson, *The Negro in Our History* (Washington, D. C., Associated Publishers, 1922).

31. New York, A. Knopf.

32. *The Negro in Our History*, Preface.

33. Alain Locke, in *Journal of Negro History*, XII, No. 1, January, 1927, pp. 99–101.

34. *The Negro in Our History,* Preface.

35. January 7, 1923, p. 18. This work was also reviewed with comments generally favorable, by *The Springfield Republican,* July 15, 1922, p. 8; *Survey,* XXXIX, October 15, 1922, p. 119; and, *American Political Science Review,* XVI, November, 1922, p. 727.

36. Woodson, *Negro Makers of History* (Washington, D.C.: Associated Publishers, 1928), 362 pp.

37. Woodson, *The Story of the Negro Retold* (Washington, D.C.: Associated Publishers, 1935), 369 pp.

38. Woodson, *African Myths, together with Proverbs* (Washington, D.C.: Associated Publishers, 1928), 184 pp.

39. Woodson, *A Century of Negro Migration* (Washington, D.C.: Association for the Study of Negro Life and History, 1918), 221 pp.

40. October 24, 1918, p. 54. *A Century of Negro Migration* was also reviewed by the *Boston Transcript,* Dec. 31, 1918, p. 6; *The Nation,* Jan. 11, 1919; *Review of Reviews,* Dec. 1918, LVIII, p. 661; and, the *Journal of Negro History,* 1918, p. 341. These critics had high praise for Woodson's objectivity and thoroughness of research.

41. Woodson, *The History of the Negro Church* (Washington, D.C.: Associated Publishers, 1921), 330 pp.: Preface. A second edition appeared in 1945. See review by F. C. Summer, *Journal of Negro History,* VII, No. 2, April, 1922. For further comment on this book see chapter on writers of Church history.

42. Woodson, *Early Negro Education in West Virginia* (Institute, W. Va.: West Virginia College, 1921. Published as "West Virginia Collegiate Institute Bulletin," Ser. 6, No. 3), 54 pp.

43. Woodson, "Fifty Years of Negro Citizenship as Qualified by the United States Supreme Court," *Journal of Negro History,* VI, No. 1, January, 1921.

44. *Ibid.,* p. 1.

45. Woodson, *The Mis-Education of the Negro* (Washington, D.C.: Associated Publishers, 1933): Preface.

46. XVIII, May 12, 1933, p. 55. This work was also similarly reviewed by Alain Locke for *Survey,* LXIX, October, 1933, p. 363.

47. *Mis-Education of the Negro,* p. xi–xii.

48. *Ibid.,* p. 1.

49. *Ibid.,* pp. 144–145.

50. *Ibid.,* p. 145 ff.

51. Woodson, ed., *Free Negro Owners of Slaves in the United States in 1830* (Washington, D.C.: The Association for the Study of Negro Life and History, 1924), 78 pp.

52. Woodson, ed., *Free Negro Heads of Families in the United States in 1830* (Washington, D.C.: The Association for the Study of Negro Life and History, 1925), 296 pp.

53. See the prefaces of both works.

54. Woodson, ed., *Negro Orators and Their Orations* (Washington, D.C.: Associated Publishers, 1926), 711 pp.

55. Woodson, ed., *The Mind of the Negro as Reflected in Letters Written During the Crisis* (Washington, D. C.: Associated Publishers, 1926), 672 pp.

56. *Negro Orators,* preface.

57. October 24, 1926, p. 26.

58. CXXIV, December, 1926, p. 427.

59. Woodson, John H. Harmon, Jr., and Arnett C. Lindsay, *The Negro as a Businessman* (Washington, D.C.: Associated Publishers, 1929), 111 pp.

60. Woodson and Lorenzo J. Greene, *The Negro Wage Earner* (Washington, D.C.: Associated Publishers, 1930), 388 pp.

61. *Ibid.,* pp. 1 ff.

62. Woodson, *The Rural Negro* (Washington, D.C.: Associated Publishers, 1930), 265 pp.

63. New York *Herald-Tribune Books,* Nov. 23, 1930, p. 14.

64. James Browning, *Journal of Negro History,* XVI, No. 2, April, 1931, p. 245. This work was also favorably reviewed by the *New York Times,* September 14, 1930, p. 16 and the *Boston Transcript,* August 16, 1930, p. 3.

65. *The Negro Professional Man and the Community* (Washington, D.C., Associated Publishers, 1934).

66. *Ibid.,* Foreword.

67. May, 1934, XXXXVII, p. 1303.

68. March 25, 1934, p. 12.

69. Woodson, *The African Background Outlined* (Washington, D.C.: Association for the Study of Negro Life and History, 1936), 478 pp.

70. *Ibid.,* pp. 217–463.

71. *Ibid.,* preface.

72. Rayford W. Logan, *Journal of Negro History,* XXI, 1936, p. 323.

73. Woodson, *African Heroes and Heroines* (Washington, D.C., Associated Publishers, 1939), 210 pp.

74. July 22, 1939, p. 3.

75. *African Heroes and Heroines,* preface.

76. *Ibid.*

77. Woodson, ed., *The Works of Francis J. Grimke,* 4 vols. (Washington, D.C.: Associated Publishers, 1942).

78. See, for example, his "The Beginnings of the Miscegenation of the Whites and Blacks," *Journal of Negro History,* III, 1918, pp.

335–353, and the following articles, all in this journal; "Some Attitudes in English Literature," XX, No. 2, April, 1935, pp. 190–243; "The Negro Washer-Woman, a Vanishing Figure," XV, No. 3, July, 1930, pp. 269–277; "Notes on the Bakongo," XXX, No. 4, October, 1945, pp. 421–431; "The Relations of Negroes and Indians in Massachusetts," V, January, 1920, pp. 45–57; "The Negroes of Cincinnati Prior to the Civil War," I, July, 1916, pp. 1–22; also "Some Things Negroes Need to Do," in *Southern Workman*, LI, January, 1922, p. 33. Woodson also wrote, "The Negro in Education," for the *Encyclopedia Americana*, XX, pp. 52–53, and biographical sketches of Richard Allen, Richard Henry Boyd, Morris Brown, Williams Wells, Brown and Blanche K. Bruce for *The Dictionary of American Biography* (See volumes I, p. 204; II, p. 528; III, pp. 145, 161, and 180 respectively).

79. Charles H. Wesley, "Carter G. Woodson—as a Scholar," *loc. cit.*, pp. 14–17.

80. Woodson, "Negro History Week," *Journal of Negro History*, XI, No. 2, April, 1926, p. 239.

81. *Ibid.*, pp. 239–240.

82. *Ibid.*, p. 239.

83. C. G. Woodson, "The Celebration of Negro History Week," *Journal of Negro History*, XII, No. 2, April, 1927, p. 103.

84. *Negro Makers of History*, preface.

85. *Journal of Negro History*, X, No. 4, October, 1925, p. 600.

86. See review of *The Negro in Our History*, in the *New York Tribune*, January 7, 1923, p. 18.

87. Kelly Miller, *loc. cit.*, p. xxvi.

88. Charles H. Wesley, "Carter G. Woodson—as a Scholar," *loc. cit.*, p. 21.

89. Melville J. Herskovits, "The Present Status and Needs of Afro-American Research," *Journal of Negro History*, XXXVI, No. 2, April, 1951, pp. 123–124.

90. John G. Van Deusen, *The Black Man in White America* (Washington, D.C., Associated Publishers, 1944), p. 284. The May, 1950 issue of the *Negro History Bulletin* was devoted exclusively to Woodson. The eight brief articles in this issue were written by persons who knew Woodson intimately.

CHAPTER 6

PIONEERS IN BLACK STUDIES

---

1. Charles H. Wesley, *Negro Labor in the United States, 1850–1925* (New York: Vanguard Press, 1927), 343 pp.

2. Wesley, *Richard Allen, Apostle of Freedom* (Washington, D.C.: Associated Publishers, 1935), 300 pp.

3. Wesley, *The Collapse of the Confederacy* (Washington, D.C.: Associated Publishers, 1937), 225 pp.

4. Wesley, *The History of Alpha Phi Alpha* (Washington, D.C.: Howard University Press, 1929), 294 pp.

5. Wesley, *A History of the I.B.P.O.E.* (Washington, D.C.: Associated Publishers, 1956).

6. For examples of these, see his: "The Participation of Negroes in Anti-Slavery Political Parties," *Journal of Negro History,* XXIX, No. 1, January, 1944, pp. 32–74; and the following articles, all in this same journal—"The Concept of the Inferiority of the Negro in American Thought," XXV, No. 4. October, 1940, pp. 540–560; "The Negro's Struggles for Freedom in its Birthright," XXX, No. 7, January, 1945, pp. 62–81; "The Negro in the West Indies," XVII, No. 1 January, 1932, pp. 51–66; "The Neglected Period of Emancipation in Great Britain," XVII, No. 2, April, 1932, pp. 156–179; "The Emancipation of the Free Colored Population in the British Empire," XIX, No. 2, April, 1934, pp. 137–170; "Negro Suffrage in the Period of the Constitution-Making, 1787–1965," XXXII, No. 2, April, 1947, pp. 143–168; "The Religious Attitudes of Negro Youth," XXI, No. 4, October, 1936, pp. 376–393; "The Reconstruction of History," XX, October, 1925, pp. 414–427; "The Employment of Negroes as Soldiers in the Confederate Army," IV, No. 3, July, 1919, pp. 239–253; "Lincoln's Plan for Colonizing the Emancipated Negroes," IV, No. 3, January, 1919, pp. 7–21; "The Struggle of Haiti and Liberia for Recognition," II, October, 1917, pp. 369–383.

7. Wesley, *The Collapse of the Confederacy,* pp. v–vi.

8. *Ibid.,* p. 168.

9. "The Reconstruction of History," *loc. cit.,* pp. 421–426.

10. Wesley, "The Concept of the Inferiority of the Negro in American Thought," *loc. cit.,* pp. 558–559.

11. Monroe Nathan Work, *Bibliography of the Negro in Africa and America* (New York: H. W. Wilson Co., 1928), 698 pp.

12. Biographical facts on Work are taken from the Introduction to his *Bibliography,* and from Jessie P. Guzman, "Monroe Nathan Work and His Contributions," *Journal of Negro History,* XXIV, October, 1940, p. 435 ff.

13. Guzman, *loc. cit.,* p. 435.

14. Introduction to his *Bibliography.*

15. *Ibid.,* p. vii.

16. *Ibid.,* p. xiii. For a favorable review of this volume see Rayford W. Logan, *Journal of Negro History,* XIII, No. 4, October, 1928, pp. 539–540.

17. Guzman, *loc. cit.*, p. 450. The Negro Yearbook was published by the Negro Yearbook Publishing Co., Tuskegee, Alabama, from 1912–1926. For a favorable review of this production see C. G. Woodson, *Journal of Negro History*, V, No. 3, July, 1920, p. 387.

18. See preface, I, of Washington's history, and Guzman, *loc. cit.*, p. 441.

19. Guzman, *loc. cit.*, p. 439.

20. For a list of published articles by Monroe Work see Guzman, *loc. cit.*, pp. 443–446. Many of these articles are listed in Work's *Bibliography*.

21. Merl R. Eppse and A. P. Foster, *An Elementary History of America, Including the Contributions of the Negro Race* (Nashville, Tenn.: National Educational Publishing Co., 1943), 299 pp.

22. *Ibid.*, p. v.

23. Merl R. Eppse, *The Negro, too, in American History* (Nashville, Tenn.: National Publishing Co., 1949), 644 pp.

24. Merl R. Eppse, *A Guide to the Study of the Negro in American History* (Nashville, Tenn.: National Educational Publishing Co., 1937), 155 pp.

CHAPTER 7
HISTORIANS WITHOUT PORTFOLIO

---

1. The best source of direct information on the activities of these societies is probably the letters and papers of the Schomburg Collection and the Carter Woodson "American Negro Papers" Collection. The latter is to be found in the Manuscript Division of the Library of Congress. This writer read many such letters to Woodson from such members of the Laymen's School as Henry A. Wallace, John R. Lynch, John Edward Bruce, and Kelly Miller. See also article by Helen Boardman, *loc. cit.*, p. 152.

2. Many of Schomburg's own writings were published by this organization as Occasional Papers. For documents illustrative of the activities of this organization see letters by Schomburg listed as Documents No. 1592, 1595, 1634, 1720, and 1736 in Schomburg Collection, 135th St. Branch of New York Public Library. For a list of the many documents in this collection bearing on the activities of this and other similar societies see the *Calendar of Manuscripts in the Schomburg Collection,* compiled by the Historical Records Survey, WPA, New York City, 1942.

3. See for example, Documents 56, 344, Schomburg Collection.

4. The period of greatest activity of this Laymen's School is roughly from 1890–1930.

5. *Who's Who of the Colored Race,* vol. I, 1915, p. 237.

6. July, 1938, vol. 45, p. 221.

7. Vol. 4, June, 1926, p. 187. For other articles on the work of Schomburg in connection with Negro history see *Opportunity*, Vol. 6, August, 1928, p. 249; *Crisis*, vol. 23, March, 1922, p. 200; and, *Opportunity*, vol. 16, July, 1938, p. 197. For a list of Schomburg's many writings, see Appendix, this study.

8. See "Letters of John W. Cromwell," in Carter Woodson "American Negro Papers" Collection, Library of Congress, Washington, D. C. Cf. also, W. J. Simmons, *op. cit.*, pp. 898–907.

9. These letters are in the Woodson Collection, Library of Congress. Also Cf. Lynch's *Some Historical Errors of James Ford Rhodes* (Boston: Cornhill Pub. Co., 1922), 115 pp; See also, *Who's Who in Colored America*, edited by F. L. Mather, Chicago 1915, p. 81. Lynch's *Facts of Reconstruction* was published in 1915 (New York: The Neale Publishing Co.), 325 pp.

10. These letters are in the Woodson Collection. See, for example, letter from James Ford Rhodes to Wallace, Seal Harbor, Maine, September 27, 1920. Facts on Wallace's life are taken from a lengthy letter which Wallace wrote to Woodson, Chester, Pennsylvania, October 26, 1922. All letters referred to in this footnote are in the Woodson Collection. Wallace's most outstanding work was his *Carpetbag Rule in Flordia* (Jacksonville: De Costa Printing Company, 1888), 444 pp. Like Lynch's study of this period, this work relies to a great extent on the author's memory.

11. There are many letters by Bruce in both the Woodson and Schomburg Collections. Facts on his life are taken from these.

12. E. A. Johnson, *School History of the Negro Race in America*, rev. ed. (New York: Isaac Goldman Co., 1911), 400 pp.

13. Helen Boardman, *loc. cit.*, p. 153. This article by Miss Boardman carries good evaluations of John R. Lynch, Archibald Grimke, Edward A. Johnson, Schomburg, Woodson, Daniel A. Payne, Charles Wesley, and others.

14. E. A. Johnson, *A History of Negro Soldiers in the Spanish American War* (Raleigh, N.C.: Capital Printing Co., 1899), 147 pp.

15. Laura E. Wilkes, *Missing Pages in American History* (Washington, D.C.: Press of R. L. Pendleton, 1919).

16. See her letter to Woodson, Washington, D.C., July 22, 1921, in the Woodson Collection, Library of Congress.

17. *The Colored Regulars in the U.S. Army, with a Sketch of the History of the Colored American* (Philadelphia: AME Book Concern, 1921), 520 pp; *The Haytian Revolution, 1791 to 1804* (N.Y.: T. Y. Crowell Co., 1914), 292 pp; and *How the Black St. Domingo Legion Saved the Patriot Army in the Siege of Savannah, 1779* (Washington, D.C.: The Negro Academy, Occasional Papers No. 5), 15 pp.

18. W. H. Crogman and J. W. Gibson, *The Colored American from Slavery to Honorable Citizenship* (Atlanta: J. L. Nichols and Co., 1902), 732 pp.

19. W. H. Crogman, and others, *Progress of a Race* (J. L. Nichols and Co., 1920), 480 pp. Ist pub. 1897, 663 pp. The Bible is quoted rather freely in this work and it is quite argumentative. For biographical facts on Crogman see *Who's Who in Colored America*, 1915, p. 81; and, W. J. Simmons, *op. cit.*, pp. 694–698.

20. Washington, D.C., 1919, 712 pp. For an example of other writings by Kelly Miller, see his: *The Everlasting Stain* (Washington, D. C.: Associated Publishers, 1924), 352 pp. and a work which he co-authored with J. R. Gay, *Progress and Achievements of the Colored People* Washington, D.C.: Austen Jenkins Co., 1917), 490 pp.

21. Quoted in "Rogers Says," column by J. A. Rogers, *Pittsburgh Courier,* December 6, 1952, p. 9.

Some of Rogers's books are: *100 Amazing Facts About the Negro, with Complete Proof: A Short Cut to the World History of the Negro* (24th rev. ed., New York: 1963), 58 pp.; *Sex and Race: Negro-Caucasion Mixing in All Ages and Lands* (New York: J. A. Rogers Publications, 1940–44, 1957–61), 3 vols.; *She Walks in Beauty* (Los Angeles: Western Publishers, 1963), 316 pp.; *As Nature Leads; An Informal Discussion of the Reason Why Negro and Caucasian Are Mixing in Spite of Opposition* (Chicago: M. A. Donohue and Co., printers, 1919), 207 pp.; *From Superman to Man* (Chicago: M. A. Donohue and Co., printers, 1917), 128 pp.; *World's Greatest Men and Women of African Descent* (New York: J. A. Rogers, 1935).

22. Miss Whiting has pioneered in adapting Negro history to the elementary level. Among the many writings which she has produced are: *Negro Art, Music and Rhyme for Young Folks, Book II* (Washington, D.C.: Associated Publishers, 1938), 38 pp. Book I was published under the title *Negro Folk Tales for Pupils in the Primary Grades* (Washington, D.C.: Associated Publishers, 1938).

23. See his *Reconstruction: The Battle for Democracy* (New York: 1937). This work was written with a very pronounced Marxist slant, following the pattern of W. E. B. Du Bois's *Black Reconstruction*. Miss Boardman takes the Marxism in Du Bois and Allen to point up "the fact that the lead in a reconsideration of certain aspects of American history is being taken by Negro historians" (*loc. cit.*, p. 166).

CHAPTER 8
CHURCH HISTORIANS

---

1. Carter Woodson, *History of the Negro Church* (Washington, D.C.: Associated Publishers, 1921), Vernon Loggins, *The Negro Author*

(N.Y.: Columbia University Press, 1931), and W. J. Simmons, *Men of Mark* (Cleveland: 1837), are fair sources for Churchmen who were writers of history. Cf., for example, Simmons's discussions of Rufus L. Perry, Alexander Crummell, and J. B. Fields, pp. 620–625, 530–535, and 1016–1021 respectively.

2. Cf., for example, A. W. Lawson, "History of the United Holiness Church of America," unpublished B.D. thesis, Shaw University, Raleigh, North Carolina, 1950. I have examined an excellent manuscript by a very competent scholar which was written over a quarter-century ago but which has never been published. This is Miles Mark Fisher's "History of Negro Baptists," c. 1925. Reverend Fisher now resides in Durham, North Carolina.

3. See Christopher Rush and George Collins, *Short Account of the Rise and Progress of the African Methodist Episcopal Church in America* (New York: Published by the author), 1843. Republished 1866, 106 pp.

4. W. Catto, *A Semi-Centenary Discourse, Delivered in the First African Presbyterian Church, Philadelphia . . . with a History of the Church* (Philadelphia, 1857).

5. William Douglass, *Annals of the First African Church in the U.S.A.* (1862). Both Catto and Douglass used mostly church minutes for their information. Both wrote in an informative, unimpassioned style.

6. Vernon Loggins, *The Negro Author*, p. 189.

7. John Hope Franklin, *From Slavery to Freedom* (New York: A. A. Knopf, 1947), p. 403.

8. B. T. Tanner, *An Outline of our History and Government* (Philadelphia: Grant, Faires and Rodgers Printers, 1884). Tanner lived from 1835–1923. Carter Woodson refers to him as "one of the most scholarly Negroes of his time." Cf. Woodson's *The History of the Negro Church* (Washington, D. C.: 1921), p. 239.

9. L. M. Hagood, *The Colored Man in the Methodist Episcopal Church* (Cincinnati: Cranston and Stowe, 1890), 327 pp.

10. *Ibid.*, p. 4.

11. *Ibid.*, p. 15.

12. Wesley J. Gaines, *African Methodism in the South* (Atlanta: Franklin Publishing Co., 1890), 305 pp.

13. *Ibid.*, preface.

14. *Ibid.*

15. J. W. Hood, *One Hundred Years of the AMEZ Church* (New York: AMEZ Book Concern, 1895), 625 pp.

16. *Ibid.*, p. xiii–xvi.

17. D. A. Payne, *Recollections of Seventy Years* (Nashville, Tennessee: A.M.E. Sunday School Union, 1888), pp. 1–33. Cf. also, W. Simmons, *Men of Mark* (Cleveland: 1887), pp. 1078–1085.

18. D. A. Payne, *History of the African Methodist Episcopal Church* (Nashville, Tennessee: A.M.E. Sunday School Union, 1891), 502 pp.

19. *Ibid.*, p. 221–222, 273 ff. and 428 ff.

20. *Ibid.*, pp. vii–viii and pp. 1–2.

21. Patrick H. Thompson, *The History of Negro Baptists in Mississippi* (Jackson, Mississippi: The R. W. Bailey Printing Co., 1898), 669 pp.

22. *Ibid.*, Introduction.

23. James A. Handy, *Scraps of Methodist Episcopal History.*

24. *Ibid.*, preface.

25. N. H. Pius, *An Outline of Baptist History.*

26. *Ibid.*, preface.

27. Charles Spencer Smith, *A History of the AME Church* (Philadelphia: Book Concern of the AME Church, 1922), 557 pp. Smith had earlier published *Glimpses of Africa, West and Southwest Coast.*

28. Lewis G. Jordan, *Negro Baptist History, U.S.A., 1750–1930.* (Published by the Sunday School Publishing Board, Nashville, Tennessee, n.d.), 395 pp.

29. *Ibid.*, Introduction.

30. *Ibid.*, p. 8.

31. *Ibid.*, p. 12.

32. Charles H. Brooks, *Official History of the First American Baptist Church, Philadelphia, Pa.* (Philadelphia: 1922), 167 pp.

33. Charles Henry Phillips, *The History of the CME Church in America* (Jackson, Tenn.: Publishing House of the CME Church), first edition, 1898, 247 pp.; third edition, 1925, 623 pp.

34. *Ibid.*, Preface. Cf. also his *From the Farm to the Bishopric: An Autobiography* (Nashville, Tenn.: The Parthenon Press, 1932), 293 pp.

35. Miles Mark Fisher, *Negro Slave Songs* (New York: Cornell University Press, 1953).

36. See also his: *A Short History of the Baptist Denomination* (Nashville, Tennessee: Townsend Sunday School Publishing Board, 1933), which integrates the story of white Baptists with that of Negroes; *The Master's Slave: Elijah John Fisher* (Philadelphia: The Judson Press, 1922), 172 pp.: *Life of Lott Carey,* (Centennial Biography, Foreign Mission Board, National Baptist Convention, 1922); "The Negro and the World War," *Journal of Religion,* vol. 7, September, 1925; and, "Life of Lott Carey," *Journal of Negro History.*

37. Benjamin E. Mays, *The Negro's God* (Boston: Chapman and Grimes, 1938), 269 pp.

38. Mays and Joseph W. Nicholson, *The Negro's Church* (New York: Institute of Social and Religious Research, 1933), 321 pp.

39. *Ibid.*, p. v.

40. Charles H. Wesley, *Richard Allen, Apostle of Freedom* (Washington, D.C.: Associated Publishers, 1935).

41. *Ibid.*, p. ix.

42. See his "The Reconstruction of History," *Journal of Negro History*, XX, No. 4, October, 1935, pp. 421–422.

43. R. R. Wright, *The Encyclopedia of the AME Church*, second edition (Philadelphia, Pa.: Book Concern of the AME Church, 1948), 688 pp.; first edition, 1916.

44. For other works in this area, see: Charles Cumner Long, Comp., *History of the AME Church in Florida* (Philadelphia: AME Book Concern, 1939), 224 pp.; Rufus Perry, *The Cushites, or The Children of Ham As Seen by the Ancient Historians and Poets* (Springfield, Massachusetts; Wiley and Co., 1893), 175 pp.; B. F. DeCosta, *Three Score and Ten—The Story of St. Phillip's Church* (New York: 1889), 57 pp.; E. K. Love, *History of the First African Baptist Church* (Savannah, Georgia, n.d.); James M. Simms, *The First Colored Baptist Church in North America* (Philadelphia, 1888), 246 pp.; William I. Hopkins, *History of the Virginia Baptist State Church School Convention*, n.d., 110 pp.; C. H. Parrish, ed., *Golden Jubilee of the General Association of Colored Baptists of Kentucky* (Louisville, Kentucky: Mayes Printing Co.) 301 pp.; Bishop H. Holsey, *Autobiography, Sermons, Addresses, and Essays* (Atlanta, Georgia: Franklin Printing Co., 1898); S. X. Floyd, *Life of Charles T. Walker, D.D.* (Nashville, Tenn.: National Baptist Publishing Board, 1902), 193 pp.; Richard Allen, *Life and Gospel Labors* (Philadelphia: Marin and Boden, 1833); G. F. Bragg, *History of Afro-American Group of the Episcopal Church* (Baltimore: Church Advocate Press, 1909); the same author's *The First Priest on Southern Soil* (Baltimore: Church Advocate Press, 1909); and his *Men of Maryland* (Baltimore: Church Advocate Press, 1914); Butt, I. L., *History of African Methodism in Virginia* (Hampton, Virginia: Hampton Institute Press, 1908); J. T. Jenifer, *Centennial Retrospect History of the AME Church* (Nashville, Tennessee: AME Church Sunday School Union, 1902); J. H. Morgan, *History of the New Jersey Conference of the AME Church, 1872–1887* (Camden, New Jersey: Chew Publishers, 1887); R. C. Ransom, *Preface to the History of the AME Church* (Nashville, Tenn.: n.d.); T. G. Steward, *Fifty Years in the Gospel Ministry* (Philadelphia: AME Book Concern, 1921); and G. A. Singleton, *Romance of African Methodism* (New York: Exposition Press, 1952).

CHAPTER 9

BLACK SCHOLARS

1. Rayford W. Logan, *The Attitude of the Southern White Press toward Negro Suffrage, 1932–1940* (Washington, D.C.: Foundation Publishers, 1940), 115 pp.

2. Logan, ed., *What the Negro Wants* (Chapel Hill: University of North Carolina Press, 1944).

3. Logan, *Diplomatic Relations between the United States and Haiti, 1776–1891* (Chapel Hill: University of North Carolina Press, 1941), 516 pp.

4. Logan, *The Senate and the Versailles Mandate System* (Washington, D.C.: The Minorities Publishers, 1945), 112 pp.

5. Logan, *The Negro and the Post-War World: A Primer* (Washington, D.C.: The Minorities Publishers, 1945), 95 pp.

6. Logan, *African Mandates in World Politics* (Washington, D.C.: Public Affairs Press, 1948), 220 pp.

7. Logan, *The Operation of the Mandate System in Africa* (Washington, D.C.: Foundation Publishers, 1942), 50 pp.

8. With Du Bois and others; see Chapter 4, note 118.

9. Logan, *The Negro in American Life and Thought: The Nadir, 1887–1901* (New York: Dial Press, 1954). Biographical facts on Logan were taken from H. W. Greene, *op. cit.*, and G. J. Fleming and C. E. Burckel, *Who's Who in Colored America*, Yonkers, N.Y., 1950 edition. For a statement on the characteristics of the New School, see Carter Woodson, "Negro Historians of our Time," *The Negro History Bulletin*, April, 1945, pp. 154 ff.

10. Review by L. L. Montague, *Journal of Negro History*, XXVI, No. 3, July, 1941, p. 389.

11. W. S. Robertson, in *American Political Science Review*, XXXV, June, 1941, p. 594. This work was also praised by D. G. Munro in *Annals of the American Academy of Political and Social Science*, July, 1941, 216:191; and by R. W. Van Alstyne in *Political Science Quarterly*, LVI, December, 1941, p. 632.

12. See review by C. G. Woodson, *Journal of Negro History*, XXVI, No. 2, April, 1941, p. 269.

13. See review by C. G. Woodson, *Journal of Negro History*, XXXI, No. 2, April, 1946, p. 236. For examples of articles by Dr. Logan see his "Liberia in the Family of Nations," *Phylon*, VII, No. 1, 1946, pp. 5–11; and the following, all in the *Journal of Negro History:* "The International Status of the Negro," XVIII, No. 1, January, 1933, pp. 33–38; "German Acquisition of Southwest Africa," XVIII, No. 4, October, 1933, pp. 369–395; "The Attitude of the Church toward Slavery Prior to 1500," XVII, No. 4, October, 1932, pp.

466–480; "Education in Haiti," XV, No. 4, October, 1930, pp. 401–460; "The Egyptian Sudan, a problem in International Relations," XVI, No. 4, October, 1931, pp. 371–381; "The Operation of the Mandate System in Africa," XIII, No. 4, October, 1928, pp. 423–477.

14. Biographical facts are taken from H. W. Greene, *op. cit.*, and G. J. Fleming and C. E. Burckel, *op. cit.*, p. 452.

15. In 1944. This work ran serially in the *Journal of Negro History.*

16. In 1939.

17. For examples of his articles, see the following, all in the *Journal of Negro History:* "The Role of Negro Soldiers in Protecting the Indian Frontier from Intruders," XXXVI, No. 1, January, 1951, pp. 25–34; "The Negro on the Mining Frontier," XXX, No. 1, January, 1945, pp. 30–46; "The Influence of John Chavis and Lunsford Lane on the History of North Carolina," XXV, January, 1940, No. 1, pp. 14–24; "The Negro in the Westward Movement," XXV, October, 1940, No. 4, pp. 531–539; "Legal Provisions for Negro Schools in Missouri from 1890–1935," XXII, No. 3, July, 1937, pp. 335–344; "The Negro in the History of the Pacific Northwest," XIII, No. 3, July, 1928, p. 255; "Legal Provisions for Negro Schools in Missouri, 1865–1890," XVI, No. 3, July, 1931, pp. 309–321.

18. L. J. Greene and Carter G. Woodson, *The Negro Wage Earner* (Washington, D.C.: The Associated Publishers, 1930), 388 pp.

19. Greene, *The Negro in Colonial New England* (New York, Columbia University Press, 1943), 404 pp.

20. Greene and Myra Colson Callis, *The Employment of Negroes in the District of Columbia* (Washington, D.C.: The Association for the Study of Negro Life and History, 1930), 89 pp.

21. *The Negro in Colonial New England,* pp. 68–69.

22. *Ibid.* For examples of scholarly articles by Dr. Greene, see his "The New England Negro as Seen in Advertisements for Runaway Slaves," *Journal of Negro History,* XXIX, April, 1944, No. 2, pp. 125–146; and, "Slaveholding New England and its Awakening," *loc. cit.*, XIII, No. 4, October, 1928, pp. 492–533.

23. In *New England Quarterly,* June, 1943, XVI, p. 346. Also reviewing the work favorably were Elizabeth Donnah, *American Historical Review,* July, 1943, XLVIII, p. 797; S. R. Harlow, *Springfield Republican,* July 31, 1943, p. 6; and C. G. Woodson, *Journal of Negro History,* XXVIII, No. 4, October, 1943.

24. Luther Porter Jackson, *A History of the Virginia State Teachers Association* (Norfolk: The Guide Publishing Company, 1937), 112 pp.

25. Jackson, *Free Negro Labor and Property Holding in Virginia* (New York: D. Appleton-Century Co., 1942), 270 pp. See also his *Virginia Negro Soldiers and Seamen in the Revolutionary War* (Norfolk: Guide Quality Press), 40 pp.

26. See, for example, review by John Hope Franklin, *Journal of Negro History*, XXVIII, No. 1, January, 1943, pp. 87–88; H. W. Greene, *Annals of the American Academy of Political and Social Science*, March, 1943, and C. G. Woodson, in *American Historical Review*, July, 1943, XLVIII, p. 811. For examples of scholarly articles by Luther Porter Jackson, see his: "Free Negroes of Petersburg, Va.," *Journal of Negro History*, XII, No. 3, July, 1927, pp. 365–388; "Religious Instruction of Negroes, 1830–1860, with Special Reference to South Carolina," *loc. cit.*, XV, No. 1, January, 1930, pp. 72–114; "Manumission in Certain Virginia Cities," *loc. cit.*, XV, No. 3, July, 1930, pp. 278–314; "The First 25 Volumes of the *Journal of Negro History* Digested," *loc. cit.*, XXV, October, 1940, No. 4, pp. 432–430; "Early Strivings of the Negro in Virginia," *loc. cit.*, XXV, January, 1940, No. 1, 25–34; "The Virginia Free Negro Farmer and Property Owner, 1830–60," *loc. cit.*, XXIV, October, 1939, No. 4, pp. 390–439; "Religious Development of the Negro in Virginia from 1700 to 1860," *loc. cit.*, XVI, No. 2, April, 1931, pp. 168–239; and, "Trends in Federal Policy Toward the Negro in the *Annual Report* of the American Historical Association, 1942, III, pp. 319–341.

27. Biographical facts taken from H. W. Greene, *op. cit.*, Taylor's dissertation was published by the Association for the Study of Negro Life and History.

28. A. A. Taylor, *The Negro in Tennessee* (Washington, D.C.: The Associated Publishers, 1941), 306 pp.

29. Taylor, *The Negro in South Carolina during the Reconstruction* (The Association for the Study of Negro Life and History, 1924), 341 pp. At this time Mr. Taylor held only the M.A. degree and was serving as an Associate Investigator of the Association for the Study of Negro Life and History.

30. Taylor et al., *A Study of the Community Life of the Negro Youth* (for the Commission on Institutions of Higher Education of the Association of Colleges and Secondary Schools, Barber-Scotia College, North Carolina, 1941), 176 pp.

31. W. M. Brewer, in *Journal of Negro History*, XXVI, No. 2, April, 1941, p. 253.

32. *Ibid.*, pp. 252–253.

33. Benjamin Quarles, *Frederick Douglass* (Washington, D.C.: Associated Publishers, 1948), 378 pp. See also his "Revisionist Negro History," *Social Education*, X, No. 3, March, 1946.

34. *Journal of Negro History*, XXXIII, July, 1948, No. 3, p. 356.

35. June 13, 1948, p. 108.

36. See also reviews by Ella Lonn, *American Historical Review*, October, 1948, p. 156; G. D. Harmon, *Annals of the American Academy of Political and Social Science*, September, 1948, p. 198.

37. For examples of his articles, see his: "The Breach between

Douglass and Garrison," *Journal of Negro History*, XXIII, No. 2, April, 1938, pp. 144–154; "Frederick Douglass and the Woman's Rights Movement," *loc. cit.*, XXV, January, 1940, No. 1, pp. 35–44.

38. John Hope Franklin, *From Slavery to Freedom* (New York: Knopf Publishers, 1947), 622 pp.

39. Franklin, *The Free Negro in North Carolina* (Chapel Hill: University of North Carolina Press, 1945), 271 pp. See Woodson's review of this work, *Journal of Negro History*, XXVII, No. 2, pp. 482–484.

40. *New York Times*, October 12, 1947, p. 40.

41. See review by George Streator, *Commonweal*, October 31, 1947, XLVII, p. 76.

42. In *Saturday Review of Literature*, November 8, 1947, XXX, p. 16. Others who reviewed the volume, generally favorably, were O. C. Cox, *American Sociological Review*, August, 1947, VIII, p. 492; W. S. Savage, *Annals of the American Academy of Political and Social Science*, September, 1947, p. 211; E. F. Frazier, *Saturday Review of Literature*, June 19, 1947, XXVI, p. 36; and, L. D. Reddick, *Library Journal*, September 15, 1947, p. 1266.

43. *The Civil War Diary of James T. Ayers* (1947).

44. See, for example, the following, all in the *Journal of Negro History*: "James Boon, Free Negro Artisan," XXX, No. 2, April, 1945, pp. 150–180; "The Enslavement of Free Negroes in North Carolina," XIX, October, 1944, No. 4, pp. 401–426; "Slaves Virtually Free in Ante-Bellum North Carolina," XXVIII, July, 1943, No. 3, pp. 284–310; "Whither Reconstruction Historiography," *Journal of Negro Education*, Fall, 1948, pp. 446–461; "History—Weapon of War and Peace," *Phylon*, 3d Qtr., 1944, pp. 249–259; and, "New Perspectives in American Negro History," *Social Education*, XIV, May, 1950, pp. 196–200.

45. Biographical data was taken from H. W. Greene, *op. cit.*, and G. J. Fleming and C. E. Burckel, *op. cit.*, p. 431.

46. For examples of his articles, see his "The Negro in the U. S. Navy during World War I," *Journal of Negro History*, XXXII, No. 2, April, 1947, pp. 201–219; "Racial Attitudes in American History Textbooks of the South," IXX, No. 3, July, 1934, pp. 225–265; "The Negro Policy of the U.S. Army, 1775–1945," XXXIV, No. 1, January, 1949, pp. 9–29; "A New Interpretation for Negro History," XXII, January, 1937, pp. 19–27, all in *Journal of Negro History*.

47. Also see his articles as follows, all in the *Journal of Negro History*: "Poor Whites and Negroes in the South Since the Civil War," XV, No. 1, January, 1930, pp. 26–37; "Lincoln and the Border States," XXXIV, No. 1, January, 1949, pp. 46–72; "The Teaching of Negro History in Secondary Schools," XXXVI, No. 1, January, 1951, pp. 71–79.

48. See also his "The Possibilities of Compromise in the Senate Committee of Thirteen and the Responsibility for Failure," *Journal of Negro History*, XVII, No. 4, October, 1932, pp. 437–467.

49. For biographical facts on Williams, see H. W. Greene, *op. cit.* Cf. *Capitalism and Slavery* (Chapel Hill: University of North Carolina Press, 1944), 285 pp.

50. Washington, D.C. The Associates in Negro Folk Education, 1942, 119 pp.

51. Port-of-Spain, Guardian Commercial Printery, 1950, 167 pp. Also, see his "The Historical Background of British Guiana's Problems," *Journal of Negro History*, XXX, No. 4, October, 1945, pp. 357–379; and, "The Golden Age of the Slave System in Britain," *Journal of Negro History*, XXV, No. 1, January, 1940, pp. 60–106.

52. C. G. Woodson, *Journal of Negro History*, XXX, No. 1, January, 1945, p. 93.

53. E. A. Williams, *Capitalism and Slavery*, p. 211.

54. Chapel Hill, University of North Carolina Press, 260 pp.

55. See review, *Journal of Negro History*, XXXVI, No. 4, October, 1951.

56. *Journal of Negro History*, XXVIII, No. 2, April, 1942. It will not be necessary, wrote Woodson of this book, p. 251, for another writer to produce a documented account of what nations did for and against disarmament from 1870 to 1907.

57. *The United States and Armaments* (1948).

58. His volumes are: *Negro Writers in American Literature* (New York: Macmillan, 1950); and, *A History of the Omega Psi Phi Fraternity* (Washington, D.C.: Published by the Fraternity); and, a novel, *Out of the Night* (1916). See also his "What Does the Innocent Teacher Impart as History," *Journal of Negro History*, XXV, No. 4, October, 1940, pp. 474–483; and, "The Education of the Negro with Respect to his Background," *loc. cit.*, XIX, No. 1, January, 1934, pp. 45–51.

59. See his "Populism and Disfranchisement in Alabama," *Journal of Negro History*, XXXIV, No. 4, Oct., 1949, pp. 410–427.

60. See, for example, his "Social and Economic Forces in Alabama Reconstruction," *Journal of Negro History*, XXIII, No. 3, July, 1938, pp. 29–348.

61. See his "Abolition and Labor," *Journal of Negro History*, XXXIII, No. 3, July, 1948, pp. 249–283; "Northern Labor and the Negro during the Civil War," *loc. cit.*, XXXIV, No. 3, July, 1949, pp. 251–273.

62. See his "African Studies," *Phylon*, first quarter, 1944, pp. 62–68, for a listing of the authorities, travellers, historians, geographers, and other sources which are essential to the study of Africa.

63. North Carolina College at Durham became the first Negro college

to offer work leading to the doctorate degree in the fall of 1952. The degree was offered in education only, but by 1969 was no longer being offered. By the latter date, while Atlanta University had a limited doctoral program, the largest of all was at Howard University where doctoral degrees offered included the field of history. The offering of work leading to the master's degree has been a marked feature of Negro college education in the last decade, and the trend seems to be continuing, despite a beginning breakdown of segregated education in southern state universities.

CHAPTER 10
SUBSTANCE AND SHADOW

---

1. Preface.

2. See chapter 6 this work on Du Bois.

3. Henry Steele Commager, *The American Mind* (New York: Yale University Press, 1950), p. 283.

4. *Ibid.*, p. 284. See also Vernon Louis Parrington, *Main Currents in American Thought*, I, Introduction.

5. Du Bois, *Souls of Black Folk*, Introduction.

6. Commager, *op. cit.*, pp. 290–308.

7. Earl E. Thorpe, "Toward A Philosophy of History," *Quarterly Review of Higher Education Among Negroes*, October, 1956; and the same author's, "Some Tendencies In Philosophy of History," *Ibid.*, July, 1956.

8. W. E. B. Du Bois, *Darkwater*, in his Credo, p. 4.

9. Witness his being tried as an unregistered agent of a foreign government because of his role in circulating the Stockholm Peace Appeal, and his overall championing of the so-called peace movement.

10. A review by Eugene Holmes of *What the Negro Wants*, edited by Rayford Logan (Chapel Hill: University of North Carolina Press), 352 pp. in *Journal of Negro History*, XXX, January, 1944, No. 1, p. 90.

11. See the several statements by Carter G. Woodson to this effect, this work.

12. Harry W. Greene, *op. cit.*, p. 48.

13. *Ibid.*, p. 49.

14. See Chapter III, this study.

15. Lowell J. Ragatz, *Fall of the Planter Class in the British Caribbean* (New York: 1928).

16. Gunnar Myrdal, *An American Dilemma* (New York: Harper and Brothers, 1944).

17. See U. B. Phillips, *Life and Labor In The Old South* (Boston: Little Brown, 1929), and other writings by Phillips. See also Kenneth Stampp, *The Peculiar Institution* (New York: A. A. Knopf, 1956).

18. "A New Interpretation for Negro History," *Journal of Negro History*, XXXII, No. 1, January, 1937, p. 20.

19. *Ibid.*

20. *Ibid.*, pp. 21–22.

21. *Ibid.*, p. 23.

22. *Ibid.*, p. 25.

23. *Ibid.*, pp. 25–26.

24. *Ibid.*, p. 27.

25. *Ibid.*, pp. 27–28.

26. Benjamin Quarles, *Frederick Douglass* (Washington, D.C.: Associated Publishers, 1948).

27. Cf., for example, her *The Story of Phillis Wheatley* (New York: Julian Messner, Inc., 1949), 170 pp.

28. See, for example, J. G. Van Deusen, *Brown Bomber: The Story of Joe Louis* (Philadelphia: Dorrance and Co., 1940); Edward Van Every, *Joe Louis* (New York: Frederick A. Stokes Co., 1936); Helen Arstein and Carlton Moss, *Lena Horne* (New York: Greenberg Publisher, 1950).

29. Commager, *op. cit.*, p. 292.

30. Also on Negro literature and historiography see: Roland C. McConnell, "Importance of Records in the National Archives on the history of the Negro," *Journal of Negro History*, XXXIV, April, 1949, pp. 135–152; Walter E. Daykin, "Nationalism as Expressed in Negro History," *Social Forces*, XIII, p. 258, December, 1934; Arthur A. Schomburg, "The Negro Digs up his Past," *Survey*, LIII, p. 670, March, 1925; John S. Lash, "On Negro Literature," *Phylon*, 3rd Qtr., 1945; J. Saunders Redding, "The Negro Writer—Shadows and Substance," *Phylon*, XI, 4th Qtr., 1950, pp. 371–377; J. Saunders Redding, "American Negro Literature," *The American Scholar*, XVIII, Spring, 1949, pp. 137–148; Benjamin Brawley, *The Negro in Literature and Art* (New York: Duffield and Co., 1918); Charles S. Johnson, "The Rise of the Negro Magazine," *Journal of Negro History*, XIII, pp. 7–21, January, 1928; John Chamberlain, "The Negro as Writer," *Bookman*, LXX, February, 1930, pp. 603–611; John G. Van Deusen, *The Black Man in White America* (Washington, D.C.: Associated Publishers, 1944); John Hope Franklin, *From Slavery to Freedom* (New York: Knopf Publishers, 1948); Carter G. Woodson, *The Negro in our History* (Washington, D.C.: Associated Publishers); Edward Franklin Frazier, *The Negro in the United States* (New York, 1949); Alain Locke, ed., *The New Negro*, (New York: Albert and Charles Boni Inc., 1925); Vernon Loggins, *The Negro Author* (New York, 1931), 457 pp; Charles Johnson,

The Negro College Graduate (Chapel Hill: University of North Carolina Press, 1937); Herman Dreer, *American Literature by Negro Authors* (New York: Macmillan, 1950); Arthur A. Schomburg, *Racial Integrity*, a Plea for the Establishment of a Chair of Negro History in our Schools and Colleges (A. V. Bernier, printer). Of the whole of American historiography, see Michael Kraus, *A History of American History* (New York: Farrar and Rinehart, 1937); John Higham, et alia, *History: The Development of Historical Studies in the United States* (New Jersey: Prentice-Hall, 1965).

SELECTED
BIBLIOGRAPHY

Allen, James S., *Reconstruction; the Battle for Democracy.* New York, International Publishers, 1937, 256 pp.

Andrews, W. T., *In Memoriam.* Washington, D. C., Howard University Press, 1891, 12 pp.

Ausubel, Herman, *Historians and their Craft: A Study of the Presidential Addresses of the American Historical Association.* Columbia University Press, 1950.

Barnes, H. E., *A History of Historical Writing.* Norman, Oklahoma, Press, 1937, 434 pp.

Bond, Horace Mann, *The Education of the Negro in the American Social Order.* New York, Prentice-Hall, 1934, 501 pp.

———, *Negro Education in Alabama; a Study in Cotton and Steel.* Washington, D. C., Associated Publishers, 1939, 358 pp.

———, *Social and Economic Influences on the Public Education of Negroes in Alabama, 1885–1930.* Washington, D. C., Associated Publishers, 1944.

Bontemps, Arna W., *Story of the Negro.* New York, Alfred A. Knopf, 1948, 239 pp.

Brawley, Benjamin, *A Social History of the American Negro.* New York, Macmillan, 1921, 420 pp.

———, *A Short History of the American Negro.* 4th rev. ed., New York, Macmillan, 1939, 288 pp.

———, *Doctor Dillard of the Jeanes Fund.* New York, F. H. Revell Co., 1930, 151 pp.

———, *Negro Builders and Heroes.* Chapel Hill, University of North Carolina Press, 1937, 315 pp.

———, *The Negro Genius; a New Appraisal of the Achievement of the American Negro in Literature and the Fine Arts.* New York, Dodd, Mead, and Co., 1937, 366 pp.

———, *The Negro in Literature and Art.* New York, Duffield and Co., 1918, 176 pp.

———, *Paul Laurence Dunbar, Poet of His People.* Chapel Hill, University of North Carolina Press, 1936, 159 pp.

———, *A Short History of the English Drama.* New York, Harcourt, Brace and Co., 1921, 260 pp.

———, *Early Negro American Writers.* Chapel Hill, University of North Carolina Press, 1935, 305 pp.

———, *History of Morehouse College.* Atlanta, Georgia, Morehouse College, 1917, 218 pp.

———, *History of the English Hymn.* New York, Abingdon Press, 1932, 256 pp.

————, *Women of Achievement*. Chicago, Woman's American Baptist Home Mission Society, 1919, 92 pp.

————, *Your Negro Neighbor*. New York, Macmillan, 1918, 100 pp.

————, *Africa and the War*. New York, Duffield and Co., 1918, 94 pp.

————, *Early Effort for Industrial Education*. Charlottesville, Virginia, 1923, 15 pp.

Brinton, Crane, *Ideas and Men*. New York, Prentice-Hall, 1950.

Brown, George W., *The Economic History of Liberia*. Washington, D. C., The Associated Publishers, 1941, 366 pp.

Brown, William Wells, *Sketches of Places and Peoples Abroad*. New York, Jewett, Proctor and Worthington, 1855, 320 pp.

————, *The Black Man: His Antecedents, His Genius, and His Achievements*. New York, 1863 editions, 288 pp. and 310 pp.

————, *The Rising Son; or the Antecedents and Advancement of the Colored Race*. Boston, Brown and Company, 1874, 555 pp.

————, *The Negro in the American Rebellion: His Heroism and Fidelity*. Boston, Lee Shepard, 1867, 380 pp.

Carpenter, Marie E., *The Treatment of the Negro in American History School Textbooks*. Menasha, Wisconsin, George Banta Publishing Co., 1941, 137 pp.

Catto, William, *A Semi-Centenary Discourse, delivered in the First African Presbyterian Church, Philadelphia, on the fourth Sabbath of May, 1857; with a history of the Church from its first organization, including a brief notice of Rev. John Gloucester, its first pastor*. *Philadelphia, J. M. Wilson, 1857*, 111 pp.

Commager, Henry S., *The American Mind*. New Haven, Yale University Press, 1950.

Crogman, W. H., and H. F. Kletzing, *Progress of a Race*. Atlanta, Georgia, J. L. Nichols, 1897, 663 pp.

————, and J. W. Gibson, *The Colored American From Slavery to Honorable Citizenship*. Atlanta, Georgia, J. L. Nichols and Co., 1902, 732 pp.

Cromwell, John W., *The Negro in American History*. Washington, D. C., The American Negro Academy, 1914, 284 pp.

Davie, Maurice R., *Negroes in American Society*. New York, Whittlesey House, 1950, 542 pp.

DeCosta, B. F., *Three Score and Ten—The Story of St. Phillip's Church, New York City*. New York, 1889, 57 pp.

Delaney, Martin R., *The Condition, Elevation, Emigration and Destiny of the Colored People of the U. S. Politically Considered*. Published by the Author, 1852, 215 pp.

Dorn, Walter L., *Competition for Empire, 1740–1763*. New York, Harper and Bros., 1940, 426 pp.

Dowd, Jerome, *The Negro in American Life*. New York, Century Co., 1926, 611 pp.

Douglass, William, *Annals of the First African Church in the U. S. A.* Philadelphia, King and Baird, 1862, 172 pp.

Dreer, Herman, *The History of Omega Psi Phi*. Washington, D. C., The Fraternity, 1940, 331 pp.

———, *Negro Writers in American Literature*. New York, Macmillan, 1950.

Du Bois, W. E. B., *Dusk of Dawn*. New York, Harcourt, Brace and Co., 1940, 334 pp.

———, *Suppression of the African Slave Trade to the United States of America, 1638–1870*. New York, Longmans, Green, 1896, 335 pp.

———, *The Philadelphia Negro*. Philadelphia, published for the University of Pennsylvania, 1899, 520 pp.

———, and Booker T. Washington, *The Negro in the South*. Philadelphia, G. W. Jacobs and Co., 1907, 222 pp.

———, *John Brown*. Philadelphia, G. W. Jacobs and Co., 1909, 406 pp.

———, *The Negro*. New York, Henry Holt and Co., 1915, 326 pp.

———, *The Gift of Black Folk*. Boston, The Stratford Co., 1924, 342 pp.

———, *Black Reconstruction*. New York, Harcourt Brace, 1935, 746 pp.

———, *Black Folk Then and Now*. New York, Henry Holt and Company, 1939, 401 pp.

———, *Color and Democracy: Colonies and Peace*. New York, Harcourt, Brace and Co., 1945, 143 pp.

———, *The World and Africa*. New York, The Viking Press, 1947, 276 pp.

———, *The Souls of Black Folk*. Chicago, A. C. McClurg and Co., 1903, 265 pp.

———, *The Quest of the Silver Fleece*. Chicago, A. C. McClurg and Co., 1911, 434 pp.

———, *Dark Princess*. New York, Harcourt, Brace, 1928, 311 pp.

———, *Darkwater*. New York, Harcourt, Brace and Howe, 1920, 276 pp.

———, ed., *From Servitude to Service*. Boston, American Unitarian Association, 1905, 232 pp.

Dunbar, Paul Laurence, *Lyrics of Lowly Life*. New York, Dodd, Mead and Co., 1896, 208 pp.

Easton, Hosea, *A Treatise on the Intellectual Character . . . of the*

Colored People of the United States. Boston, Isaac Knapp, 1837, 56 pp.

Edmonds, Helen G., *The Negro and Fusion Politics in North Carolina, 1894–1901.* Chapel Hill, University of North Carolina Press, 1950, 260 pp.

Embree, Edwin R., *Thirteen Against the Odds.* New York, The Viking Press, 1944, 261 pp.

Eppse, Merl R., and A. P. Foster, *An Elementary History of America, Including the Contributions of the Negro Race.* Nashville, Tennessee, National Educational Publishing Co., 1943, 312 pp.

————, *The Negro, Too, in American History.* Nashville, Tennessee, National Publishing Co., 1949, 644 pp.

————, *A Guide to the Study of the Negro in American History.* Nashville, Tennessee, National Educational Publishing Co., 1937, 115 pp.

Fisher, Eric, *The Passing of the European Age.*

Fisher, Miles M., *The Evolution of Slave Songs in the United States.* Unpublished doctoral dissertation, Chicago, University of Chicago Library, 1949, 350 pp. Microfilm copy at Fisk University, Nashville, Tennessee.

————, *The Master's Slave: Elijah John Fisher.* Philadelphia, The Judson Press, 1922, 172 pp.

Franklin, John Hope, *The Free Negro in North Carolina.* Chapel Hill, University of North Carolina Press, 1946, 271 pp.

————, *From Slavery to Freedom.* New York, Knopf Publishers, 1947, 622 pp.

————, ed., *The Diary of James T. Ayers, Civil War Recruiter.* Springfield, 1947, 138 pp.

Frazier, Edward F., *The Negro in the United States.* New York, Macmillan, 1949.

Greene, H. W., *Holders of Doctorates Among American Negroes.* Boston, Meador Publishing Co., 1946, 275 pp.

Greene, Lorenzo J., and C. G. Woodson, *The Negro Wage Earner.* Washington, D. C., Associated Publishers, 1930, 388 pp.

————, *The Negro in Colonial New England, 1620–1776.* New York, Columbia University Press, 1943, 404 pp.

————, and M. C. Callis, *The Employment of Negroes in the District of Columbia.* Washington, D. C., The Association for the Study of Negro Life and History, 1930, 88 pp.

Grimes, Joseph, *A Study of the Negro Historian, 1844–1920.* Unpublished master's thesis, University of Iowa, 1935, 78 pp.

Grimke, Archibald H., *The Life of Charles Summer; the Scholar in Politics.* New York, Funk and Wagnalls Co., 1892, 415 pp.

———, *William Lloyd Garrison, the Abolitionist.* New York Funk and Wagnalls, 1891, 405 pp.

———, *Papers of the American Negro Academy.* Washington, D. C., The Academy, 1915, 78 pp.

Hagood, L. M., *The Colored Man in the Methodist Church.* Cincinnati, Ohio, 1880, 327 pp.

Herskovits, M. J., *The Myth of the Negro Past.* New York, Harper and Brothers, 1941.

Holly, James Theodore, *A Vindication of the Capacity of the Negro Race for Self-Government and Civilized Progress,* 48 pp.

Hutchinson, Will T., ed., *The Marcus W. Jernegan Essays in American Historiography.* Chicago, Chicago University Press. 1937.

Jackson, Luther Porter, *A History of the Virginia State Teachers Association.* Norfolk, The Guide Publishing Co., 1937, 112 pp.

———, *Free Negro Labor and Property Holding in Virginia.* New York, D. Appleton-Century Co., 1942, 270 pp.

———, *Virginia Negro Soldiers and Seamen in the Revolutionary War.* Norfolk, Guide Quality Press, 46 pp.

Jameson, J. F., *The History of Historical Writing in America.* New York, Houghton Mifflin Co., 1891.

Johnson, Charles S., *The Negro College Graduate.* Chapel Hill, The University of North Carolina Press, 1938, 399 pp.

Johnson, Edward A., *School History of the Negro Race in America from 1619 to 1890.* Rev. ed., New York, Isaac Goldman Co., 1911, 400 pp.

———, *History of Negro Soldiers in the Spanish-American War.* Raleigh, North Carolina, Capital Printing Co., 1899, 147 pp.

Kraus, Michael, *A History of American History.* New York, Farrar and Rinehart, 1937.

Lawson, Elizabeth, *Study Outline History of the American Negro People, 1619–1918.* New York, Workers Book Shop, 1939, 100 pp.

Lewis, Robert B., *Light and Truth.* 1st edition, 1836, Boston, Massachusetts, 176 pp.; 2d edition, Portland, Maine, B. C. Colesworthy, 1844, 400 pp.

Locke, Alain, ed., *The New Negro.* New York, Albert and Charles Boni, 1925, 446 pp.

———, comp., *A Decade of Negro Self-Expression.* Charlottesville, Virginia, 1928.

Logan, Rayford W., ed., *The Attitude of the Southern White Press Toward Negro Suffrage, 1932–1940.* Washington, D. C., The Foundation Publishers, 1940, 115 pp.

———, ed., *What the Negro Wants.* Chapel Hill, University of North Carolina Press, 1944, 352 pp.

————, *The Diplomatic Relations of the United States with Haiti, 1776–1891*. Chapel Hill, The University of North Carolina Press, 1941, 516 pp.

————, *The Senate and the Versailles Mandate System*. Washington, D. C., The Minorities Publishers, 1945, 112 pp.

————, *The Negro and the Post-War World*. Washington, D. C., The Minorities Publishers, 1945, 95 pp.

————, *The African Mandates in World Politics*. Washington, D. C., Public Affairs Press, 1948, 220 pp.

————, *The Operation of the Mandate System in Africa*. Washington, D. C., Foundation Publishers, 1942, 50 pp.

————, *The Negro in American Life and Thought; The Nadir, 1877–1901*. New York, Dial Press, 1954, 380 pp.

Love, E. K. *History of the First African Baptist Church*. Savannah, Georgia, 360 pp.

Lynch, John R., *The Facts of Reconstruction*. New York, Neale Pub. Co., 1915, 325 pp.

————, *Some Historical Errors of James Ford Rhodes*. Boston, Cornhill Pub. Co., 1922, 115 pp.

Matthews, Basil, *Booker T. Washington, Educator and Racial Interpreter*. Cambridge, Harvard University Press, 1948, 350 pp.

Mazyck, W. H., *George Washington and the Negro*. Washington, D. C., Associated Publishers, 1932, 180 pp.

Miller, Kelly, *The Everlasting Stain*. Washington, D. C., Associated Publishers, 1924, 352 pp.

————, and J. R. Gay, *Progress and Achievements of the Colored People*. Washington, D. C., Austen Jenkins Co., 1917, 490 pp.

————, *Kelly Miller's History of the World War for Human Rights*. Published by the Author, Washington, D. C., n.d.

Myrdal, Gunnar, *An American Dilemma: Negro Problem and Modern Democracy*. New York, Harper and Brothers, 1944, 1483 pp.

Nell, William Cooper, *Colored Patriots of the American Revolution*. Boston, R. F. Wallcut, 1855, 396 pp.

————, *Services of Colored Americans in the Wars of 1776 and 1812*. Boston, Prentiss and Sawyer, 1855, 24 pp.

————, *Property Qualification or No Property Qualification*. New York, T. Hamilton and W. H. Leonard, 1860, 24 pp.

Ottley, Roi, *Black Odyssey: the Story of the Negro in America*. New York, C. Scribner's Sons, 1948, 340 pp.

Ovington, Mary W., *Portraits in Color*. New York, The Viking Press, 1927, 241 pp.

Palmer, R. R., *A History of the Modern World*. New York, Knopf Pubs., 1950.

Parrington, Vernon L., *Main Currents in American Thought*. New York, Harcourt Brace, 1927–30.

Payne, Daniel A., *Recollections of Seventy Years*. Nashville, Tennessee, A. M. E. Sunday Union, 1888, 355 pp.

——, *History of the African Methodist Episcopal Church*. Nashville, Tennessee, A.M.E. Sunday School Union, 1891, 502 pp.

Pennington, James W. C., *The Fugitive Blacksmith*. 3d ed. London, C. Gilpin, 1850, 84 pp.

——, *A Textbook of the Origin and History of the Colored People*. Hartford, Connecticut, 1841, 96 pp.

Perry, Rufus, *The Cushites, or, the Children of Ham as Seen by the Ancient Historians*. Springfield, Massachusetts, Wiley and Co., 1893, 175 pp.

Phillips, C. H., *The History of the Colored Methodist Episcopal Church in America*. Jackson, Tennessee, 1898, 247 pp.

Phillips, Ulrich B., *Life and Labor in the Old South*. Boston, Little, Brown and Co., 1929, 375 pp.

Quarles, Benjamin, *Frederick Douglass*. Washington, D. C., Associated Publishers, 1948, 378 pp.

Ragatz, Lowell J., *The Fall of the Planter Class in the British Caribbean, 1763–1833*. New York, the Century Co., 1928, 520 pp.

Randall, John Herman Jr., *Making of the Modern Mind*. Rev. ed., Boston, Houghton, Mifflin Co., 1940.

Redding, J. S., *They Came in Chains*. Philadelphia, Lippincott, 1950, 320 pp.

Reid, Ira De A., *The Negro Immigrant*. New York, Columbia University, 1939, 261 pp.

Rush, Christopher, and George Collins, *Short Account of the Rise and Progress of the A. M. E. Church in America*. New York, Published by the Author, 1843, 106 pp.

Savage, William S., *The History of Lincoln University*. Jefferson City, Missouri, 1939, 302 pp.

——, *The Controversy over the Distribution of Abolition Literature, 1830–1860*. Washington, D. C., Associated Publishers, 1938, 141 pp.

Scott, Emmett J. and Lyman Beecher Stowe, *Booker T. Washington*. New York, Doubleday, Page and Co., 1918, 331 pp.

Simms, James M., *The First Colored Baptist Church in North America*. Philadelphia, 1888, 246 pp.

Simmons, W. J., *Men of Mark*. Cleveland, Ohio, G. M. Rewell & Co., 1887, 1141 pp.

Steward, Theophilus G., *The Colored Regulars in the U. S. Army, with a Sketch of the History of the Colored American*. Philadelphia, A. M. E. Book Concern, 1921, 540 pp.

————, *The Haitian Revolution, 1791 to 1804.* New York, T. Y. Crowell, 1914, 292 pp.

————, *How the Black St. Domingo Legion Saved the Patriot Army in the Siege of Savannah, 1779.* Washington, D. C., The Negro Academy, Occasional Papers No. 5, 15 pp.

Still, William, *The Underground Railroad.* Philadelphia, Porter and Coats, 1872, 788 pp.

Tate, Merze, *The Disarmament Illusion.* New York, The Macmillan Company, 1942, 398 pp.

Taylor, Alrutheus A., *The Negro in Tennessee, 1865–1880.* Washington, D. C., Associated Publishers, 1941, 306 pp.

————, *The Negro in South Carolina During the Reconstruction.* Washington, D. C., The Association for the Study of Negro Life and History, 1924, 341 pp.

————, et al., *A Study of the Community Life of the Negro Youth.* Barber-Scotia College, North Carolina, 1941, 176 pp.

————, *The Negro in the Reconstruction of Virginia.* Washington, D. C., The Association for the Study of Negro Life and History, 1926, 300 pp.

Toynbee, Arnold J., *A Study of History.* Vol. IV, London, Oxford University Press, 1939.

Van Deusen, John G., *The Black Man in White America.* Washington, D. C., Associated Publishers, 1944.

Wallace, Henry A., *Carpetbag Rule in Florida.* Jacksonville, De Costa Printing Co., 1888, 444 pp.

Washington, Booker T., *Tuskegee and Its People.* New York, D. Appleton and Co., 1905, 354 pp.

————, *Working with the Hands.* New York, Doubleday, 1904, 246 pp.

————, *The Negro in Business.* Chicago, Hertel, Jenkins and Co., 1907, 379 pp.

————, *Education of the Negro.* New York, J. B. Lyon Co., 1900, 44 pp.

————, and W. E. B. Du Bois, et al., *The Negro Problem.* New York, J. Pott and Co., 1903, 324 pp.

————, *Putting the Most into Life.* New York, Crowell, 1906, 35 pp.

————, *The Future of the American Negro.* Boston, Small, Maynard, 1899, 244 pp.

————, *Sowing and Reaping.* New York and Boston, H. M. Caldwell Co., 1900, 29 pp.

————, et al., *The Negro Problem.* New York, J. Pott and Co., 1903, 234 pp.

————, et al., *A New Negro for a New Century*. Chicago, American Publishing House, 1900, 428 pp.

————, *My Larger Education*. New York, Doubleday, Page and Co., 1911, 313 pp.

————, *The Story of My Life and Work*. Atlanta, J. L. Nichols and Co., 1901, 452 pp.

————, *Up from Slavery*. Boston, Houghton Mifflin Co., 1928, School edition; first published, New York, A. L. Burt Co., 1900, 330 pp.

————, *Frederick Douglass*. Philadelphia, George W. Jacobs and Co., 1906, 355 pp.

————, *The Story of My Life and Work*. Atlanta, J. L. Nichols and Co., 332 pp.; II, 437 pp.

Wesley, Charles H., *Negro Labor in the United States, 1850–1925*. New York, Vanguard Press, 1927, 343 pp.

————, *A Manual of Research and Thesis Writing*. Washington, D. C., Howard University Press, 1941, 80 pp.

————, *Richard Allen, Apostle of Freedom*. Washington, D. C., Associated Publishers, 1935, 300 pp.

————, *The Collapse of the Confederacy*. Washington, D. C., Associated Publishers, 1937, 225 pp.

————, *The History of Alpha Phi Alpha*. Washington, D. C., Howard University Press, 1929, 294 pp.

————, *A History of the Improved Benevolent and Protective Order of Elks of the World, 1898–1954*. Washington, D. C., Association for the Study of Negro Life and History, 1955, 503 pp.

Whiting, Helen A., *Negro Art, Music and Rhyme, for Young Folks*. Book II, Washington, D. C., Associated Publishers, 1938.

————, *Negro Folk Tales for Pupils in the Primary Grades*. Washington, D. C., Associated Publishers, 1938.

Wilkes, Laura E., *Missing Pages in American History*. Washington, D. C., Press of R. L. Pendleton, 1919, 91 pp.

Williams, Eric, *Capitalism and Slavery*. Chapel Hill, University of North Carolina Press, 1944, 285 pp.

————, *The Negro in the Caribbean*. Washington, D. C., The Associated in Negro Folk Education, 1942, 119 pp.

————, *Education in the British West Indies*. Port-of-Spain, Guardian Commercial Printery, 1950, 167 pp.

Williams, George W., *A History of the Negro Race in America from 1619 to 1880*. New York, Putnam and Sons, 1883, 481 pp., 611 pp.

————, ed., *The Negro in the Americas*. Howard University, 1940, 86 pp.

————, *A History of the Negro Troops in the War of the Rebellion, 1861–1865.* New York, Harper and Brothers, 1888, 353 pp.

Wilson, Joseph T., *Emancipation: Its Course and Progress from 1481 B.C. to A.D. 1875.* Hampton, Virginia, 1882, 242 pp.

————, *The Black Phalanx.* Hartford, Conn., American Publishing Company, 1887, 528 pp.

————, *Voice of a New Race.* Hampton, Virginia, 1882, 43 pp.

Woodson, Carter G., *Education of the Negro Prior to 1861.* New York, G. P. Putnam's Sons. 1915, 454 pp.

————, *The Negro in Our History.* Washington, D. C., The Association for the Study of Negro Life and History, 1922, 393 pp.

————, *A Century of Negro Migration.* Washington, D. C., The Association for the Study of Negro Life and History, 1918, 221 pp.

————, *The History of the Negro Church.* Washington, D. C., Associated Publishers, 1921, 330 pp.

————, *Early Negro Education in West Virginia.* West Virginia College, Institute, West Virginia, 1921, 54 pp.

————, *The Mis-Education of the Negro.* Washington, D. C., Associated Publishers, 1923.

————, ed., *Free Negro Owners of Slaves in the United States in 1830.* Washington, D. C., The Association for the Study of Negro Life and History, 1924, 78 pp.

————, ed., *Free Negro Heads of Families in the United States in 1830.* Washington, D. C., The Association for the Study of Negro Life and History, 1925, 296 pp.

————, ed., *Negro Orators and their Orations.* Washington, D. C., Associated Publishers, 1926, 711 pp.

————, ed., *The Mind of the Negro as Reflected in Letters Written During the Crisis, 1800–1860.* Washington, D. C. Associated Publishers, 1926, 672 pp.

————, *The Story of the Negro Retold.* Washington, D. C., Associated Publishers, 1935, 369 pp.

————, *African Myths, together with Proverbs.* Washington, D. C., The Associated Publishers, 1928, 184 pp.

————, et al., *The Negro as a Businessman.* Washington, D. C., Associated Publishers, 1929, 111 pp.

————, *The Rural Negro.* Washington, D. C., Associated Publishers, 1930, 265 pp.

————, *The Negro Professional Man and the Community.* Washington, D. C., Associated Publishers, 1934, 365 pp.

————, *The African Background Outlined.* Washington, D. C. Association for the Study of Negro Life and History, 1936, 478 pp.

———, *African Heroes and Heroines*. Washington, D. C., Associated Publishers, 1939, 210 pp.

———, ed., *The Works of Francis J. Grimke*. Washington, D. C., The Associated Publishers, 1942, 4 vols.

Wright, R. R., *The Encyclopedia of the A. M. E. Church*. 2d ed., Philadelphia, The Book Concern of the A. M. E. Church, 1948, 688 pp.

Zook, George F., *The Company of Royal Adventures Trading Into Africa*. Lancaster, Pa., The New Era Printing Co., 1919, 105 pp.

———, *Higher Education for American Democracy*. New York, Harper and Bros., 1948, 475 pp.

Index